KJV-KJW

Law of France

Library of Congress Classification
2008

Prepared by the Cataloging Policy and Support Office
Library Services

LIBRARY OF CONGRESS
Cataloging Distribution Service
Washington, D.C.

This edition cumulates all additions and changes to subclasses KJV-KJW through Weekly List 2008/03, dated January 16, 2008. Additions and changes made subsequent to that date are published in weekly lists posted on the World Wide Web at

<http://www.loc.gov/aba/cataloging/classification/weeklylists/>

and are also available in *Classification Web*, the online Web-based edition of the Library of Congress Classification.

Library of Congress Cataloging-in-Publication Data

Library of Congress.
Library of Congress classification. KJV-KJW. Law of France / prepared by the Cataloging Policy and Support Office, Library Services. — 2008 ed.
p. cm.
"This edition cumulates all additions and changes to subclasses KJV-KJW through Weekly list 2008/03, dated January 16, 2008. Additions and changes made subsequent to that date are published in weekly lists posted on the World Wide Web at <http://www.loc.gov/aba/cataloging/classification/weeklylists/> and are also available in *Classification Web*, the online Web-based edition of the Library of Congress classification." — T.p. verso.
Includes index.
ISBN-13: 978-0-8444-1195-8
ISBN-10: 0-8444-1195-7
1. Classification, Library of Congress. 2. Classification—Books—Law. 3. Classification—Books—France. 4. Law—France—Classification. I. Library of Congress. Cataloging Policy and Support Office. II. Title. III. Title: Law of France.
Z696.U5K65 2008 025.4'634944—dc22 2008001166

For sale by the Library of Congress Cataloging Distribution Service,
101 Independence Avenue, S.E., Washington, DC 20541-4912.
Product catalog available on the Web at **www.loc.gov/cds**.

PREFACE

The first edition of subclasses KJV-KJW, *Law of France*, was published in 1985. A 1999 edition cumulated all additions and changes that had been made to the schedule between 1985 and 1999. This 2008 edition cumulates additions and changes made since the publication of the 1999 edition.

Classification numbers or spans of numbers that appear in parentheses are formerly valid numbers that are now obsolete. Numbers or spans that appear in angle brackets are optional numbers that have never been used at the Library of Congress but are provided for other libraries that wish to use them. In most cases, a parenthesized or angle-bracketed number is accompanied by a "see" reference directing the user to the actual number that the Library of Congress currently uses, or a note explaining Library of Congress practice.

Access to the online version of the full Library of Congress Classification is available on the World Wide Web by subscription to *Classification Web*. Details about ordering and pricing may be obtained from the Cataloging Distribution Service at:

<http://www.loc.gov/cds/>

New or revised numbers and captions are added to the L.C. Classification schedules as a result of development proposals made by the cataloging staff of the Library of Congress and cooperating institutions. Upon approval of these proposals by the weekly editorial meeting of the Cataloging Policy and Support Office, new classification records are created or existing records are revised in the master classification database. Weekly lists of newly approved or revised classification numbers and captions are posted on the World Wide Web at:

<http://www.loc.gov/aba/cataloging/classification/weeklylists/>

Paul Weiss and Jolande Goldberg, senior cataloging policy specialists in the Cataloging Policy and Support Office, are responsible for coordinating the overall intellectual and editorial content of subclasses KJV-KJW. Kent Griffiths, assistant editor of classification schedules, is responsible for creating new classification records, maintaining the master database, and creating index terms for the captions.

This printed edition of KJV-KJW must be used in conjunction with the separately published K Tables: Form Division Tables for Law, available for purchase from the Cataloging Distribution Service. This classification schedule includes references to form division tables within the range K1 to K24, which are found only in that publication.

Barbara B. Tillett, Chief
Cataloging Policy and Support Office

January 2008

OUTLINE

- KJV2-9158 Law of France
  - KJV2-4 Bibliography
  - KJV9-18 Official gazettes
  - KJV30-70 Legislation
  - KJV80-108 Court decisions and related materials
  - KJV112 Encyclopedias
  - KJV115 Law dictionaries. Terms and phrases
  - KJV121-123 Judicial statistics
  - KJV124-127 Directories
  - KJV128-135 Trials
  - KJV140-144 Legal research. Legal bibliography
  - KJV147 Legal reporting
  - KJV150-166 Legal education
  - KJV170-228 The legal profession
  - KJV230 Law societies and associations
  - KJV233 General works. Treatises
  - KJV235 Popular works. Civics
  - KJV237 Addresses, essays, lectures
  - KJV245-282 History
    - KJV247-250 Auxiliary sciences
    - KJV251-251.5 Biography
    - KJV254-281 Sources
      - KJV256-268 Coutumes. Droit coutumier. Custumals
  - KJV284-318 Philosophy and theory of French law
  - KJV320 Law reform. Criticism
  - KJV322 Concepts applying to several branches of law
  - KJV323-333 Works on diverse aspects of a special subject and falling within several branches of the law
  - KJV334-336 Private law
  - KJV360-428 Private international law
    - KJV373-378 Nationality
    - KJV382-386 Status of aliens in France
    - KJV388-397 Conflict of laws
    - KJV401-428 Conflict of jurisdictions
      - KJV403-410 Court procedure
      - KJV417 Arbitration and award
      - KJV425-428 Effects of foreign judgments
  - KJV441-2168 Civil law
    - KJV474-479 Rights created by civil law
    - KJV480-520 Juristic facts and acts
    - KJV525-527 Evidence

OUTLINE

Law of France

Civil law - Continued

KJV1461-1498	Gratuities
KJV1467-1468	Charitable gratuities
KJV1480-1488	Gifts inter vivos
KJV1491	Gifts causa mortis
KJV1529-2100	Choses in action. Obligations
KJV1571-1617	Creditor and debtor. Performance
KJV1650-1666	Extinction of obligations
KJV1668-1970	Contracts
KJV1791-1970	Individual contracts and obligations
KJV1978-1987	Quasi contracts. Unjust enrichment
KJV2001-2100	Civil liability
KJV2059-2071	Presumption of fault. Liability without fault. Strict liability
KJV2087-2100	Particular faults and injuries
KJV2111-2168	Security
KJV2122-2123	Suretyship and guaranty
KJV2130-2168	Rights in rem upon debtor's property
KJV2134-2143	Rights in rem upon debtor's personal property. Pledges
KJV2151-2168	Privileges and mortgages
KJV2185-3237	Commercial law
KJV2218-2226	Commercial courts and procedure
KJV2228-2231	Chambers of commerce
KJV2232	Commercial register
KJV2235-2283	Business interprises and merchants
KJV2301-2720	Commercial transactions and contracts
KJV2312-2317	Commercial mandate
KJV2317	Brokerage. Brokers
KJV2320-2338	Commercial sale
KJV2340-2361	Commercial leases
KJV2371-2415	Negotiable instruments. Titles of credit
KJV2391-2395	Bill of exchange
KJV2397-2405	Check
KJV2410	Promissory note
KJV2412-2415	Documents of title. Warrants
KJV2420-2466	Banking
KJV2437-2447	Bank deposits. Bank accounts
KJV2456-2464	Credit. Documentary credit. Advances on goods
KJV2470-2480	Commercial pledges and liens

OUTLINE

OUTLINE

Law of France - Continued

KJV5396-5404	Veterinary medicine and hygiene
KJV5406-5425.5	Environmental law. Environmental pollution
KJV5426-5530	Cultural affairs
KJV5434-5468	Education
KJV5468	Social advancement
KJV5470-5528	Science and the arts. Public collections. Historic buildings
KJV5530	Educational, scientific, and cultural exchange
KJV5541-5685	Economic law
KJV5560-5614	Government control and policy
KJV5562-5568	National planning
KJV5570	Distribution
KJV5575-5586	Prices and price control
KJV5595-5610	Competition rules. Horizontal and vertical combinations. Unfair competition
KJV5614	Standards. Norms. Quality control
KJV5620-5685	Regulation of industry and trade
KJV5622	Consumer protection
KJV5630-5634	Foreign trade
KJV5638-5682	Domestic trade
KJV5687-5860	Primary production
KJV5687-5820	Agricultural law
KJV5822-5828	Fisheries and fishing
KJV5830-5860	Mining. Quarrying
KJV5862-5980	Particular industrial and trade lines
KJV5862-5890	Manufacturing industries
KJV5892-5899	Building and construction industry
KJV5900-5938	Food processing industries. Food products
KJV5941-5972	Power production and supply. Energy policy
KJV5973-5980	Publishing. Printing. Book trade
KJV5981-6200	Transportation
KJV5997-6010	Transport by land. Road transport
KJV6012-6024	Railroads
KJV6029	Pipelines
KJV6035-6140	Water transportation. Administrative maritime law
KJV6145-6200	Air law. Civil aviation
KJV6220-6328	Communication. Mass media
KJV6251-6283	Press law
KJV6290-6325	Radio and television communications
KJV6328	Information services

OUTLINE

Law of France
Bibliography
For bibliography of special topics, see the topic
For manuals on legal bibliography, legal research and the use of law books see KJV140+
2 Bibliography of bibliography
3 General bibliography
3.5 Library catalogs
3.6 Sales catalogs
3.7 Indexes to periodical literature, society publications, collections
For indexes to particular publications, see the publication
Indexes to festschriften see KJV238
4.A-Z Special classes or groups of writers, A-Z
<6> Periodicals
For periodicals consisting predominantly of legal articles, regardless of subject matter and jurisdiction, see K
For periodicals consisting primarily of informative material (Newsletters, bulletins, etc.) relating to a particular subject, see subject and form division for periodicals
For law reports, official bulletins or circulars, and official gazettes intended chiefly for the publication of laws and regulations, see appropriate entries in the text or form division tables
7 Monographic series
Official gazettes
For city gazettes, see the issuing province or city
For departmental gazettes, see the issuing department or agency
9 Indexes (General)
12 Moniteur universal (1869-1870)
14 Journal officiel de l'Empire français
17 Journal officiel de la République française
Including Editions de Londres (1941-1943), Editions d'Algér (1943-1944)
18 Indexes
Legislative documents
see J
Legislation
Class here legislation beginning ca. 1789, and earlier legislation if included in collections or compilations extending beyond 1789
For legislation on a particular subject, see the subject
For legislation limited to a particular province, department, or locality, see the province, department or locality
For legislation prior to 1789 see KJV254+
Indexes and tables. By date
For indexes to a particular publication, see the publication
30 General

Legislation
Indexes and tables. By date -- Continued
34 Chronological indexes
40 Abridgements and digests
Statutes
Including statutory orders, administrative regulations, etc.
Sessional volumes. Annual volumes
50 Serials
56 Monographs. By date of initial session
Collections. Compilations. Selections
Including official and private editions
60 Serials
Monogaphs. By date
Including unannotated and annotated editions
65 General
68 Collected codes
Class here works consisting of both private and public law codes
For codes on a particular branch of law, see the subject
For works consisting of civil and commercial codes see KJV314+
Collections of bills submitted at individual sessions see J
70.A-Z Collections for particular groups of users, A-Z
Law enforcement officers see KJV70.P65
70.P65 Police and other law enforcement officers
Treaties
Treaties on international public law see KZ
Treaties on international uniform law not limited to a region see K
Treaties on international uniform law of the European region see KJC and KJE
Court decisions and related materials
Including authorized and private editions
Class here decisions beginning 1789, and earlier decisions if included in collections or compilations extending beyond 1789
For decisions relating to a particular subject, see the subject
For collections of decisions covering periods prior to 1789 see KJV275+
For collections of civil and commercial decisions see KJV314+

Court decisions and related materials -- Continued

80 Several courts

Class here collections of decisions or courts of different jurisdictions

For courts (several or individual) of an individual jurisdiction, see the region, municipality, etc.

Particular courts

90 Tribunal des conflits. Competence conflict court (Table KJV-KJW1)

95 Cour de cassation. Court of cassation (Table KJV-KJW1)

For collections related to a particular division of that court, see the pertinent branch of law, e.g., decisions by Civil Divisions, see KJV446

100 Regional courts of appeal. Cours d'appel (Table KJV-KJW1)

For collections of decisions related to particular court sittings (Civil, criminal, etc.), see the subject

105 Tribunaux de grande instance (Table KJV-KJW1)

For collections of decisions related to particular court-sittings (e.g. Tribunaux civils, Tribunaux correctionnels, Tribunaux de commerce), see the subject

108 Tribunaux d'instance (Table KJV-KJW1)

Class here decisions of both justice of the peace (Tribunaux de paix; Juges de paix) and magistrate courts (Tribunaux de simple police)

For decisions of Police courts (Tribunaux de simple police) see KJV8464

Conseil constitutionnel see KJV4390+

Administrative decisions on a particular subject see the subject

112 Encyclopedias

115 Law dictionaries. Terms and phrases

For law dictionaries on a particular subject, see the subject

Bilingual and multilingual dictionaries see K52.A+

118 Legal maxims. Quotations

119 Form books

For form books on a particular subject, see the subject

120 Yearbooks

Class here publications issued annually, containing information, statistics, etc. about the year just past

For other publications appearing yearly, see K1+

Judicial statistics

121 General

122 Criminal statistics

123.A-Z Other. By subject, A-Z

Directories

124 National

Directories -- Continued
125.A-Z Regional. By region, A-Z
126.A-Z Local. By department, county or city, A-Z
127.A-Z By specialization, A-Z
Barristers see KJV173+
Notaries see KJV187+
Trials
Criminal trials and judicial investigations
For military trials see KJV7578+
Collections. Compilations
128 General
129.A-Z Particular offenses, A-Z
Assassination see KJV129.M87
129.H47 Heresy
129.M87 Murder. Assassination
129.P65 Political offenses
129.T74 Treason
War crimes see KJV132+
129.W57 Witchcraft
Individual trials
Including records, briefs, commentaries, and stories on an individual trial
130.A-Z By defendant, A-Z
Chevalier, Michèle see KJV131.B63
Morgan, Claude see KJV131.K73
Wurmser, André see KJV131.K73
131.A-Z By best known (popular) name, A-Z
131.A78 Assassinat de Sadi Carnot
131.A79 Association internationale des travailleurs, Procès de l'
131.A98 Avril, Affaire d'
Bill see KJV131.M65
131.B63 Bobigny, Affaire de
Carnot, Sadi see KJV131.A78
131.C68 Courrier de Lyon, Affaire du
131.F83 Fualdès Affaire
131.F85 Fuites, Affaire des
131.G56 Glozel, Affaire de
131.G83 Guadeloupéens, Procès des
131.I58 Instituteur Lesnier, Histoire de l'
131.K73 Kravchenko, Procès
Lesnier see KJV131.I58
131.L98 Lyon, Procès de
131.M37 Marie Walewska, Affaire
131.M65 Monsieur Bill, Procès de
Ornano-Jean Savant see KJV131.M37
Sadi Carnot see KJV131.A78
Savant, Ornano-Jean see KJV131.M37

Trials
Criminal trials and judicial investigations
Individual trials
By best known (popular) name, A-Z -- Continued
131.V54 Vidocq, Procès de
Walewska, Marie see KJV131.M37
War crime trials
Class here trials of French nationals by French courts
For trials by international military tributnals or trials of foreigners by French courts see KZ1168+
132 Collections. Compilations
133.A-Z Individual trials. By first named defendant or best known (popular) name, A-Z
Other trials
134 Collections. Compilations
135.A-Z Individual trials. By plaintiff, defendant, or best known (popular) name, A-Z
Legal research. Legal bibliography
Including methods of bibliographic research and how to find the law
140 General (Table K11)
Electronic data processing. Information retrieval systems
142 General (Table K11)
143.A-Z By subject, A-Z
Subarrange each by Table K12
144 Systems of citation. Legal abbreviations
145 Legal composition
147 Law reporting
Legal education
150 General (Table K11)
Study and teaching
General works see KJV150
153 Students' guides and textbooks
Including textbooks for particular academic degrees and diplomas in law
For students' guides and textbooks on a particular subject, see the subject
For introductory surveys of the law see KJV252
155 Law students
Law schools
Statutes, rules, and regulations
Class here collections
For particular law schools see KJV166.A+
156 General
158 Legal education at Catholic schools of higher learning
159 Studies and requirements for a Certificate of Capacity in Law

Legal education
Law schools
Statutes, rules, and regulations -- Continued
Studies and requirements for academic degrees in law
160 General
162 Licence en driot. Degree of Licence in Law
163 Diplome d'études supèrieures. Diploma of Advanced Study
164 Doctorat en droit. Doctorate in law
166.A-Z Particular law schools. By name, A-Z
Under each:

.xA2	*History. By date*
.xA4-.xA49	*Journals*
.xA5-.xA59	*Outlines of study, catalogs, bulletins, etc.*
.xA6	*Administration reports. By date* *Including organization and policy*
.xA7	*Anniversaries. Special celebrations, etc. By date*
.xA8-.xZ	*General works*

The legal profession
Including law as a career
Cf. KJV3831+ Judicial personnel
170 General (Table K11)
172 Admission to the profession. Accès à la profession (Table K11)
Including works on admission to magistracy
Barristers. Avocats
173 General (Table K11)
174 Liability. Responsabilité civile des avocats (Table K11)
175 Women barristers. Femmes-avocats (Table K11)
176 Avocats aux conseil (Table K11)
Class here works on the lawyers entitled to practice before the Court of Cassation and the Council of State and performing the function of both barristers and solicitors
Bar associations. Barreaux
178 General (Table K11)
Discipline. Disbarment see KJV224+
180 Association nationale des avocats de France et de Communauté
184.A-Z Individual bars. By place, A-Z
Notaries. Notaires
187 General (Table K11)
Notarial acts. Actes notariés
189 General (Table K11)

The legal profession
Notaries. Notaires
Notarial acts. Actes notariés -- Continued
190 Notaries' liability. Responsabilité civile des notaires (Table K11)
Including professional secrets
192 Forms. Form books
196 Professional partnerships of notaries. Sociétés civiles professionnelles notariales (Table K11)
Associations of notaries
198 General (Table K11)
202.A-Z Particular associations. By place, A-Z
204 Honoraria. Fees (Table K11)
Solicitors. Avoués
212 General (Table K11)
Avocats aux conseil see KJV176
214 Solicitors' liability. Responsabilité civile des avoués (Table K11)
216 Fees (Table K11)
Practice of law
218 General (Table K11)
219 Lawyers' liability. Responsabilité civile des hommes de loi (Table K11)
Legal ethics. Devoir légal
Including barristers, notaries, or solicitors
220 General (Table K11)
222 Professional secrets. Secret professionnel (Table K11)
223 Unauthorized practice (Table K11)
Discipline. Disbarment
224 General (Table K11)
226.A-Z Particular disciplinary cases
By first named person subjected to disciplinary action or by best known (popular) name, A-Z
228 Costs. Fees (Table K11)
229 Legal aid. Assistance judiciaire (Table K11)
230.A-Z Law societies and associations. By name, A-Z
Including the journals, proceedings, annual reports, etc., of such societies
232.A-Z Congresses. Seminars. By name, A-Z
233 General works. Treatises
234 Compends, outlines, etc.
235 Popular works. Civics
237 Addresses, essays, lectures
Including single essays, collected essays of several authors, festschriften, etc.
238 Indexes to festschriften, etc.

240.A-Z Manuals and other works for particular groups of users. By user, A-Z
240.B87 Businesspeople. Foreign investors
Foreign investors see KJV240.B87
Law and lawyers in literature
see PB-PZ
Relation of law to other topics see K486+
History of law
Class here general works on legal history including works on both legal history and constitutional history
For constitutional history see KJV4080.5+
245 Bibliography
246 Encyclopedias
246.3 Law dictionaries. Terms and phrases. Vocabularies
Including early works
Methodology see KJV254
Auxiliary sciences
247 General works
247.3 Paleography
248 Linguistics. Semantics
248.3 Archaeology. Symbolism in law
Class here general works on various manifestations of legal symbolism
For early works, including schemata, stemmata, arbores, etc., see the author in KJV257+
249 Inscriptions
250 Heraldry. Seals. Flags. Insignia. Armory
250.3 Proverbs
Clauses and formulae see KJV278+
Biography
251 Collective
251.5.A-Z Individual, A-Z
Under each:
.xA3 *Autobiography. Reminiscences. By date*
.xA4 *Letters. Correspondence. By date*
Including individual letters, general collections, and collections of letters to particular individuals
.xA6 *Knowledge. Concept of law. By date*
.xA8-.xZ *Biography and criticism*
252 General works. Treatises
252.3 Popular works

History of law -- Continued
253 Addresses, essays, lectures
Including single essays, collected essays of several authors, festschriften, etc.
253.3 Indexes to festschriften
By period
Gaul see KJ155.A2+
Early period. Germanic tribes see KJ160+
Frankish period, ca. 500-ca. 900 see KJ320+
Ancien Régime (to 1789)
Sources
For the sources of a particular territory or town, see the appropriate territory or town
254 Studies on sources
Including history of sources and methodology
255 Collections. Compilations (General)
Individual sources or groups of sources
Coutumes. Droit coutumier. Custumals
256 Bibliography
General coutumiers of France
257 Les grand covstvmier de France (Jacques d'Ableiges, fl. 1391, comp.) (Table K20b)
257.3 Le grâdes coustumes generalles et particulieres du royaulme de France (Table K20b)
258 La somme rural (par Jean Boutillier) By date
258 La somme rural (Jean Boutillier, comp.) (Table K20b)
259 Des covstvmes generalles et particvlieres dv royavme de France & des Gaulles (Charles Du Moulin, comp.) (Table K20b)
260 Les coustumes et statutz particuliers de la pluspart des bailliages, seneschaucees et preuostez royaulx de royaulme de France (Table K20b)
260.3 Nouveau coutumier general, ou Corps des coutumes generales et particulieres de France, et des provinces connues sous de nom des Gaules (Charles A. Bourdot de Richebourg, comp.) (Table K20b)
263 General works. Treatises
Including early works on the droit coutumier
Pays de coutume. Coutume regions
Bibliography see KJV256+
264.A-K264.Z Coutumes of the Central Region. By jurisdiction, A-Z
264.A87 Auvergne (Table KJV-KJW2)
264.A88 Auxerre (Table KJV-KJW2)

History of law
By period
Ancien Régime (to 1789)
Sources
Individual sources or groups of sources
Coutumes. Droit coutumier. Custumals
Pays de coutume. Coutume regions
Coutumes of the Central Region. By jurisdiction, A-Z -- Continued

264.B43 Beauvaisis (Table KJV-KJW2)
264.B47 Berry (Table KJV-KJW2)
264.B55 Blois (Table KJV-KJW2)
264.B67 Bourbonnais (Table KJV-KJW2)
264.B68 Bourges (Table KJV-KJW2)
264.C43 Chartres (Table KJV-KJW2)
264.C45 Chasteau-neuf en Thymerais (Table KJV-KJW2)
264.C54 Clermont-en-Beauvaisis (Table KJV-KJW2)
264.E83 Etampes (Table KJV-KJW2)
264.L64 Loir-et-Cher (Table KJV-KJW2)
264.L67 Lorris (Table KJV-KJW2)
264.M35 Mantes (Table KJV-KJW2)
264.M37 Marche (Table KJV-KJW2)
264.M43 Meaux (Table KJV-KJW2)
264.M45 Melun (Table KJV-KJW2)
264.M65 Montargis (Table KJV-KJW2)
264.M67 Montfort-l'Amaury (Table KJV-KJW2)
264.N58 Nivernais (Table KJV-KJW2)
264.O74 Orléans (Table KJV-KJW2)
264.P37 Paris (Table KJV-KJW2)
264.P47 Perche (Table KJV-KJW2)
264.S45 Senlis (Table KJV-KJW2)
264.T67 Touraine (Table KJV-KJW2)
264.T68 Tours (Table KJV-KJW2)
265.A-Z Coutumes of the Western Region. By jurisdiction, A-Z
265.A54 Angers (Table KJV-KJW2)
265.A56 Angoumois (Table KJV-KJW2)
265.A57 Anjou (Table KJV-KJW2)
e. g. Le Coutumier daniou et du maine (1486)
265.B74 Brittany (Table KJV-KJW2)
265.L37 La Rochelle (Table KJV-KJW2)
265.L68 Loudun (Table KJV-KJW2)
265.M34 Maine (Table KJV-KJW2)
Cf. KJV265.A57 Anjou
265.M67 Morbihan (Table KJV-KJW2)

History of law
By period
Ancien Régime (to 1789)
Sources
Individual sources or groups of sources
Coutumes. Droit coutumier. Custumals
Pays de coutume. Coutume regions
Coutumes of the Western Region. By jurisdiction, A-Z -- Continued

265.N67 Normandy (Table KJV-KJW2)
e. g. Coutumes du pais de Normandie (1483)
265.P64 Poitou (Table KJV-KJW2)
265.R68 Roville (Table KJV-KJW2)
266.A-Z Coutumes of the Northern Region. By jurisdiction, A-Z
266.A33 Abbeville (Table KJV-KJW2)
266.A65 Amiens (Table KJV-KJW2)
266.A77 Arras (Table KJV-KJW2)
266.A78 Artois (Table KJV-KJW2)
266.B34 Bailleul (Table KJV-KJW2)
266.B68 Bouillon (Table KJV-KJW2)
266.C35 Cambrai (Table KJV-KJW2)
266.C53 Chalons (Table KJV-KJW2)
266.C58 Chauny (Table KJV-KJW2)
266.F53 Flanders (Walloon) (Table KJV-KJW2)
266.G67 Gorgue (Table KJV-KJW2)
266.G85 Gumes (Table KJV-KJW2)
266.H34 Hainaut (French) (Table KJV-KJW2)
266.L55 Lille (Table KJV-KJW2)
266.L88 Luxembourg (French) (Table KJV-KJW2)
266.M65 Mons (Table KJV-KJW2)
266.P47 Peronne (Table KJV-KJW2)
266.P52 Picardy (Table KJV-KJW2)
266.P65 Ponthieu (Table KJV-KJW2)
266.R44 Reims (Table KJV-KJW2)
266.S35 Saint-Amand (Table KJV-KJW2)
266.S36 Saint-Bauzeil (Table KJV-KJW2)
266.S38 Saint-Omer (Table KJV-KJW2)
266.S44 Sedan (Table KJV-KJW2)
266.T68 Tournan (Table KJV-KJW2)
266.V47 Vermandois (Table KJV-KJW2)
267.A-Z Coutumes of the Eastern Region. By jurisdiction, A-Z
267.A48 Alsace (Table KJV-KJW2)
267.B37 Bar-le Duc (Table KJV-KJW2)
267.B38 Bassigny (Table KJV-KJW2)
267.B68 Bourgogne (Table KJV-KJW2)

History of law
By period
Ancien Régime (to 1789)
Sources
Individual sources or groups of sources
Coutumes. Droit coutumier. Custumals
Pays de coutume. Coutume regions
Coutumes of the Eastern Region. By jurisdiction, A-Z -- Continued

267.B74 Bresse (Table KJV-KJW2)
267.C53 Champagne (Table KJV-KJW2)
267.C55 Chaumont-en-Bassigny (Table KJV-KJW2)
267.F47 Ferrette (Table KJV-KJW2)
267.F73 Franche-Comte (Table KJV-KJW2)
267.L66 Lorraine (Table KJV-KJW2)
267.L67 Lorraine and Bar (Table KJV-KJW2)
267.M37 Marsal (Table KJV-KJW2)
267.M48 Metz (Table KJV-KJW2)
267.O72 val d'Orbey (Table KJV-KJW2)
267.S35 Saint-Mihiel (Table KJV-KJW2)
267.S46 Sens (Table KJV-KJW2)
267.T76 Troyes (Table KJV-KJW2)
267.V38 Vaudémont (Table KJV-KJW2)
267.V47 Verdun (Table KJV-KJW2)
267.V58 Vitry-en-Perthois (Table KJV-KJW2)
268.A-Z Pays de droit écrit. Coutumes of Written Law Regions. By jurisdiction, A-Z
268.A54 Agen (Table KJV-KJW2)
268.A64 Andorre (Table KJV-KJW2)
268.B43 Béarn (Table KJV-KJW2)
268.B67 Bordeaux (Table KJV-KJW2)
268.C36 Castel-Amouroux (Table KJV-KJW2)
268.C37 Castelsagrat (Table KJV-KJW2)
268.D38 Dauphine (Table KJV-KJW2)
268.G37 Garonne (Table KJV-KJW2)
268.L37 Laroque-Timbaut (Table KJV-KJW2)
268.P73 Prayssas (Table KJV-KJW2)
268.P76 Provence (Table KJV-KJW2)
268.R68 Roussillon (Table KJV-KJW2)
268.S34 Saint-Gauzens (Table KJV-KJW2)
268.S344 Saint-Gilles (Table KJV-KJW2)
268.S35 Saint-Jean-d'Angély (Table KJV-KJW2)
268.T68 Toulouse (Table KJV-KJW2)
269 Etablissements de Saint Louis
Ordonnances royales. Royal ordinances
270 Collections. Compilations
271 Individual. By date

History of law
By period
Ancien Régime (to 1789)
Sources
Individual sources or groups of sources -- Continued
Remonstrances du Parlement de Paris. Remonstrances of the Sovereign Court of Paris
273 Collections. Compilations
274 Individual. By date
Recueil d'arrêts. Law reports
275 Collections. Compilations
For remonstrances of the Sovereign Court of Paris see KJV273+
Contemporary legal literature
277 Compends. Digests. Indexes
Formularies
278 General
279 Particular clauses and formulae
280 Handbooks
Including handbooks for advocates, public officers, private persons, court (trial) practice, pleading, etc.
Law dictionaries see KJV246.3
Encyclopedic works see KJV246
281 General works. Treatises
Including quaestiones, responsae, observationes, etc.
282.A-Z Special topics, A-Z
Class here subjects not provided for otherwise in the schedule
282.W57 Witchcraft
Philosophy and theory of French law
Class here works on doctrines peculiar to French legal institutions
For works on the philosophy of a particular branch of law (e.g. constitutional law or criminal law), see the branch
For works by French authors on the philosophy of law in general see K237+
284 General works
The object of law. Law and justice
285 General works
286 Principles of natural justice and equity. Principes généraux
Public policy and good morals. Ordre public et bonnes moeurs
287 General works
Ordre public (Conflict of laws) see KJV393
288 Equity. Fairness
Effectiveness and validity of law see KJV314+

Philosophy and theory of French law -- Continued
289 Certainty of law
289.3.A-Z Other topics, A-Z
The law. Droit objectif
290 General works
Sources of law. Sources de la règle juridique
291 General works
Sources emanating from State authorities. Sources étatiques
292 General works
Treaties and executive agreements as a source of statutory law. La Loi
Cf. KJV4324+ Legislative power
295 General works
Decree laws see KJV4357
296 Statutory laws as an expression of the general will. Volonté générale
297 Promulgation and publication
298 Repeal of law. Abrogation d'une loi
Non-legislated law. Droit non légiféré
299 General works
301 Jurists' law. La doctrine
Cf. KJV303 Interpretation and construction of the law
Case law. Judge-made law
302 General works
302.2 Res judicata. Chose jugée
302.3 Precedent. Stare decisis. Jurisprudence constante
International law see KJV304+
303 Interpretation and construction of law
International and municipal law. Droit international et droit interne français
304 General (Table K11)
304.2 Application of international law by French courts. Application du droit international par le juge français
Territorial and temporal applicability of laws. Application de la loi dans l'espace et dans le temps
For works limited to a particular branch of law or subject, see the branch of law or the subject
Cf. KJV388+ Conflict of laws
305 General works
306 Interprovincial conflict of laws and jurisdictions. Conflit interprovincial
For both interprovincial conflict of laws and international conflict of laws see KJV388+
307.2 Retroactive law. Principle of nonretroactivity. Principe de la nonrétroactivité des lois

Philosophy and theory of French law
The law. Droit objectif
Territorial and temporal applicability of laws. Application de la loi dans l'espace et dans le temps -- Continued
307.3 Intertemporal law. Droit transitoire
Rights of the individual. Droits subjectifs
308 General works
Rights of civil law see KJV474+
Civil rights see KJV4204+
308.2 Abuse of rights. Abus des droits
Juristic facts and acts. Causalité juridique
Class here works on juristic facts and acts in general
For works limited to a particular branch of law or the subject, see the branch of law or the subject
310 General works
Prescription see KJV322.P73
Birth see KJV556+
Death see KJV560+
Juristic acts. Actes juridiques
Cf. KJV3898+ Judicial decisions
Cf. KJV4711+ Administrative acts
311 General works
312 Declaration of intention. Déclaration de volonté
312.4 Declaratory and constitutive acts. Actes declaratifs et actes constitutifs
Evidence. La preuve
Class here works on evidence of juristic facts and acts in both private and public law
For works limited to a particular branch of law or subject, see the branch of law or subject
313 General works
Recording and registration see KJV527
Validity, nullity, and effectiveness of law. Validité, nullité, et efficacité ou effectivité
Including droit objectif, droits subjectifs, et causalité juridique
314 General works
Time. Period of time see KJV322.T56
Prescription see KJV322.P73
316 Legal advertising. Publicité légale
317 Théorie de l'apparence
318 Classification of French law. Distinction between public law and private law
319.A-Z Relation of French law to other disciplines, subjects, or phenomena, A-Z
Catholic ethics see KJV319.E84
319.E84 Ethics, Catholic

319.4 Influence of other legal systems on French law
e.g. reception of Roman and canon law
320 Law reform. Criticism
Including reform of the administration of justice in general
For reform of criminal justice and administration see KJV7967
322.A-Z Concepts applying to several branches of law, A-Z
Deadlines see KJV322.T56
322.D65 Domicile
322.G66 Good faith. Bonne foi
322.L53 Liability. Responsabilité
322.N68 Notice. Notification. Avis
322.P73 Prescription
322.P74 Presumption
322.R58 Risk
322.T56 Time periods. Deadlines. Le terme. Délai
Works on diverse aspects of a special subject and falling within several branches of the law
323 Accounting, auditing, inventories
Animals. Animaux
324 General (Table K11)
Domestic animals. Animaux domestiques
325 General (Table K11)
326 Dogs. Chiens (Table K11)
327 Horses. Chevaux (Table K11)
328 Automobiles (Table K11)
329 Private mail. Correspondence privée (Table K11)
330 Sundays and holidays. Dimanches et fêtes (Table K11)
Cf. KJV5646 Sunday legislation
331 Children. Mineurs (Table K11)
332 Women. Femmes (Table K11)
333.A-Z Other aspects, A-Z
Subarrange each by Table K12
333.C65 Computers (Table K12)
333.H85 Human body. Corps humain (Table K12)
Private law. Droit privé
Class here works on all aspects or private law
334 History
Class here works on private law prior to 1804
For works on droit civil (jus civile; lois civiles, including both private and public law) as distinguished from Canon law prior to 1700 see KJV254+
336 General (Table K11)

Private international law. Droit international privé
Including works on acquisition and loss of French nationality, and works on status of aliens in France
For works limited to Overseas France, French colonial law, or to the French community see KJV4530+

360 General (Table K11)

Nationality. Nationalité

373 General (Table K11)

374.A-Z Special topics, A-Z
Subarrange each by Table K12
Aliens see KJV382+
Associations see KJV1881+
Companies see KJV1881+

374.C65 Concurrence of nationality. Conflits de nationalité (Table K12)

374.J87 Juristic persons, Nationality of. Nationalité de personnes morales (Table K12)

374.M4 Married women, Nationality of. Nationalité de la femme mariée (Table K12)

French nationality. Nationalité française
Including acquisition and loss of French nationality

376 General (Table K11)

377 Naturalization

378.A-Z Special topics, A-Z
Subarrange each by Table K12
Aliens see KJV382+

378.R54 Rights and duties of Frenchmen residing abroad (Table K12)

Citizenship in the French Union see KJV4650.C57

Status of aliens in France. Condition des étrangers en France
Including status of foreign juristic persons in France, and both private and public law aspects
Cf. KJV4198.A55 Aliens

382 General (Table K11)

383.A-Z Special topics, A-Z
Subarrange each by Table K12

383.A44 Alien property (Table K12)
Including real property, commercial property, etc.
Aliens as parties to action see KJV407+
Businesspeople, Foreign see KJV2276+
Capacity to inherit see KJV1337.A65
Employment see KJV3477.A55

383.N35 Name (Table K12)
Including names of both natural and juristic persons
Notarial acts drawn up for aliens see KJV422

Private international law. Droit international privé
Status of aliens in France. Condition des étrangers en France -- Continued
384.A-Z By nationality, A-Z
e.g.
384.B75 British
British associations and companies in France see KJV1894.B75
384.R87 Russians
Russian associations and companies in France see KJV1894.R87
Associations and juristic persons of aliens in France. Associations et personnes morales des étrangers en France
Including foreign juristic persons (general) in France, and including works on nationality of such associations and juristic persons
For both nationality of foreign juristic persons and French nationality of juristic persons see KJV1893+
Cf. KJV1894.B75 Foreign associations and companies
Cf. KJV3185+ Foreign commercial companies
385 General (Table K11)
386 Foundations. Fondations (Table K11)
Conflict of laws. Conflits de lois
For conflict rules of branches other than private law (e.g. criminal law), see the subject
For conflict of rules of procedure see KJV401+
388 General (Table K11)
Qualifications
390 General (Table K11)
391 By lex fori. Par la loi du for (Table K11)
Including general works on lex fori
391.2 By lex causae. Par la lex causae
392 Points of contact. Renvoi (Table K11)
393 Public policy. Ordre public (Table K11)
Form of juristic acts. Forme des actes juridiques
394 General (Table K11)
395 Locus regit actum (Table K11)
397.A-Z Particular branches and subjects of law, A-Z
Subarrange each by Table K12
397.A33 Agency (Table K12)
Aircraft see KJV397.S55
Aliens. Etrangers see KJV382+
Aliens' capacity to inherit see KJV397.S83
Boats see KJV397.S55
Capacity see KJV397.S73
397.C58 Civil liability. Responsabilité civile (Table K12)

Private international law. Droit international privé
Conflict of laws. Conflits de lois
Particular branches and subjects of law, A-Z -- Continued

397.C76 Contracts. Obligations (Table K12)
397.D59 Divorce and separation (Table K12)
Estates of foreign decedents see KJV1425
Extra-contractual obligations see KJV397.C76
397.F35 Family property (Table K12)
397.F55 Filiation. Conflits de lois en matière de filiation (Table K12)
Foreign insurance companies in France see KJV2882+
Foreign investments see KJV5572
397.G66 Goods in transit. Marchandises en transit (Table K12)
397.I53 Incapables, Protection of. Protection des incapables (Table K12)
Incapacity see KJV397.S73
397.I56 Insurance. Assurances (Table K12)
Insurance policies see KJV397.I56
Insurance policies signed on foreign currencies see KJV2878
397.I57 Intangible personal property. Meubles incorporels (Table K12)
397.I58 Intellectual and industrial property (Table K12)
Labor law see KJV3409
397.L54 Life insurance. Assurances sur la vie (Table K12)
397.L57 Liquidation and partition (Ownership; Co-ownership) (Table K12)
397.M37 Marriage (Table K12)
397.M38 Matrimonial property relationships. Régimes matrimoniaux (Table K12)
397.N36 Name (Table K12)
Including names of both natural and juristic persons
Nationality see KJV374.C65
397.N85 Nullity and ineffectiveness (Table K12)
Obligations see KJV397.C76
397.P37 Parent and child. Rapports entre les parents et les enfants (Table K12)
Parental authority see KJV397.P37
Partition of estate in private international law see KJV397.L57
397.P76 Property. Biens (Table K12)
Protection of incapables see KJV397.I53
397.S43 Security (Table K12)
397.S55 Ships, boats, and aircraft. Navires, bateaux de rivière, et aéronefs (Table K12)
397.S73 Status and capacity of persons. Etat et capacité des personnes (Table K12)

Private international law. Droit international privé
Conflict of laws. Conflits de lois
Particular branches and subjects of law, A-Z -- Continued
397.S83 Succession upon death (Table K12)
397.T35 Tangible personal property. Meubles corporels (Table K12)
397.T67 Tortious liability. Responsabilité civile extra-contractuelle (Table K12)
Wills made in foreign countries see KJV1350
Conflict of jurisdictions. Procedure. Conflits de juridictions
401 General (Table K11)
Court procedure. Procédure judiciaire
403 General (Table K11)
404 Letters rogatory. Commissions rogatoires (Table K11)
Including letters rogatory in civil and criminal matters
Parties to action. Parties dans un procès
405 General (Table K11)
Aliens. Etrangers
Including works on civil and criminal jurisdiction (competence) of French courts
407 General (Table K11)
409 Security for costs. Caution judicatum solvi (Table K11)
410 Foreign states (Table K11)
417 Arbitration and award. Jurisdiction arbitrale. Sentences arbitrale (Table K11)
For execution of foreign arbitral awards see KJV427+
Acts of public officials. Actes des officiers publics
418 General (Table K11)
Notarial acts. Actes notariés
420 General (Table K11)
422 Notarial acts drawn up for aliens. Actes notariés passés à l'étranger
Execution see KJV427+
Effects of foreign judgments. Protection of vested rights. Effets des jugements étrangers. Respect des droits acquis
425 General (Table K11)
Execution of foreign judgments, awards and notarial acts. Exécution des judgements étrangers, sentences étrangers et actes notariés étrangers
427 General (Table K11)
428.A-Z Special topics, A-Z
Subarrange each by Table K12
428.E93 Execution of Swiss civil judgments in France
Civil law. Droit civil
441 Bibliography

Civil law. Droit civil -- Continued

441.2 Periodicals

For periodicals consisting predominantly of legal articles, regardless of subject matter and jurisdiction, see K

For periodicals consisting primarily of informative material (Newsletters, bulletins, etc.) relating to a particular subject, see subject and form division for periodicals

For law reports, official bulletins or circulars, and official gazettes intended chiefly for the publication of laws and regulations, see appropriate entries in the text or form Division Tables

442 Monographic series

Legislation

Statutes

Class here legislation beginning in 1804, and earlier legislation if included in collections or compilation extending beyond 1804

For legislation on a particular subject of private law, see the subject

For legislation limited to a particular province, department, or locality, see the province, department or locality

For legislation enacted prior to 1804 see KJV447.7

Collections. Compilations

443 Serials

443.2 Monographs. By date

Particular acts. Codes

Collections see KJV443+

444.2<date> Individual codes

Arrange chronologically by appending date of original enactment or revision of code to KJV444.2 and deleting any trailing zeros, e.g., the number KJV444.21804 is used for the Code Napoléon enacted in 1804. Subarrange each code by Table K16

446 Court decisions

447 Encyclopedias. Dictionaries

447.4 Formbooks

447.5 Yearbooks

447.7 History

Including source materials (i.e., laws and legislation enacted prior to 1804, and early works)

450 General works. Treatises

472 Theory of equivalence. Theorie d'équivalence

Rights created by civil law. Droits civil

474 General (Table K11)

Rights appreciable in money see KJV1112+

Rights non-appreciable in money see KJV533

Civil law. Droit civil
Rights created by civil law. Droits civil -- Continued
Rights in rem. Droits réels
476 General (Table K11)
Rights in rem upon property see KJV1170+
Rights in personam see KJV1529+
Intellectual rights see KJV3248+
479 Tangible and intangible rights. Droits corporels et droits incorporels (Table K11)
For a particular right or a group of rights, see the appropriate subject
Juristic facts and acts. Causalité juridique
480 General (Table K11)
Birth or conception see KJV556+
Consanguinity see KJV870+
Majority see KJV565
Physical and mental deficiencies see KJV941+
Death see KJV560+
482 Fortuitous events and acts of God. Cas fortuit ou de force majeure (Table K11)
Quasi contracts see KJV1978+
Possession see KJV1160+
Prescription
483 General (Table K11)
Acquisitive prescription see KJV1162
Extinctive prescription. Prescription extinctive
For works on extinctive prescription pertaining to a particular right or obligation, see the right or the obligation
484 General (Table K11)
Duration of extinctive prescription. Dureé de la prescription extinctive
485 General (Table K11)
486 Statutory periods of time. Délais légaux
Limitation of actions see KJV3944
Juristic acts. Actes juridiques
For both juristic acts of private law and of public law see KJV310+
487 General (Table K11)
489 Unilateral and bilateral acts. Actes unilatéraux et actes bilatéraux (Table K11)
Gratuitous and onerous acts. Actes à titre gratuit et actes à titre onereux
For a particular onerous act or contract, see the act or contract
Cf. KJV1670 General classification of contracts
490 General (Table K11)

Civil law. Droit civil
Juristic facts and acts. Causalité juridique
Juristic acts. Actes juridiques
Gratuitous and onerous acts. Actes à titre gratuit et actes à titre onereux -- Continued
Gratuities see KJV1461+
Commutative contracts see KJV1687
Aleatory contracts see KJV1970+
493 Acte d'administration (Table K11)
494 Disposition. Acte de disposition (Table K11)
For works on a particular type of disposition, see the subject, e.g. KJV1340+, Wills
Acte conservatoire see KJV1114
495 Agency. Representation. Mandat légal (Table K11)
For contractual agency (mandate) see KJV1930+
For negotiorum gestio see KJV1980
Requirements for validity. Nullity and ineffectiveness. Conditions de validité. Nullité et inefficacité
497 General (Table K11)
Capacity to perform juristic acts see KJV564
Intention and declaration of intention. Volonté. Déclaration de volonté
499 General (Table K11)
Private autonomy see KJV1544
Defects of consent. Vices de consentement
500 General (Table K11)
500.4 Mental reservation (Table K11)
Simulation see KJV1750
501 Error. Erreur (Table K11)
Deceit see KJV2095
Duress. Violence. Dol
502 General (Table K11)
Lesion see KJV1748
Unilateral declaration of intention see KJV1545.2+
Form
503 General (Table K11)
Conflict of laws relating to the form of juristic acts see KJV394+
505 Acts under private signature. Actes sous signe privé (Table K11)
Including both acts under private signature and simple contracts (Conventions verbales)
506 Acts in solemn form. Actes solennels (Table K11)
Cf. KJV189+ Notarial acts
507 Certification. Forme probante (Table K11)
Recording and registration see KJV527
Legal advertising see KJV316

Civil law. Droit civil
Juristic facts and acts. Causalité juridique
Juristic acts. Actes juridiques -- Continued
510 Terms of time. Terme (Table K11)
Including termination of term. Terme extinctif
Cf. KJV322.T56 Time periods
Conditions
Cf. KJV1584+ Performance
512 General (Table K11)
513 Retroactivity of conditions. Rétroactivité de la condition (Table K11)
514 Suspensive conditions. Condition suspensive (Table K11)
515 Resolutory conditions. Condition résolutoire (Table K11)
520 Renunciation. Renonciation (Table K11)
Consolidation see KJV1172
Merger of rights see KJV1662
Evidence. Preuve
For works on evidence in procedure see KJV3949+
525 General (Table K11)
526 Presumption in private law. Présomption en droit privé (Table K11)
527 Recording and registration. Enregistrement (Table K11)
For a particular register, see the subject, e.g. KJV580 Register of civil status
For data protection see KJV2094
Acts under private signature see KJV505
Persons. Personnes
532 General (Table K11)
533 Personality and personality rights (Table K11)
Including both natural and juristic persons
Natural persons. Personnes physiques
534 General (Table K11)
Civil status. Etat civil
History
536 General works
Noblemen see KJV4090+
Clergymen (Ecclesiastiques) see KJV4089.2+
Serfs see KJV4095
541-545.8 General (Table K10)
550 Retroactivity of law in regard to civil status (Table K11)
Personality. Personnalité
553 General (Table K11)
Commencement of personality. Commencement de la personnalité
555 General (Table K11)

Civil law. Droit civil
Persons. Personnes
Natural persons. Personnes physiques
Civil status. Etat civil
Personality. Personnalité
Commencement of personality. Commencement de la personnalité -- Continued
Birth. Naissance
Including birth registration (acte de naissance)
556 General (Table K11)
558 Unborn children. Nasciturus. Personalité anterieure à la naissance (Table K11)
Including their capacity to enjoy rights (capacité de jouissance des droits)
End of personality. Fins de la personnalité
559 General (Table K11)
Death. Décès
Including missing persons and declaration and registration of death
560 General (Table K11)
Civil death see KJV8123
Capacity and incapacity. Capacité
562 General (Table K11)
Capacity to enjoy rights. Capacité de jouissance des droits
563 General (Table K11)
Unborn children see KJV558
564 Capacity to perform juristic acts. Capacité d'exercice
Class here general works
For a special limitation of this capacity or limitation for a special group of persons, see the subject or the group of persons, e.g. KJV567 Women
Minors see KJV974+
565 Majority. Majorité (Table K11)
Illegitimate children see KJV898+
Mentally ill and people with mental disabilities see KJV995+
Aliens. Etrangers see KJV382+
Women. Femmes
For legal status in both private and public law see KJV332
567 General (Table K11)
Married women see KJV673+
568 Single women. Femme seule (Table K11)
Personality rights. Droits de la personnalité

Civil law. Droit civil
Persons. Personnes
Natural persons. Personnes physiques
Civil status. Etat civil
Personality rights. Droits de la personnalité -- Continued
Name. Nom
Including registration of name, and works on protection of name
570 General
Family name. Nom de famille
572 General (Table K11)
Family name of legitimate children see KJV894+
Family name of illegitimate children see KJV899
573 Married and divorced woman's name. Nom de la femme mariée et nom de la divorcée (Table K11)
574 Change of name. Changement de nom (Table K11)
575 Pseudonyms. Pseudonymes (Table K11)
Title of nobility see KJV4091+
Dignity, honor, and reputation see KJV2090
Privacy see KJV2093+
Life, body, and health see KJV2026+
Nationality and citizenship see KJV373+
Family status see KJV608+
578 Domicile (Table K11)
Acts of civil status. Actes de l'état civil
Class here required records of facts comprising a person's civil status
579 General (Table K11)
580 Civil register. Registres de l'état civil (Table K11)
Including registration (acte de naissance), marriage (acte de mariage), and death (acte de déces), and family name
Cf. KJV527 Recording and registration
582 Action of civil status. Actions d'état civil (Table K11)
Juristic persons of private law. Personnes morales de droit privé
For business corporations see KJV2985+
For juristic persons of public law see KJV4897
584 General (Table K11)
Juristic personality. Legal capacity. Personnalité
585 General (Table K11)
587 Limited legal capacity (Table K11)
588 Personality rights. Droits de la personnalité (Table K11)

Civil law. Droit civil
Persons. Personnes
Juristic persons of private law. Personnes morales de droit privé -- Continued
589 Liability. Responsabilité (Table K11)
Including criminal and civil liability
Nationality. Nationalité
590 General (Table K11)
Nationality of juristic persons in private international law see KJV373+
Foreign companies see KJV1893+
Associations, companies, and foundations of public benefit. Etablissements d'utilité publique
594 General (Table K11)
596 Distinction of associations, companies, and foundations of public benefit from public institutions. Distinction des établissements d'utilité publique et des établissements publics
Juristic persons of mixed private and public character
600 General (Table K11)
Companies partly owned or controlled by government see KJV5592+
Domestic relations. Family law. La famille
608 History
609 Criticism. Reform
611-619 General (Table K9b)
Marriage. Husband and wife. Mariage. Les époux
622 Criticism. Reform
History
Including the history of civil marriage
623 General works
624 Marital power. Autorité maritale (Table K11)
Class here all aspects of husband's power over his wife
Cf. KJV673+ Legal status of married woman
626 Indissolubility of marriage. Indissolubilité du mariage
628 Secretly contracted marriages. Mariages clandestinement contractés
630 Marriages of dissenters. Mariages de dissidents
Including marriages of protestants
Criticism. Reform see KJV609
631-639 General (Table K9b)
Requirements for contracting a marriage. Impediments. Conditions de formation du mariage. Empêchements
642 General (Table K11)
Betrothal. Promise of marriage. Fiançailles. Promesse de mariage

Civil law. Droit civil
Persons. Personnes
Domestic relations. Family law. La famille
Marriage. Husband and wife. Mariage. Les époux
Requirements for contracting a marriage.
Impediments. Conditions de formation du mariage. Empêchements
Betrothal. Promise of marriage. Promise of marriage. Fiançailles. Promesse de mariage -- Continued
645 General (Table K11)
646 Breach of promise of marriage. Rupture de promesse de mariage (Table K11)
Including fraud
Nuptial capacity. Capacité nuptiale
Including marriage license (Certificat prénuptial)
649 General (Table K11)
650 Age (Table K11)
For marriage of minors or incapable majors see KJV860
651 Soldiers. Militaires (Table K11)
652 Aliens. Etrangers (Table K11)
Dissenters see KJV630
653 Prohibited degrees of consanguinity or affinity. Parenté ou alliance au degré prohibé (Table K11)
654 Exemptions. Dispenses (Table K11)
Mutual consent of spouses. Consentement des époux
655 General (Table K11)
Mentally ill and people with mental disabilities see KJV861
656 Simulated marriage. Mariage simulé (Table K11)
657 Posthumous marriage. Mariage posthume (Table K11)
Parental consent. Consent by the family. Consentement des parents. Consentement familial
658 General (Table K11)
Secretly contracted marriage see KJV628
Performance of marriage. Celebration du mariage
659 General
660 Publicity. Publicité
For register of marriages see KJV580
Secretly contracted marriages see KJV628
661 Marriage by proxy. Mariage par procuration (Table K11)

Civil law. Droit civil
Persons. Personnes
Domestic relations. Family law. La famille
Marriage. Husband and wife. Mariage. Les époux
Performance of marriage. Celebration du mariage -- Continued

661.2 Civil marriage and religious marriage. Le mariage civil et le mariage religieux (Table K11)

662 Deathbed marriages. Mariages en extremis (Table K11)

Cf. KJV657 Posthumous marriage

Quasi-matrimonial relationships. Concubinage. Union libre

663 General (Table K11)

Concubinage and conjugal domicile see KJV680

664 Liquidation and partition of concubinage property. Liquidation et partage des biens des concubins (Table K11)

Void and voidable marriages. Nullités du mariage. Annulation de mariage

For impediments see KJV642+

For dissolution of marriage (dissolution du mariage) see KJV811+

665 General (Table K11)

666 Putative marriage. Mariage putatif (Table K11)

668.A-Z Special topics, A-Z

Subarrange each by Table K12

Marriage bond. Droits et devoirs respectifs des époux

672 General (Table K11)

Legal status of married women. Statut juridique de la femme mariée

673 General (Table K11)

Marital power see KJV624

Name. Nom see KJV573

Choice of nationality (Option de nationalité) see KJV374.M4

Choice of profession of her own. Exercice de la profession séparée

676 General (Table K11)

677 Married businesswoman. Femme mariée commerçante (Table K11)

Married woman's power over her children see KJV918

Conjugal domicile. Domicile conjugal

679 General (Table K11)

680 Conjugal domicile and concubinage. Domicile conjugal et concubinage (Table K11)

Civil law. Droit civil
Persons. Personnes
Domestic relations. Family law. La famille
Marriage. Husband and wife. Mariage. Les époux -- Continued
Matrimonial property and regime. Régimes matrimoniaux

681 History
691-699 General (Table K9b)
Administration of spouse's property by other spouse
701 General (Table K11)
Administration of wife's property. Administration des biens de la femme mariée
702 General (Table K11)
703 Equitable conversion and reinvestment of wife's property by husband. Emploi et remploi (Table K11)
Including bonds and shares (Valeurs mobilières)
704 Wife's right of recompense from husband or community property. Droit de reprise de la femme sur les biens du mari ou de la communauté (Table K11)
704.5 Wife's statutory mortgage on husband's property. Hypothèque légale de la femme mariée (Table K11)
Antenuptial contracts. Contrats de mariage
Class here works on both conventional community property and other types of antenuptial contracts
History
705 General
706.A-Z Special topics, A-Z
711-715.8 General (Table K10)
718 Immutability of antenuptial contracts. Immutabilité des conventions matrimoniales
Systems of community property. Régimes communautaires
722 History
731-735.8 General (Table K10)
Statutory system of community property. Régime de la communauté légale
744 General (Table K11)
745 Equality of husband and wife. Egalité des époux (Table K11)
745.5 Propre mobilier (Table K11)
Conventional community property. Communauté conventionnelle
746 General (Table K11)

Civil law. Droit civil
Persons. Personnes
Domestic relations. Family law. La famille
Marriage. Husband and wife. Mariage. Les époux
Matrimonial property and regime. Régimes matrimoniaux
Systems of community property. Régimes communautaires
Conventional community property. Communauté conventionnelle -- Continued

747 Community of personality and acquêts. Communauté de meubles et acquêts

Community reduced to acquêts. Communauté réduite aux acquêts see KJV800

748 General community property. Communauté universelle

Separate property of either spouse in systems of community property. Propre

749 General (Table K11)

750.A-Z Special topics, A-Z

Subarrange each by Table K12

Administration of wife's property see KJV702+

Fonds de commerce see KJV804.F65

Gratuities between husband and wife see KJV1471

750.I58 Intellectual property. Propriété intellectuelle (Table K12)

Life annuity see KJV1294.L54

750.S46 Separate earnings of either spouse. Wife's personal belongings. Biens réservés. Biens personnels (Table K12)

Wife's right of recompense from husband or community property see KJV704

Liquidation, renunciation, and partition of community property. Liquidation, renonciation et partage de communauté conjugale

751 General (Table K11)

Judicial separation of property see KJV774

System of separation of property. Régimes de séparation de biens

770 General (Table K11)

771 Joint expenditures. Joint debts. Dépenses communes. Dettes communes

Including housekeeping expenditures (Dépenses de ménage)

771.3 Wife's separate property exclusive of dowry. Biens paraphernaux

Civil law. Droit civil
Persons. Personnes
Domestic relations. Family law. La famille
Marriage. Husband and wife. Mariage. Les époux
Matrimonial property and regime. Régimes matrimoniaux
System of separation of property. Régimes de séparation de biens -- Continued
Conventional separation of property. Séparation de biens contractuelle
772 General (Table K11)
773 Dissolution of conventional separation of property. Dissolution de la séparation de biens contractuelle (Table K11)
774 Judicial separation of property. Séparation de biens judiciaire (Table K11)
Dotal system. Régime dotal
780 General (Table K11)
Wife's separate property exclusive of dowry see KJV771.3
791 Inalienability of dowry. Inaliénabilité de la dot (Table K11)
792 Wife's liability regarding contracts. Responsabilité de la femme dotale de l'occasion d'un contrat (Table K11)
800 System of sharing in acquêts. Régime de participation aux acquêts
Contracts between husband and wife. Conventions entre époux
For antenuptial contracts see KJV705+
801 General (Table K11)
801.3 Contract of employment. Contrat de travail (Table K11)
Associations and companies between husband and wife. Associations et sociétés entre époux
802 General (Table K11)
803 Commercial companies. Sociétés commerciales (Table K11)
Including family companies (Sociétés de famille)
For fonds de commerce in matrimonial property relationships see KJV804.F65
804.A-Z Special topics, A-Z
Subarrange each by Table K12

Civil law. Droit civil
Persons. Personnes
Domestic relations. Family law. La famille
Marriage. Husband and wife. Mariage. Les époux
Matrimonial property and regime. Régimes matrimoniaux
Special topics, A-Z -- Continued

804.B35 Bankruptcy. Faillite et banqueroute
Including insolvency of either spouse and its effect on other spouse's rights and duties, and including Benefice d'émolument (wife's liability limited to a community property)

Equitable conversion and reinvestment of wife's property see KJV703

804.F65 Fonds de commerce on stock in trade or on business concerns exclusive of real property

Life insurance between spouses see KJV2887

804.P47 Personal property. Meubles

804.P76 Proceeds of husband's and wife's work. Produits du travail des époux

804.R43 Real property. Immeubles
Including leases affecting wife's real property

Dissolution and disintegration of marriage

811-K819 General (Table K9b)

Divorce
Including both divorce and adultery

831 General (Table K11)

834.A-Z Special topics, A-Z
Subarrange each by Table K12

Separation

840 General (Table K11)

851 Separation from bed and board. Séparation de corps (Table K11)

852 De facto separation. Séparation de fait

Separate maintenance see KJV933+

Rights of surviving spouse. Droits de l'époux survivant

855 General (Table K11)

856.A-Z Special topics, A-Z
Subarrange each by Table K12

856.D68 Dower. Douaire

860 Marriages of minors. Married minors. Mariages des mineurs. Epoux mineurs (Table K11)
For parental consent and consent by the family see KJV658+

861 Marriages of incapable majors. Mariages des incapables majeurs (Table K11)

Civil law. Droit civil
Persons. Personnes
Domestic relations. Family law. La famille
Marriage. Husband and wife. Mariage. Les époux -- Continued
Criminal aspects of marriage. Adultery. Bigamy see KJV8238

865 Same-sex marriage. Mariage des homosexuels (Table K11)
Including quasi-marital relationships

Consanguinity and affinity. Parenté

870 General (Table K11)

Parent and child. Filiation. Rapports entre les parents et les enfants
Including parental liability toward third persons

881-889 General (Table K9b)

Legitimacy. Filiation légitime
Including works on legitimation

894 General (Table K11)

Determination of legitimacy. Determination de la filiation légitime

895 General (Table K11)

896 Action for a status of a legitimate child. Action en réclamation d'état (Table K11)
Including disclaiming paternity (Désaveu de paternité)

897.A-Z Special topics, A-Z
Subarrange each by Table K12

Adoptive legitimation see KJV910+

897.C45 Children of divorced or separated parents. Les enfants de parents divorcées ou separés (Table K12)

Legitimation of children born in adultery or of incest see KJV900

Legitimation as a matter of accommodation see KJV904

Illegitimacy. Filiation naturelle

898 General (Table K11)

899 Legal status of illegitimate child (Table K11)
Including capacity and disability of illegitimate children in old French law

900 Children born in adultery, or incest. Enfants adultérins (Table K11)
Including legitimation incestueuse

Affiliation. Etablissement de la filiation naturelle

901 General (Table K11)

Civil law. Droit civil
Persons. Personnes
Domestic relations. Family law. La famille
Consanguinity and affinity. Parenté
Parent and child. Filiation. Rapports entre les parents et les enfants
Illegitimacy. Filiation naturelle
Affiliation. Etablissement de la filiation naturelle -- Continued
Acknowledgment of illegitimate children. Reconnaissance volontaire de la filiation naturelle

903 General (Table K11)
904 Accommodation acknowledgements and accommodation legitimation of children et legimations (Table K11)

Affiliation proceedings. Judicial establishment of parentage. Recherché de la maternité et la paternité naturelles. Reconnaissance judiciaire de la maternité et de la paternité naturelles

905 General (Table K11)
906 Proof of natural parentage. Preuve de la filiation naturelle (Table K11)

Succession rights of affiliated children see KJV1400+

Adoption. Adoptive filiation. Filiation adoptive
Including procedures

910 General (Table K11)
912 Adoptive legitimation. Légitimation adoptive (Table K11)

Parental power. Autorité parentale

917 General (Table K11)
918 Married woman's power over her children. Droits de la femme mariée sur la personne des enfants (Table K11)

Choice of religion see KJV975

919 Custody. Garde (Table K11)
920 Parental power of punishment. Correction paternelle (Table K11)
921 Visiting rights. Droits de visite (Table K11)
Including children of divorced or separated parents

Parental consent for marriage see KJV658+
Parental administration of child's property see KJV952

922 Employment relations between parents and children. Relations de travail entre les parents et les enfants (Table K11)

Civil law. Droit civil
Persons. Personnes
Domestic relations. Family law. La famille
Consanguinity and affinity. Parenté
Parent and child. Filiation. Rapports entre les parents et les enfants
Parental power. Autorité parentale -- Continued
Parental obligation for support and education of children see KJV931+
925 Parental liability. Responsabilité des parents (Table K11)
Including works on both civil and criminal liability
926 Judicial control of parental power. Controle judiciaire de la puissance parentale (Table K11)
927 Loss of parental power and of right of custody. La déchéance de la puissance parentale et la privation du droit de garde (Table K11)
Obligation of support. Obligation alimentaire
931 General (Table K11)
Desertion and non-support see KJV8237
Alimony. Pensions alimentaires
Including separate maintenance
933 General (Table K11)
935 Inalienability of alimony. Incessibilité de la pension alimentaire (Table K11)
936 Actions for support. Actions alimentaires (Table K11)
937.A-Z Special topics, A-Z
Subarrange each by Table K12
937.S63 Social security. Sécurité sociale (Table K12)
939 Domestic relations courts and procedure. Juridictions familiales (Table K11)
Protection of incapables. Protection des incapables
941-945.8 General (Table K10)
947 Liability. Responsabilité (Table K11)
Including liability of incapables, their curators, counsels, and of property administrators
For parental liability see KJV925
952 Property management. Administration légale (Table K11)
953 Minors. Mineurs
Tutorship. Tutelle
Class here protection of unemancipated minors or interdicted insane persons
961-965.8 General (Table K10)
972 Family council. Conseil de famille (Table K11)
973 De facto tutorship. Tutelle de fait (Table K11)
Unemancipated minors. Mineurs non émancipés

Civil law. Droit civil
Persons. Personnes
Protection of incapables. protection des incapables
Tutorship. Tutelle
Unemancipated minors. Mineurs non émancipés -- Continued
974 General (Table K11)
Homeless children as wards of public assistance see KJV3632
975 Choice of religion. Option religieuse (Table K11)
Juvenile courts see KJV3635
976 Interdiction (Table K11)
Including provisional administration over interdicted insane persons' property
Curatorship. Curatelle
985 General (Table K11)
986 Emancipated minors. Mineurs émancipés (Table K11)
Including emancipation
Incapable majors. Incapables majeurs
Cf. KJV565 Majority
987 General (Table K11)
988 The sick. Les malades (Table K11)
Including both curatorship over the sick, and social or medical legislation on the sick
Cf. KJV5314+ Public health
Cf. KJV5336 Medical law
Mentally ill and people with mental disabilities. Malades mentaux et faibles d'esprit
Including social or medical legislation on the mentally ill and people with mental disabilities
995 General (Table K11)
1000 Provisional administrators. Administrateur provisoire (Table K11)
1001 Institutional care. Internement (Table K11)
Including provisional administration of property of interned persons
Interdiction see KJV976
1002 Non-interdicted mentally ill or people with mental disabilities. Malades mentaux non interdits (Table K11)
Including provisional administration of their property
1003 Liability of mentally ill or people with mental disabilities and their guardians. Responsabilité des malades mentaux et de leur gardiens (Table K11)
For criminal liability see KJV8043

Civil law. Droit civil
Persons. Personnes -- Continued
1010 Judicial counsel and curator of prodigals. Conseil judiciaire et curateur des prodigues (Table K11)
Property. Biens
1099 History
1101-1109 General (Table K9b)
Patrimony. Patrimoine
Class here works on a person's assets, liabilities and rights appreciable in money (droits patrimoniaux)
1112 General (Table K11)
1113 Usufruct of patrimony. Usufruit d'un patrimoine (Table K11)
1114 Act conservatoire (Table K11)
Ownership and possession. Propriété et possession
Class here works on both ownership and possession of real property, and of personal property
1117 General (Table K11)
Ownership. Propriété
Class here works on ownership of personal property, and on ownership of both personal property and real property
History see KJV1099+
1121-1129 General (Table K9b)
1130.3 Private and public property. Propriété privée et propriété publique (Table K11)
Right of ownership. Droit de propriété
Class here works on protection of ownership (garanties de la propriété), proof of ownership (preuve du droit de propriété) and non-contractual loss of ownership (perte de la propriété)
1131 General (Table K11)
1133 Recovery of property by the owner. Revendication (Table K11)
Including the owner's actions for recovery of property
Disappearance of a thing. Disparition de la chose
1134 General (Table K11)
1135 Substituted property (Table K11)
Co-ownership. Copropriété
For works on co-ownership of real property see KJV1236+
1137 General (Table K11)
Syndic see KJV3001
Community property see KJV722+
1139-1141.2 Liquidation and partition. Liquidation et partage
Including works on both liquidation of co-ownership and partition of indivisum

Civil law. Droit civil
Property. Biens
Ownership and possession. Propriété et possession
Ownership. Propriété
Co-ownership. Copropriété
Liquidation and partition. Liquidation et partage -- Continued
1139 General (Table K11)
1141 Lésion (Table K11)
Court-ordered licitation see KJV3990
1143 Collective ownership. Propriété collective (Table K11)
Including works on collective ownership of personal and real property
Acquisition and transfer of ownership. Acquisition et transfert de la proprieté
Including both the acquisition (or transfer) of real property and of personal property
Cf. KJV1238+ Acquisition and transfer of real property ownership
1145 General (Table K11)
Sale and exchange see KJV1791+
Gifts inter vivos see KJV1488
Inheritance and succession see KJV1310+
1154 Accessions (Table K11)
Including both the accession to real property (accession au profit d'un immeuble) and the accession to personal property (accession au profit d'un meuble)
Cf. KJV1247+ Accession to real property
Possession
Including works on possession of both real property and personal property
1160 General (Table K11)
Indivisum see KJV1165+
Acquisition of ownership by possession. Acquisition de la propriété par la possession
Including possession as a proof of ownership
1161 General (Table K11)
1162 Adverse possession. Prescription acquisitive (Table K11)
1163 Occupancy. Occupation (Table K11)
Indivisum. Partage
1165 General (Table K11)
Partition. Partage
For liquidation of co-ownership and partition of indivisum see KJV1139+
1166 General (Table K11)

Civil law. Droit civil
Property. Biens
Ownership and possession. Propriété et possession
Indivisum. Indivision
Partition. Pargage
Court ordered licitation see KJV3990
Rights in rem upon another's property. Démembrements de la propriété
For rights in rem upon another's real property see KJV1271+
1170 General (Table K11)
Usufruct. Use. Habitation. Usufruit. Usage. Habitation
Including usufruct of both real property and personal property
For both usufruct and servitudes see KJV1271+
1171 General (Table K11)
1172 Consolidation (Table K11)
Repairs of building incumbent upon the usufructuary see KJV1237.R46
Rights in rem upon debtor's property see KJV2130+
Real property. Immeubles
History
Cf. KJV5690+ Agricultural law
1174 General works
Feudal tenure. Tenure féodale. Fief
Cf. KJV4094+ Constitutional history
1177 General works
1180 Livery of seisin. Saisine
For seisin of heirs-by-law see KJV1384
Copyhold. Censive
1182 General works
1185 Roture. Villenage
Offices ministériels see KJV5022+
1191-1195.8 General (Table K10)
Real property by nature. Immeubles par nature
1202 General (Table K11)
1203 Edifices (Table K11)
1204 Real property by destination. Immeubles par destination (Table K11)
Real property by its object. Immeubles par l'objet auquel ils s'appliquent
1205 General (Table K11)
Usufruct see KJV1171+
Servitudes see KJV1277+
Entail see KJV1359

Civil law. Droit civil
Property. Biens
Real property. Immeubles -- Continued
Real property by declaration. Immeubles par déclaration
Class here works on incorporeal things, being real property by declaration of their owner
1205.5 General (Table K11)
Shares of stock of the Bank of France see KJV2433+
State bonds see KJV6528
1206.A-Z Special topics, A-Z
Aliens' real property. Propriété immobilière des étrangères see KJV383.A44
1206.S34 Second homes. Résidences secondaires (Table K12)
1206.U73 Urban real property. Immeubles urbains (Table K12)
Rights in rem upon real property see KJV1271+
Ownership and possession. Land tenure. Propriété et possession. Régime foncier
1208 History
Including propres réels et acquêts réels
1211-1219 General (Table K9b)
Public and private restraints on real property
1226 General works
Entailed estate see KJV1359
Farmland ownership and possession. Farmland tenure see KJV5692+
Rights incident to ownership of land. Régime du sol
1227 General (Table K11)
Adjoining landowners. Propriétaires voisins
1228 General (Table K11)
Boundary and inclosure. Bornage et clôture
1229 General (Table K11)
1230 Party walls. Mitoyenneté (Table K11)
1230.3 Murs privatifs (Table K11)
1231 Building across boundaries. Construction empiétant sur le terrain voisin (Table K11)
1231.5 Riparian rights (Table K11)
Cf. KJV5166 Public property
Commonage and pasture see KJV5694
Consolidation of rural land holdings see KJV5696
Emphyteusis see KJV5713
Property above and below surface. Buildings. Propriété dessus et du dessous. Bâtiments
1232 General (Table K11)
Superficies. Buildings erected upon another's land. Constructions élevées sur le terrain d'autrui
Cf. KJV1271+ Encumbrances
1235 General (Table K11)

Civil law. Droit civil
Property. Biens
Real property. Immeubles
Ownership and possession. Land tenure. Propriété et possession. Régime foncier
Property above and below surface. Buildings. Propriété dessus et du dessous. Bâtiments
Superfices. Buildings erected upon another's land. Constructions élevées sur le terrain d'autrui
Telecommunication lines see KJV6300+
Mines and quarries see KJV5832+
Co-ownership. Copropriété
1236 General (Table K11)
1236.3 Building partnerships. Condominium. Horizontal property. Copropriété des immeubles divisés par étage ou par appartements (Table K11)
Including buildings under construction
1237.A-Z Special topics, A-Z
Subarrange each by Table K12
1237.R46 Repair, Keeping in. Réparation d'entretien (Table K12)
Acquisition and transfer of real property. Acquisition et transfert de la propriété immobiliere
1238 General (Table K11)
1239 Title deeds. Certificat du propriété (Table K11)
Cf. KJV1283+ Land registry
Sale and exchange of real property. La vente et l'échange de biens immobiliers
Including actions pertaining to vendors and purchasers
For sale and exchange of real property and of personal property see KJV1791+
1241 General (Table K11)
1243 Judicial sales of real property. Ventes judiciaires d'immeubles
Including actions in resolution of sales of real property
1246 Exchange of real property. Echange de biens immobiliers (Table K11)
Acquisitive prescription see KJV1254
Accession to real property. Accession au profit d'un immeuble
1247 General (Table K11)
1248 Natural accession. Accession naturelle (Table K11)
Including alluvium and accessions
Artificial accession. Accession artificielle
1249 General (Table K11)

Civil law. Droit civil
Property. Biens
Real property. Immeubles
Ownership and possession. Land tenure. Propriété et possession. Régime foncier
Acquisition and transfer of real property. Acquisition et transfert de la propriété immobiliere
Accession to real property. Accession au profit d'un immeuble
Artificial accession. Accession artificielle -- Continued

1249.3.A-Z Special topics, A-Z
Subarrange each by Table K12
Building across boundaries see KJV1231

Possession
For both possession of real property and of personal property see KJV1160+

1252 General (Table K11)

1254 Adverse possession. Prescription acquisitive (Table K11)

Possessory actions. Action or writ of ejectment. Actions possessoires. Réintégrande

1256 General (Table K11)

1257 Complainte. Possessory action after one year of possession (Table K11)

1258 Action against disturbance of possession. Dénonciation de nouvel oeuvre (Table K11)

1260 Proof of ownership. Recovery of property by the owner. Preuve du droit de propriété. Revendication (Table K11)
For land registry see KJV1283+

Encumbrances. Démembrements de la propriété immobilière
Including right in rem upon real property in general

1271-1275.8 General (Table K10)

Usufruct. Use. Habitation see KJV1171+

Servitudes
Including both servitudes in private law and servitudes in public law

1277 General (Table K11)

Personal servitudes see KJV1171+

Real servitudes. Servitudes réelles

1278 General (Table K11)

1279 Right of way. Droit de passage (Table K11)

1280.A-Z Special topics, A-Z
Subarrange each by Table K12
Aerial servitudes see KJV6302

Civil law. Droit civil
Property. Biens
Real property. Immeubles
Encumbrances. Démembrements de la proprieté immobilière
Servitudes
Special topics, A-Z -- Continued
Servitudes concerning roads and waterways see KJV5130
Servitudes for public interest see KJV5129+
1280.S73 Statutory servitudes. Servitudes légales (Table K12)
Concession immobilière
Class here long-term lease of urban property
1281 General (Table K11)
Lease of land for erection of building. Bail à construction see KJV1235+
Rights in rem upon debtor's real property see KJV2130+
Land register. Registration of rights upon real property. Publicité fonciere
1283 General (Table K11)
Registration of charges upon real property. Transcription hypothecaire
1284 General (Table K11)
Registration of privileges on real property see KJV2165
1285 Mortgage registration. Inscription hypothecaire (Table K11)
1287 Cadastral survey. Cadastre (Table K11)
Personal property. Meubles
Including tangible property
1290 General (Table K11)
1294.A-Z Special topics, A-Z
Subarrange each by Table K12
1294.A66 Annuities. Rentes (Table K12)
1294.B85 Building materials. Materiaux de construction (Table K12)
Choses in action see KJV1529+
Fonds de commerce see KJV2241+
1294.F86 Fungibles. Choses fongibles (Table K12)
Intellectual property see KJV3248+
1294.L54 Life annuity. Rente viagère (Table K12)
1294.P47 Personal property by anticipation. Quasi-personality. Meubles par anticipation (Table K12)

Civil law. Droit civil
Property. Biens
Personal property. Meubles
Special topics, A-Z -- Continued
1294.P48 Personal property of historic or artistic interest. Meubles presentant un intérêt historique ou artistique (Table K12)
1294.R45 Registered personal property. Meubles immatricules (Table K12)
1294.R46 Rentes foncières (Table K12)
Rights in rem upon debtor's personal property see KJV2134
Securities see KJV2371+
Succession upon death. Successions
1310 History
1321-1329 General (Table K9b)
Capacity and disability to inherit. Qualités requises pour succéder
For both capacity (or disability) to inherit and capacity (or disability) to receive gifts inter vivos or mortis causa see KJV1480+
1333 General (Table K11)
1335 Unworthiness. Indignité (Civil penalty) (Table K11)
1337.A-Z Particular types of persons, A-Z
1337.A65 Aliens. Etrangers
1337.M56 Minors. Mineurs
Testamentary succession. Wills. Succession testamentaire. Testaments
For testamentary succession of a class of heirs, see the class
For both wills and gifts inter vivos or mortis causa see KJV1461+
1340 General (Table K11)
1341 Capacity to make a will. Freedom of testation. Capacité du testateur. Liberté de tester (Table K11)
Forms of wills
1342 General (Table K11)
1343 Holographic wills. Testaments olographes (Table K11)
1344 Notarial wills. Testaments notariés (Table K11)
1345 Mystic wills. Testaments mystiques (Table K11)
Privileged wills. Testaments privilégiés
1346 General (Table K11)
1347 Military wills. Testaments aux armées (Table K11)
1348 Maritime wills. Testaments au cours d'un voyage en mer (Table K11)
1349 Codicil. Codicille (Table K11)
1350 Wills made in foreign countries (Table K11)

Civil law. Droit civil
Succession upon death. Successions
Testamentary succession. Wills. Succession testamentaire. Testaments -- Continued

1351 Effectiveness of a lost or fraudulently destroyed will. Efficacité du testament perdu ou frauduleusement detruit (Table K11)

Testamentary dispositions. Legacies. Dispositions testamentaires. Legs

1352 General (Table K11)

1354 Residuary legacies. Legacies by universal title. Legs à titre universel (Table K11)

Prohibited legacies. Legs interdits

1356 General (Table K11)

Appointment of a reversionary heir see KJV1359

Revocation and nullity of gifts and legacies see KJV1498

Legatees' security. Sûrétés des légataires

1356.2 General (Table K11)

Separation of patrimonies see KJV1418

1356.3 Legatee's mortgage. Hypothèque du légataire (Table K11)

Legitime and disposable portion of an estate see KJV1372+

1359 Substitution of heirs. Entail. Entailed estate. Substitution d'heritiers. Majorat (Table K11)

Charitable bequests. Legs de charité

1360 General (Table K11)

1361 Bequest for the benefit of the poor. Legs en faveur des pauvres (Table K11)

1362 Disinheritance. Exhérédation (Table K11)

1363 Testamentary execution. Exécution testamentaire

1364 Lapse and revocation of legacies. Caducité et revocation des legs

Acceptance and renunciation of inheritance see KJV1405+

Relations among heirs see KJV1416+

Probate law. Ouverture et vérification des testaments

For both probate law and administration of estates see KJV1420+

1370 General (Table K11)

1371 Probate courts. Tribunaux en matière testamentaire (Table K11)

Including procedure

Civil law. Droit civil
Succession upon death. Successions -- Continued
Legitime and disposable portion of an estate. Réserve héréditaire et biens disponibles
Including freedom of testation
For both disposable portion of an estate and abatement of gifts and legacies see KJV1428+
1372 General (Table K11)
Legitime in kind. Réserve en nature
1374 General (Table K11)
Attribution integrale see KJV1433+
Disposable portion of estate between husband and wife see KJV1486
1376 Cumulation of a legitime and a disposable portion of an estate. Cumul de la réserve et de la portion disponible (Table K11)
Estates of deceased soldiers. Successions de militaires décédés
1376.3 General (Table K11)
Military wills see KJV1347
Inheritance of farms. Rural succession upon death see KJV5702+
1377 Intestate succession. Succession intestate (Table K11)
1380 Contracts of inheritance. Successions contractuelles (Table K11)
Order of succession. Classes of heirs. Ordre successif. Ordres d'héritiers
1381 General (Table K11)
Heirs by law. Regular successors. Héritiers légitimes. Successeurs légitimes
1383 General (Table K11)
1384 Seisin of heirs by law. Saisine héréditaire (Table K11)
Descendants
Including their legitime (réserve héréditaire)
1385 General (Table K11)
Principle of equality of descendants of the same degree and class. Principe du partage égal
1387 General (Table K11)
Attribution integrale see KJV1433+
Succession by right of representation see KJV1404.R46
Legitimate descendants. Descendants légitimes
1388 General (Table K11)
1388.5 Birthright. Droit d'ainesse (Table K11)
1389 Legitimate children. Enfants légitimes (Table K11)
Illegitimate descendants see KJV1398+

Civil law. Droit civil
Succession upon death. Successions
Order of succession. Classes of heirs. Ordre successif. Ordres d'héritiers
Heirs by law. Regular successors. Héritiers légitimes. Successeurs légitimes
Ascendants
Including works on their legitime (réserve héréditaire)
1390 General (Table K11)
1391 Mothers. Mères (Table K11)
Natural parents see KJV1401
Collaterals. Collatéraux
Including works on their legitime (réserve héréditaire)
1392 General (Table K11)
1393.A-Z Special topics, A-Z
Subarrange each by Table K12
Succession by right of representation see KJV1404.R46
Surviving spouse see KJV1403+
Irregular successors. Successeurs irreguliers
1394 General (Table K11)
Illegitimate children see KJV1400+
Surviving spouse see KJV1403+
1396 The state. Escheat. Etat (Table K11)
Cf. KJV1442 Administration of estates in abeyance
1397.A-Z Special topics, A-Z
Subarrange each by Table K12
1397.W75 Writ of possession. Envoi en possession (Table K12)
Natural heirs. Héritiers naturels
Including works on their legitime (réserve héréditaire)
1398 General (Table K11)
Natural children. Enfants naturels
1400 General (Table K11)
Principle of equality of descendants of the same degree and class see KJV1387
1401 Natural parents. Parents naturels (Table K11)
1402.A-Z Special topics, A-Z
Subarrange each by Table K12
Seisin of heirs by law see KJV1384
Writ of possession see KJV1397.W75
Surviving spouse. Epoux survivant
Including works on his or her legitime (réserve héréditaire)
Cf. KJV855+ Right of surviving spouse
1403 General (Table K11)
Writ of possession see KJV1397.W75
Seisin of heirs by law see KJV1384

Civil law. Droit civil
Succession upon death. Successions
Order of succession. Classes of heirs. Ordre successif. Ordres d'héritiers -- Continued

1404.A-Z Special topics, A-Z
Subarrange each by Table K12
1404.R46 Representation, Succession by right of. Répresentation successorale (Table K12)

Acceptance and renunciation of inheritance. Acceptation et renonciation de la succession. Option
Including legacies
1405 General (Table K11)
Contracts of inheritance see KJV1380
Acceptance pure and simple
1407 General (Table K11)
1408 Forced acceptance as result of fraudulent concealment. Acceptation forcée résultant du recel (Table K11)
Acceptance with the benefit of inventory. Acceptation sous benéfice d'inventaire
1409 General (Table K11)
1410 Separation of patrimonies. Séparation des patrimoines (Table K11)
For separation of patrimonies related to inheritance in indivisum see KJV1417+
1411 Renunciation. Renonciation (Table K11)

Creditors of the deceased. Liabilities of the estate. Créanciers du défunt. Passif des successions
Including third parties
1412 General (Table K11)
Gross estate of succession see KJV1420+
1413.A-Z Special topics, A-Z
Subarrange each by Table K12
Advances of reimbursements due to co-heirs see KJV1427+
Assignment of inheritance rights see KJV1440+
1413.C53 Claim (title) to an inheritance held by a third party. Pétition d'héredité (Table K12)
1413.E97 Expenses of the last sickness. Frais de dernière maladie (Table K12)
1413.F86 Funeral expenses. Frais funéraires (Table K12)
Heir apparent see KJV1413.C53
Liabilities of the estate and acceptance pure and simple see KJV1407+
Liabilities of the estate and acceptance with the benefit of inventory see KJV1409+
1413.N87 Nursing expenses, Privilege of. Privilege des nourrices (Table K12)

Civil law. Droit civil
Succession upon death. Successions
Creditors of the deceased. Liabilities of the estate. Créanciers du défunt. Passif des successions
Special topics, A-Z -- Continued
Separation of patrimonies see KJV1410
Relations among heirs. Rapports des successeurs entre eux
1416 General (Table K11)
Inheritance in indivisum. Indivision héréditaire
1417 General (Table K11)
1418 Separation of patrimonies. Séparation des patrimoines (Table K11)
Inheritance of personality rights
1419 General (Table K11)
Inheritance of partner's rights see KJV3034
Gross estate of succession. Masse successorale
Including administration and liquidation of estates
For probate law see KJV1370+
1420 General (Table K11)
1425 Estates of foreign decedents (Table K11)
Testamentary executor see KJV1363
Indivisum see KJV1165+
Liabilities of the estate see KJV1412+
Property given (received) in advance of future inheritance. Advances of reimbursements due to co-heir. Avancement d'hoire. Prélevements
1427 General (Table K11)
Abatement of gifts and legacies. Reduction de dons et legs
1428 General (Table K11)
Cumulation of a legitime and disposable portion of inheritance see KJV1376
1429 Collation. Rapport à masse successorale
Partition of estates. Partage des successions
Including partition of inheritance in indivisum
1430 General (Table K11)
Principle of equal shares see KJV1387
Partition by an ascendant see KJV1437
Forms of partition. Formes du partage
1431 General (Table K11)
1432 Partition by court. Partage judiciaire (Table K11)
Attribution integrale. Attribution préférentielle
Class here exceptions to the principle of equal shares
1433 General (Table K11)
1434.A-Z Particular, A-Z
Subarrange each by Table K12

Civil law. Droit civil
Succession upon death. Successions
Gross estate of succession. Masse successorale
Partition of estates. Partage des successions
Forms of partition. Formes du partage
Attribution integrale. Attribution préférentielle
Particular, A- -- Continued
Business concerns see KJV1434.B87
1434.B87 Business enterprise. Entreprise commerciale ou industrielle. Fonds de commerce (Table K12)
1434.D94 Dwelling, Inexpensive. Habitations à bon marché (Table K12)
Family farm see KJV5704
1434.H45 Heirlooms. Souvenirs de famille (Table K12)
1437 Partition by an ascendant. Self-liquidation of an estate. Partage d'ascendant
Assignment of inheritance rights. Cession des droits successifs
1440 General (Table K11)
1441 Retrait successoral. Retrait lignager (Table K11)
Class here works on taking back of a family property by ancestor in case of its alienation by descendant and reimbursement of the buyer
1442 Administration of estates in abeyance. Administration des successions vacantes (Table K11)
Including court procedure (Tribunaux des successions)
For probate courts see KJV1371
Civil penalty. Pénalité civile
1448 General (Table K11)
Unworthiness see KJV1335
Forced acceptance as a result of fraudulent conversion see KJV1408
Estate and inheritance tax see KJV6924+
Gratuities. Libéralités
1461-1465.8 General (Table K10)
1466 Consideration. Cause (Table K11)
Charitable gratuities. Liberalités pieuses
1467 General (Table K11)
Charitable bequests see KJV1360+
Foundations. Fondations
1468 General (Table K11)
Foundations of public benefit see KJV594+
1469 Disguised gifts. Donations déguisées. Simulations (Table K11)
Including renunciation
1471 Gratuities with charges and conditions. Charges et conditions des liberalités (Table K11)

Civil law. Droit civil
Gratuities. Libéralités -- Continued
1473 Remunerative gifts. Donations rémunératoires (Table K11)
1474 Gifts of future property. Donations de biens a venir (Table K11)
Including gifts of future property by antenuptial contract and gifts of future property between husband and wife
1476 Capacity to make a gratuitous disposition or to receive it. Capacité de disposer et de recevoir à titre gratuit (Table K11)
Including both capacity to receive gratuitous dispositions, and capacity to inherit
Gifts inter vivos. Donations entre vifs
1480 General (Table K11)
1482 Manual gifts. Dons manuels (Table K11)
Including manual gifts mortis causa
Gifts by antenuptial contracts. Donations par contrats de mariage
1484 General (Table K11)
Gift of future property by an antenuptial contract see KJV1474
Gifts between husband and wife. Donations entre époux
Including mutual and reciprocal gratuities and gifts
For gifts of future property see KJV1474
1485 General (Table K11)
1486 Disposable portion of estate. Quotité disponible entre époux (Table K11)
1488 Usufruct and life annuity. Usufruit et rente viagère (Table K11)
For usufruct of patrimony see KJV1113
For life annuities see KJV1294.L54
1491 Gifts causa mortis. Donations à cause de mort (Table K11)
1496 Acceptance of gifts. Acceptation des dons (Table K11)
Including acceptance and legacies in favor of incapables
For acceptance of legacies see KJV1405+
1498 Revocation and nullity of gifts and legacies. Revocation et nullité des donations et legs (Table K11)
Including ingratitude, unworthiness, simulation, etc.
For nullity of gifts and legacies because of incapacity see KJV1476
Choses in action. Créances. Obligations
1529 History
1531-1539 General (Table K9b)
Sources of obligations. Les sources des obligations
1543 General (Table K11)
1544 Autonomy. Autonomie de la volonté (Table K11)
Including liberty of contract (liberté contractuelle)

Civil law. Droit civil
Choses in action. Créances. Obligations
Sources of obligations. Les sources des obligations -- Continued
Voluntary sources. Consideration. Sources volontaires. Cause
1545 General (Table K11)
Contracts see KJV1668+
Unilateral engagement. L'engagement unilatéral
1545.2 General (Table K11)
1546.A-Z Particular, A-Z
Subarrange each by Table K11
Stipulation for a third party see KJV1604
1548 Involuntary sources. Sources non volontaires (Table K11)
For quasi-contracts see KJV1978+
For quasi-delicts see KJV2019+
Types of obligations
1549 Civil and natural obligations. Obligations civiles ou naturelles (Table K11)
Obligations to give. Obligations de donner
1550 General (Table K11)
1550.2 Obligations in kind. Obligations de donner des choses de genre (Table K11)
Money obligations. Obligations pécuniaires
1551 General (Table K11)
Payment of money debts. Tender. Paiement des dettes de sommes d'argent. Offres réeles
1552 General (Table K11)
Monetary clauses. Clauses monétaires
1553 General (Table K11)
1553.2 Gold clause. La clause-or (Table K11)
Valuta clause see KJV1554.2
1553.3 Index adjustment clauses. Clauses d'indexation (Table K11)
Cf. KJV5575+ Price control
Payment in foreign currency. Paiement en monnaie étrangère
For works on foreign exchange regulations see KJV6510+
1554 General (Table K11)
1554.2 Valuta clause. La clause de paiement en monnaie étrangère (Table K11)
1555 Revalorization of debts. Revalorisation des dettes
Interest. Intéret
1556 General (Table K11)
Usury see KJV8260

Civil law. Droit civil
Choses in action. Créances. Obligations
Types of obligations -- Continued
1557 Obligation to do or refrain from doing. Obligations de faire ou de ne pas faire (Table K11)
Including pertinent actions
1560 Divisible and indivisible obligations. Obligations divisibles et indivisibles (Table K11)
1561 Positive obligations. Obligations positives (Table K11)
For obligations to give see KJV1550+
For obligations to do see KJV1557
Negative obligations see KJV1557
1562 Obligations de résultat et les obligations de moyens (Table K11)
1563 Obligations patrimoniales ou extra-patrimoniales (Table K11)
Obligations rélles see KJV2130+
Plural obligations. Obligations plurales
1564 General (Table K11)
1565 Obligations with a multiple object. Obligations à objet complexe (Table K11)
Including conjunctive obligations, alternative obligations, and facultative obligations
Correality and solidarity see KJV1576+
Conditional obligations see KJV512+
1567 Statutory obligations. Obligations legislatives (Table K11)
Creditor and debtor. Créancier et débiteur
1571-1575.8 General (Table K10)
Correality and solidarity. Obligations à sujets complexes
1576 General (Table K11)
Obligations conjointes
Including the obligation with several creditors of equal part of the claim, and the obligation with several debtors of an equal part of the debt
1578 General (Table K11)
Obligations in solidum see KJV1582
Solidary obligations. Joint and several obligations. Obligations solidaires
1579 General (Table K11)
1580 Solidarity between creditors. Solidarité active (Table K11)
1582 Joint and several liability. Solidarité passive (Table K11)
Including imperfect solidarity
Successors of the creditor or debtor see KJV1620+
Mortgages see KJV2166+
Pledges see KJV2140+

Civil law. Droit civil
Choses in action. Créances. Obligations
Creditor and debtor. Créancier et débiteur -- Continued
1583 Unsecured creditors. Créanciers chirographaires (Table K11)
For enforcement see KJV1606+
Personal subrogations see KJV1594
Performance. Payment. Exécution
1584 General (Table K11)
Suretyship see KJV2122+
Promise of a third party's performance see KJV1605
Time and place of performance. Le temps et le lieu du paiement
1588 General (Table K11)
1590 Days of grace. Moratorium. Délai de grace. Moratoire (Table K11)
1591 Payment in goods other than money. Exécution en nature (Table K11)
Subrogation
Including contractual and statutory subrogation (subrogation conventionnelle et légale)
1592 General (Table K11)
1594 Personal subrogations (Table K11)
Substituted payment see KJV1656
Discharge of plural obligations see KJV1564+
1598 Formal request to fulfill an obligation. Mise en demeure (Table K11)
1600 Wartime performance. Exécution pendant la guerre (Table K11)
Third parties. Tiers
1602 General (Table K11)
Successors to the parties see KJV1620+
1604 Third party beneficiary. Stipulations pour autrui (Table K11)
1605 Promise of a third party's performance. Promesse de porte-fort (Table K11)
For suretyship see KJV2122+
Negotiorum gestio see KJV1980
Enforced performance. Exécution forcée
1606 General (Table K11)
Gage commun
1610 General (Table K11)
Possessory lien see KJV2143
1616 Oblique action. Action oblique (Table K11)
1617 Paulian action. Action paulienne (Table K11)
Constraint against the debtor's person see KJV3985
Astreinte see KJV3980

KJV

Civil law. Droit civil
Choses in action. Créances. Obligations
Performance. Payment. Exécution -- Continued
Impossibility of performance see KJV1666
Non-merchant's insolvency see KJV4002
Transfer of obligations. Transmission des obligations
1620 General (Table K11)
1622 Théorie générale de l'inopposabilité (Table K11)
1624 Successors by universal or particular title. Ayants cause universels ou particuliers (Table K11)
Cf. KJV1321+ Succession upon death
Successors of the creditor. Ayants cause du créancier
1628 General (Table K11)
Successors of the creditor by universal or particular title. Ayants cause universels ou particuliers du créancier
1630 General (Table K11)
Assignment. Cession de créance
1634 General (Table K11)
Personal and statutory subrogation see KJV1592+
Transfer of debt. Successors of the debtor. Transfert des dettes. Ayants cause du débiteur
1640 General (Table K11)
1642 Successors of the debtor by universal or particular title. Ayants cause universels ou particuliers du débiteur (Table K11)
Extinction of obligations. Extinction des obligations
1650 General (Table K11)
Performance see KJV1584+
1656 Substituted payment. Dation en paiement (Table K11)
1658 Novation (Table K11)
1660 Set-off. Compensation
1661 Unforeseeability. Rebus sic stantibus clause. Imprévision
1662 Merger of rights. Confusion
Termination of a term see KJV510
Compromise and arbitration-clause see KJV4000
1663 Delegation
Non performance. Extinction without satisfaction of creditor. Extinction d'une créance sans désintéressement du créancier
1664 General (Table K11)
1665 Release of debt. Remise de la dette
1666 Impossibility of performance. Impossibilité d'exécutor (Table K11)
Including original and supervening impossibility
Extinctive presecription see KJV484+

Civil law. Droit civil
Choses in action. Créances. Obligations
Extinction of obligations. Extinction des obligations
Non performance. Extinction without satisfaction of creditor ...
Dissolving condition see KJV515
Contracts. Contrats
1668 General (Table K11)
1670 Contracts and wartime or emergency measures
Classification of contracts
Consensual, formal and real contracts. Contrats consensuels, contrats solennels et contrats réel
Including simple contracts (Conventions verbales)
For both simple contracts and acts under private signature see KJV505
1674 General (Table K11)
Offer and acceptance see KJV1710+
Synallagmatic and unilateral contracts. Contrats synallagmatiques et contrats unilatéraux
1675 General (Table K11)
1676 Special rules in case of nonperformance. Régles particulières en cas d'inexécution (Table K11)
Including exception non adimpleti contractu, and risk
1677 Imperfect synallagmatic contracts. Contrats synallagmatiues imparfaits (Table K11)
1678 Unilateral contracts. Contrats unilatéraux (Table K11)
1680 Contracts de gré à gré (Table K11)
1682 Contracts of adhesion. Contrats d'adhesion (Table K11)
1683 Standardized terms of contracts. Contrats-types (Table K11)
For a particular type of standardized contract, see the type, e.g. KJV2815+ Bills of lading
1684 Contracts imposed by the law. Contrats forcés (Table K11)
1686 Individual contracts and collective agreements. Contrats individuels et conventions collectives (Table K11)
Gratuitous and onerous contracts see KJV490+
1687 Commutative and aleatory contracts. Contrats commutatifs et contrats aléatoires (Table K11)
1688 Instantaneous and successive contracts. Contrats à exécution instantanée et contrats successifs (Table K11)
1689 Nominate and innominate contracts. Contrats nommés et contrats innomés (Table K11)

Civil law. Droit civil
Choses in action. Créances. Obligations
Contracts. Contrats
Classification of contracts -- Continued
1690 Contracts of record. Contrats enregistrés (Table K11)
Contracts of unspecified duration. Contrats a durée indéterminée
1691 General (Table K11)
1692 Breach of contract of unspecified duration. Rupture du contrat à durée indéterminée (Table K11)
Relativity of contracts. Relativité des conventions
1695 General (Table K11)
1696 Object of contracts (Table K11)
Liberty of contract see KJV1544
Formation of contracts. Formation des contrats
1702 General (Table K11)
Precontractual obligations. Obligations précontractuelles
1704 General (Table K11)
Promise of contract. Promesse de contrat
Including preliminary contract (avant-contrat)
1705 General (Table K11)
1706 Option (Table K11)
Invitation to offer see KJV1718
1707 Culpa in contrahendo (Table K11)
Offer and acceptance. Consent. L'offre et l'acceptation. Consentement
1710 General (Table K11)
1718 Invitation to offer. Pollicitation (Table K11)
Including contract to keep the offer open
1721 Offer with a term for acceptance. Offre avec délai d'acceptation (Table K11)
1724 Contracts by mail. Contrats par correspondance (Table K11)
Including contracts by telegram, teletype, telephone
Contracts with oneself see KJV1737
Vices of consent see KJV500+
1725 Consideration. Cause (Table K11)
1726 Earnest. Arrhes (Table K11)
1727 Form of contract (Table K11)
Cf. KJV503+ Juristic acts
Parties to contract. Les contractants
1730 General (Table K11)
1736 Capacity to contract. Capacité de contracter (Table K11)
Agency see KJV495

Civil law. Droit civil
Choses in action. Créances. Obligations
Contracts. Contrats
Parties to contract. Les contractants -- Continued
1737 Contract with oneself. Contrat avec soi-même (Table K11)
Agent of undisclosed principal see KJV1939
Successors of the parties see KJV1620+
Assignment see KJV1634+
Correality and solidarity see KJV1576+
1738 Intuitu personae. Strictly personal obligation (Table K11)
Third party beneficiary see KJV1604
Void and voidable contracts. Nullités absolues et nullités relatives des contrats
Including pertinent actions
1740 General (Table K11)
Immoral and unlawful contracts. Contrats immoraux et contrats illicites
1746 General (Table K11)
1748 Lesion (Table K11)
1750 Simulation. Defeasance. Contre-lettres (Table K11)
Including resolutory clause (clause résolutoire) and fiscal aspects of defense
Effects of contract. Effets du contrat
1756 General (Table K11)
1757 Interpretation of contract (Table K11)
1758.A-Z Collateral provisions. Modalités de la force obligatoire, A-Z
Subarrange each by Table K12
Arbitration clause. Clause commissoire see KJV4000
Contractual guaranties of payment see KJV2122+
Contractual penalty. Clause pénale see KJV2081
1758.E93 Exclusive rights clause. Clause d'exclusivité (Table K12)
Jurisdiction clause. Clause de competence see KJV3938
Liability limitation clause see KJV2082
Monetary terms see KJV1551+
Non-competition clause see KJV3412
Term of time and condition see KJV510
Time and place of performance see KJV1588+
Breach of contract. Inexécution du contrat
1760 General (Table K11)
1766.A-Z Special topics, A-Z
Subarrange each by Table K12

Civil law. Droit civil
Choses in action. Créances. Obligations
Contracts. Contrats
Effects of contract. Effets du contrat
Breach of contract. Inexécution du contrat
Special topics, A-Z -- Continued
Breach of a contract of unspecified duration see KJV1692
Contractual penalty see KJV2081
Enforced performance see KJV1606+
1766.M57 Misuse of one's right. Abus de droit en matière de contrat (Table K12)
Negligence see KJV2019+
1766.R47 Rescission. Resiliation des contrats (Table K12)
1770 Revision of contract. Révision du contrat (Table K11)
Individual contracts and obligations. Contrats spéciaux
For commercial contracts see KJV2301+
Sale and exchange. La vente et l'échange
1791-1795.8 General (Table K10)
1797 Redhibitory action. Redhibition. Action rédhibitoire (Table K11)
Right of unpaid seller
1798 General (Table K11)
1799 Privilège du vendeur de meubles (Table K11)
1800 Stoppage in transitu. Saisies-arrêts sur les marchandises en courts de transport (Table K11)
Judicial sale see KJV3989+
Exchange see KJV1791+
Gifts see KJV1461+
Lease. Louage des choses
For commercial leases see KJV2340+
1804 History
1806-1810.8 General (Table K10)
Landlord and tenant. Bail
1814 General (Table K11)
Lease of rural property see KJV5710+
1822 Lease of urban property. Bail urbain (Table K11)
Lease of business premises see KJV2341+
Concession immobilière see KJV1281+
Lease of land for erection of a building see KJV1235+
1824 Housing, apartments, or professional premises. Bail d'habitation ou professionnel (Table K11)
Including exchange of apartments
1825 Sublease. Subtenancy. Sous-louage. Sous-location (Table K11)

Civil law. Droit civil
Choses in action. Créances. Obligations
Contracts. Contrats
Individual contracts and obligations. Contrats spéciaux
Lease. Louage des choses
Landlord and tenant. Bail -- Continued

1826 Tenantable repairs. Réparations locatives (Table K11)

Protection of tenants. Protection des locataires

1827 General (Table K11)

1827.2 Rent control. Réglementation des loyers (Table K11)

1827.3 Lease litigation. Juges des loyers (Table K11)

Wartime and emergency measures. Mesures exceptionnelles

1828 General (Table K11)

Rent control see KJV1827.2

1829 Moratorium. Moratoire (Table K11)

1830 Lease of personal property. Louage de meubles (Table K11)

Lease-purchase see KJV2327

Hire. Contract of service and labor. Louage d'ouvrage et louage de services

1837 General (Table K11)

Locatio operis see KJV1841+

Master and servant see KJV3410+

Contract for work and labor. Contrat d'entreprise

For both contract for work and labor and contract of service and labor see KJV1837+

1841-1845.8 General (Table K10)

1852 Special rules for work on personal property. Regles spéciales aux travaux mobiliers (Table K11)

1853 Sub-contracting. Sous-entreprise (Table K11)

Mechanic's lien see KJV2143

1855 Liability. Responsabilité (Table K11)

Including liability for faulty work

1856.A-Z Particular types of contracts, A-Z

1856.C65 Computer contracts (Table K12)

Deposit. Dépôt

Including irregular depost (dépôt irregulier)

1860 General (Table K11)

1867 Voluntary deposit. Dépôt volontaire (Table K11)

1868 Necessary deposit. Dépôt nécessaire (Table K11)

Class here works on deposits made in haste because of imminent danger, e.g. fire

Sequestration. Séquestre

1869 General (Table K11)

Civil law. Droit civil
Choses in action. Créances. Obligations
Contracts. Contrats
Individual contracts and obligations. Contrats spéciaux
Deposit. Dépôt
Sequestration. Séquestre -- Continued
1870 Conventional sequestration. Séquestre conventionnel (Table K11)
1874 Judicial sequestration. Séquestre judiciaire (Table K11)
Cf. KJV3232 Trustee in bankruptcy. Syndic
1875 Legal deposit. Dépôt legal
Mutuum see KJV1959+
Association and civil company. Association et société civile
Including commercial companies
1881-1889 General (Table K9b)
1892 Nationality of associations and companies. Nationalité des associations et sociétés (Table K11)
Foreign associations and companies. Sociétés étrangères
1893 General (Table K11)
1894.A-Z By nationality, A-Z
Subarrange each by Table K12
1894.B75 British associations and companies in France. Sociétés brittanniques en France (Table K12)
1894.R87 Russian associations and companies in France. Sociétés russes en France (Table K12)
1902 Registered associations. Associations déclarées (Table K11)
Associations of public benefit see KJV594+
1904 Unregistered associations. Associations non déclarés (Table K11)
Associations under special rule. Associations
1905 General (Table K11)
Trade and professional associations see KJV3429+
1906 Approved associations. Associations agrées
Friendly societies see KJV2879.M87
Religious societies, congregations, etc. see KJV4248
Associations syndicales des proprietaires see KJV5754
Co-operative associations see KJV3174+
1907 Partnerships de facto. Invalid companies. Sociétés de fait. Nullités de sociétés
Civil companies. Sociétés civiles

Civil law. Droit civil
Choses in action. Créances. Obligations
Contracts. Contrats
Individual contracts and obligations. Contrats spéciaux
Association and civil company. Association et société civile
Associations under special rule. Associations
Civil companies. Sociétés civiles -- Continued
1910 General (Table K11)
1912 Universal property partnership. Société universelle de tous biens présents (Table K11)
1914 Universal profit partnership. Société universelle gains (Table K11)
1916 De facto companies (Table K11)
1917 Civil partnership. Société particuliere (Table K11)
Partner's shares see KJV3035+
Mandate. Mandat
For both mandate and non-contractual agency see KJV495
For commercial mandate see KJV2312+
1930 General (Table K11)
1937 Power of attorney. Procuration (Table K11)
Negotiorum gestio see KJV1980
Effects in regard to third parties. Effets à l'égard des tiers
1938 General (Table K11)
1939 Agent of undisclosed principal. Convention de prête-nom (Table K11)
Loan. Prêt
1950 General (Table K11)
Loan for use. Prêt à usage
1957 General (Table K11)
Onerous loan for use see KJV1830
1958 Commodatum. Commodat (Table K11)
Mutuum. Prêt a consommation
1959 General (Table K11)
Loan of money. Prêt d'argent
1960 General (Table K11)
Loan on interest. Prêt à intérêt see KJV2456+
Compromise see KJV3998
Aleatory contracts. Contrats aléatoires
1970 General (Table K11)
Gaming and betting see KJV5296+
Insurance policy see KJV2876+
Contract of life annuity see KJV1294.L54
Bottomry and respondentia see KJV2861

Civil law. Droit civil
Choses in action. Créances. Obligations -- Continued
Quasi contrats. Quasi-contracts
1978 General (Table K11)
1980 Negotiorum gestio. Gestion d'affaires (Table K11)
Unjust enrichment. Enrichissement sans cause
1985 General (Table K11)
1986 Recovery of the payment of a thing not due. Restoration. Restitution. Répétition de l'indu. Relevement (Table K11)
1987 Action in rem verso. Action de in rem verso (Table K11)
Civil liability. Responsabilité civile
Class here civil liability in general
For civil liability related to a particular subject, see the subject
2001-2009 General (Table K9b)
Offense. Quasi offense. Delicts. Faute. Dommage
2013 General (Table K11)
2015 Intentional and unintentional faults. Faute intentionnelle et faute nonintentionnelle (Table K11)
Misfeasance and negligent omission. Imprudence et négligence
Class here both negligence in contracts (faute non dolosive) and tortious negligence (quasi délict)
2019 General (Table K11)
2020 Unwarranted negligence, gross negligence, and ordinary negligence. Faute inexcusable, faute lourde, et faute légère (Table K11)
2021 Objective and subjective negligence. Faute in abstracto et faute in concreto (Table K11)
Contributory negligence see KJV2045
Redress see KJV2072+
Material and moral injuries. Préjudice matériel et préjudice moral. Dommage moral
2022 General (Table K11)
2023 Material damage to corporeal things. Dommage matériel à des biens corporels (Table K11)
2024 Pecuniary damage. Dommage pécuniaire (Table K11)
Class here general works on material damage not resulting from injury to, or loss of, a corporeal object
2025 Moral injury. Préjudice moral. Dommage moral (Table K11)
Personal injury. Préjudice corporel
Including both personal injury and préjudice esthétique
For injuries limited to a person's esthetic appearance see KJV2087+
2026 General (Table K11)

Civil law. Droit civil
Choses in action. Créances. Obligations
Civil liability. Responsabilité civile
Material and moral injuries. Préjudice matériel et préjudice moral. Dommage moral
Personal injury. Préjudice corporel -- Continued
Evaluation of personal injury see KJV5332
Tort liability. Delicts. Responsabilité civile extra-contractuelle. Délits
2030 General (Table K11)
Quasi-delict see KJV2019+
Causality. Causalité
2040 General (Table K11)
2042 Direct and indirect injuries. Dommage direct et dommage indirect (Table K11)
Factors relieving from liability. Causes d'exonération de responsabilité
2043 General (Table K11)
2045 Contributory negligence. Comparative negligence. Faute de la victime (Table K11)
Contractual agreement excluding liability see KJV2080+
2045.2 Assumption of risk by injured (Table K11)
2046 Necessity. Necessité (Table K11)
2047 Superior orders. Ordre d'un supérieur (Table K11)
2048 Liability for one's own action. Responsabilité du fait personnel (Table K11)
Presumption of fault. Liability without fault. Strict liability. Presomption de faute. Responsabilité sans faute
2059 General (Table K11)
Liability of the acts of animals (responsabilité du fait des animaux) see KJV2062+
2061 Vicarious liability. Respondeat superior doctrine. Responsabilité du fait d'autrui
Liability for the acts of things. Responsabilité du fait des choses (animées et inanimées)
2062 General (Table K11)
2066.A-Z Particular, A-Z
Subarrange each by Table K12
2066.D65 Dogs. Chiens (Table K12)
Electric current see KJV5269
Elevators see KJV5270
Game see KJV5795+
2071.A-Z Special topics, A-Z
Civil actions before criminal courts in cases of vicarious liability or liability for the acts of things see KJV3943

Civil law. Droit civil
Choses in action. Créances. Obligations
Civil liability. Responsabilité civile
Presumption of fault. Liability without fault. Strict liability. Presomption de faute. Responsabilité sans faute
Special topics, A-Z -- Continued

2071.E66 Employer's liability. Responsabilité de l'employer
Including works on both employer's civil liability and criminal liability

Redress. Damages. Réparation

2072 General (Table K11)

2073 Restitution. Réparation en nature

Compensation. Réparation en equivalent

2074 General (Table K11)

2076 Non-pecuniary compensation. Equivalents non pécuniaires

Compensation in money. Indemnité

2077 General (Table K11)

Evaluation of damages see KJV2079+

2078 Cumulation of indemnity with actual performance. Cumul de l'indemnité avec l'exécution effective (Table K11)
Including damages for delay (dommages moratoires)

Evaluation of damages. Evaluation des dommages-intêrets

2079 General (Table K11)

2079.2 Fixing of indemnity by the court. Evaluation de l'indemnité par la justice (Table K11)

Fixing of indemnity by contractual penalty see KJV2081

Contributory negligence see KJV2045

Liability limitation and non-liability clauses see KJV2082

Agreements on civil liability. Conventions de responsabilité

2080 General (Table K11)

2081 Contractual penalties. Clauses pénales (Table K11)
Including penalty for a breach of contract or delict

2082 Liability limitation and non-liability clauses. Clause limitative de responsabilité et clause de non-responsabilité (Table K11)

Arbitration clause see KJV4000

Jurisdiction clause (clause de competence) see KJV3938

Particular faults and injuries

2087 Damage to the aesthetic physical appearance of a person. Préjudice esthétique (Table K11)

Civil law. Droit civil
Choses in action. Créances. Obligations
Civil liability. Responsabilité civile
Particular faults and injuries -- Continued
Physical injuries. Death by wrongful act
2088 General (Table K11)
2088.2.A-Z Particular, A-Z
Subarrange each by Table K12
2088.2.M44 Medical malpractice (Table K12)
2089 Injury to a rightful authority. Atteinte à une autorité légitime (Table K11)
2090 Injury to reputation. Atteinte à la reputation (Table K11)
Injury to a name see KJV570+
2091 Injury to modesty. Atteinte à la pudeur (Table K11)
2092 Injury to sentiments of affection. Atteinte aux sentiments d'affection (Table K11)
Violation of privacy. Violation de secret
Cf. KJV6346 Professional secret
Cf. KJV8206+ Offenses against privacy (Criminal law)
2093 General (Table K11)
2093.5 Right in one's own picture. Droit de la personne sur son image (Table K11)
2094 Protection of personal data in information retrieval systems (Table K11)
Including public and private records register, statistics, etc.
2094.3 Property damage. Responsabilité aquilienne (Table K11)
Including action aquilienne
Cf. KJV2023 Material injury
2095 Tortious deceit and deceit related to contracts. Fraude et dol (Table K11)
Abuse of contractual rights. Abus de droit en matiere de contrat
2097 General (Table K11)
2098 Concealment in contracts relating to patrimony. Hidden defect. Réticence dans les contrats relatifs au patrimoine. Vice caché (Table K11)
2099 Nuisances. Atteintes (Table K11)
Cf. KJV1228+ Adjoining landowners
2100.A-Z Accidents, A-Z
Subarrange each by Table K12
2100.A88 Automobile accidents (Table K12)
2100.S36 School accidents (Table K12)
2100.S66 Sports accidents (Table K12)
Security. Sûretés

Civil law. Droit civil
Security. Sûretés -- Continued
2111-2115.8 General (Table K10)
Suretyship and guaranty. Sûretés personnelles. Cautionnement
2122 General (Table K11)
Joint and several liability see KJV1582
2123 Joint and several suretyship-bond. Cautionnement solidaire (Table K11)
Rights in rem upon debtor's property. Sûretés réelles
2130 General (Table K11)
Commercial pledges and liens see KJV2470+
2132 Rights in rem upon debtor's real property. Sûretés réelles sur les immeubles (Table K11)
For a particular right, see the subject, e.g. KJV2166 Mortgage
2134 Rights in rem upon debtor's personal property. Sûretés réelles sur les meubles
For a particular right, see the subject, e.g. KJV2140+ Pledge
Pledges. Nantissements
2140 General (Table K11)
2141 Antichresis. Antichrèse (Table K11)
2142 Pledge on personal property. Gage (Table K11)
2143 Possessory lien. Droit de rétention (Table K11)
Pledges on public contracts see KJV4732
Privileges and mortgages. Privilèges et hypothèques
2151-2155.8 General (Table K10)
Priority of claims. Civil law privilege. Privilèges
Cf. KJV3216 Commercial law
2156 General (Table K11)
2157 Privileges and bankruptcy. Privilèges en matière de faillite (Table K11)
Registration of privileges on real property see KJV2165
2160 General privileges on personal property (not requiring registration). Privilèges generaux sur les meubles) (Table K11)
2162 General privileges with a subsidiary charge on real property. Privilèges generaux portant subsidiairement sur les immeubles (Table K11)
2163.A-Z Particular, A-Z
Subarrange each by Table K12
Privilege of nursing and funeral expenses see KJV1413.F86
Privilege of the fiscus see KJV6536+

Civil law. Droit civil
Security. Sûretés
Rights in rem upon debtor's property. Sûretés réeles
Privileges and mortgages. Privilèges et hypotheques
Priority of claims. Civil law privilege. Privilèges
Particular, A-Z -- Continued
Privilege of a seller of personal property see KJV1799
2163.S86 Suppliers of provisions to debtor and his family. Fournisseurs de subsistances faites au debiteur et à sa famille (Table K12)
2165 Registration of privileges on real property. Inscription en matière de priviléges sur les immeubles (Table K11)
For both registration of privileges on real property and registration of mortgages see KJV1284+
Mortgages. Hypothèques
2166 General (Table K11)
Chattel mortgages. Hypothèques mobilières
Cf. KJV2134 Rights in rem upon debtor's personal property
2167 General (Table K11)
Hypothecation of ships see KJV2859
Hypothecation of aircraft see KJV2696.3
Statutory mortgage. Hypothèque légale
2168 General (Table K11)
Wife's statutory mortgage on husband's property see KJV704.5
Mortgage registration see KJV1285
Commercial law. Droit commercial
2185 History
Including early works
2191-2199 General (Table K9b)
Commercial debts and claims. Créances commerciales
2201 General (Table K11)
Collection of commercial debts see KJV2226+
2202 Marketing. Distribution (Table K11)
For marketing of a particular good, see the good, e.g. KJV2491+, Marketing of securities
Means of payment. Moyens de paiement
2203 General (Table K11)
Credit on security see KJV2456+
Effets de commerce see KJV2371+
Commercial courts and procedure. Tribunaux de commerce et procedure commerciale
2218 General (Table K11)

Commercial law. Droit commercial
Commercial courts and procedure. Tribunaux de commerce et procedure commerciale -- Continued

2219 Jurisdiction (Table K11)

Consular courts. Local courts. Juridictions consulaires

2220 General (Table K11)

2221.A-Z By place, A-Z

e.g.

2221.L97 Lyon (Table K12)

2221.P38 Paris (Table K12)

2222 Attorneys or solicitors before commercial courts. Agréés (Table K11)

2223 Expert evidence. Expertise judiciaire (Table K11)

Including accountants

2225 Default proceedings. Procédure par défaut (Table K11)

Arbitration and award see KJV4000

Execution

2226 General (Table K11)

Judicial sale (General) see KJV3989+

Judicial sale and attachment of business see KJV2251

Attachment (General) see KJV3984

Chambers of commerce. Chambres de commerce

2228 General (Table K11)

2229.A-Z By place, A-Z

Subarrange each by Table K12

2231 Guilds of commerce and artisanship (Table K11)

Commercial register. Régistre de commerce

2232 General (Table K11)

Registration of business concerns see KJV2254+

Registration of commercial companies see KJV3005+

Business enterprises and merchant. Entreprise commerciale ou industrielle et commerçant

2235 General (Table K11)

Fonds de commerce

Class here works on stock in trade or on business concerns exclusive of real property

2241-2245.8 General (Table K10)

2251 Attachment and judicial sale of business concerns. Saisie et vente judiciaire des fonds de commerce (Table K11)

Business concern in matrimonial property relationships see KJV804.F65

2251.2 Charge registered against debtor's business. Nantissement de fonds de commerce (Table K11)

Employee ownership see KJV3454

2251.3 Valuation of business concerns. Evaluation des fonds de commerce (Table K11)

Commercial law. Droit commercial
Business enterprises and merchant. Entreprise commerciale ou industrielle et commerçant
Fonds de commerce -- Continued
Goodwill. Achalandage. Clientèle
2252 General (Table K11)
2252.2 Business names. Nom commercial (Table K11)
2252.3 Contracts of transfer of clientele. Contrats de transfert de clientèle (Table K11)
Management of business concerns. Gérance des fonds de commerce
Cf. KJV3006+ Managers and directors
2253 General (Table K11)
2253.2 Contracts of management of business concerns. Contrats de gérance des fonds de commerce (Table K11)
Registration and transfer of business concerns. Enregistrement et transmission de fonds de commerce
2254 General (Table K11)
Sale of business concern. Vente de fonds de commerce
Including promises of sale
2256 General (Table K11)
2256.3 Price regulation. Réglement de prix (Table K11)
2256.4 Billet de fonds (Table K11)
Class here works on a bill of exchange given for the sale on credit of a business concern
Judicial sale of business concern see KJV2251
2257 Assignment of business concern. Cession de fonds de commerce (Table K11)
2258 Lease of business concern. Location de fonds de commerce (Table K11)
Accounting. Comptabilité
Including works on accounting in both commercial law and tax law
2261-2265.8 General (Table K10)
Financial statement. Bilan
2271 General (Table K11)
2272 Hidden reserves. Réserves latentes (Table K11)
2274 Depreciation. Amortissements (Table K11)
Including works on both commercial law aspects and tax law aspects
2275 Inventories. Inventaires (Table K11)
Including forms (Formulaires)
Middlemen (Intermédiaires) see KJV2312+
Liability. Responsabilité

Commercial law. Droit commercial
Business enterprises and merchant. Entreprise commerciale ou industrielle et commerçant
Liability. Responsabilité -- Continued
2276 General (Table K11)
Criminal liability. Responsabilité pénale
2281 General (Table K11)
2283.A-Z Particular, A-Z
Subarrange each by Table K12
2283.F83 Fraud in balance sheets. Fraude dans les bilans (Table K12)
2283.I55 Illegal speculation. Spéculation illicite (Table K12)
Profiteering see KJV2283.I55
Commercial transactions and contracts. Actes de commerce. Contrats de commerce
2301-2305.8 General (Table K10)
2311 Théorie de l'apparence (Table K11)
Commercial mandate. Mandat commercial
2312 General (Table K11)
Commercial agency. Trustees. Agence commerciale
Including independent and dependent middlemen (intermédiaires)
2313 General (Table K11)
2314 Breach of contract of commercial agency. Rupture du contrat d'agent commercial (Table K11)
2315 VRP (Voyageur, representant, placier). Trading agent (Table K11)
2316 Commission merchants (Table K11)
Class here works on factors (commissionaire) for undisclosed principal
2317 Brokerage. Brokers. Courtage. Courtiers (Table K11)
Bonders and depositaries see KJV2362+
Commercial sale. Vente commerciale
2320 General (Table K11)
2321 C.I.F. clause. Vente C.A.F. (Table K11)
Including documentary credit (crédit documentaire)
2322 Delivery of goods. Délivrance dans la vente de meubles corporels (Table K11)
Warranty. Damages. Garantie. Dommages-intérêts
2323 General (Table K11)
2323.5 Warranty of title. Garantie en cas d'eviction (Table K11)
2324 Products liability. Responsabilité du fait des produits (Table K11)
Commission see KJV2316
Franchise. Licensing contract. Concession commerciale
2325 General (Table K11)

Commercial law. Droit commercial
Commercial transactions and contracts. Actes de commerce. Contrats de commerce
Commercial sale. Vente commerciale
Franchise. Licensing contract. Concession commerciale -- Continued
2326 Exclusive license. Concession exclusive (Table K11)
2327 Credit sale. Lease-purchase. Vente à crédit. Location-vente (Table K11)
Auction. Enchère
2329 General (Table K11)
2330 Highest bid. Surenchère (Table K11)
Sale by public auction. Ventes publiques
2332 General (Table K11)
Judicial sale see KJV3989+
Maritime sales see KJV2830+
Export sales. Contrats d'exportation
2333 General (Table K11)
2335 Payment. Paiement (Table K11)
For C.I.F. clause see KJV2321
2337 Conditional sale. Vente sous condition (Table K11)
Stoppage in transitu see KJV1800
2338 Criminal provisions (Table K11)
Commercial leases. Locations commerciales
2340 General (Table K11)
Lease-purchase see KJV2327
Lease of business concern see KJV2258
Lease of business premises. Bail commercial
2341 General (Table K11)
2350 Propriété commerciale (Table K11)
2358 Lease renewal. Renouvellement de bail (Table K11)
2359 Eviction (Table K11)
Including compensation for eviction (indemnité d'eviction)
2360 Industrial equipment leases. Credit-bail-mobilier (Table K11)
2361 Automobiles and trucks (Table K11)
Deposit. Dépôt
2362 General (Table K11)
Bank deposits see KJV2434
2364 Warehousing. Dépôt de merchandises (Table K11)
For récépissé-warrants see KJV2413
2365 Safe-deposit companies. Location des coffres-forts (Table K11)
2366 Consignation (Table K11)
2367 Consignment. Expédition (Table K11)
Negotiable instruments. Titles of credit. Effets
2371-2375.8 General (Table K10)

Commercial law. Droit commercial
Commercial transactions and contracts. Actes de commerce. Contrats de commerce
Negotiable instruments. Titles of credit. Effets -- Continued
Bearer certificates. Titres au porteur
For works on a particular type of bearer certificate, see the type
2381 General (Table K11)
2382 Loss and reconstruction of bearer certificates. Perte et restitution des titres au porteur (Table K11)
Instruments made out to order. Titres à ordre
2383 General (Table K11)
Endorsement. Endossement
2384 General (Table K11)
2384.3 Blank endorsement. Endossement en blanc (Table K11)
2385 Registered certificates. Titres nominatifs (Table K11)
2386 Transfer. Transmission (Table K11)
Including endorsement
Marketing of securities see KJV2491+
Issuance of securities see KJV3085+
2387 Loss and reconstruction of securities. Perte et restitution des titres (Table K11)
Bill of exchange. Lettre de change
2391-2395.8 General (Table K10)
Billet de fonds see KJV2256.4
Check. Chèque
2397 General (Table K11)
2398 Crossed check. Chèque barré (Table K11)
2399 Funds transfer between postal current accounts by check. Chèque de virement (Table K11)
2400 Drawer's bankruptcy or compulsory liquidation of his liabilities. Faillité ou liquidation judiciaire du tireur (Table K11)
2403 Bank liability regarding payment of checks. Responsabilité des banques à l'occasion du paiement des cheques (Table K11)
Infractions
2404 General (Table K11)
2405 Uncovered checks. Chèques sans provision (Table K11)
2410 Promissory note. Billet à ordre (Table K11)
Documents of title. Warrants
2412 General (Table K11)

Commercial law. Droit commercial
Commercial transactions and contracts. Actes de commerce. Contrats de commerce
Negotiable instruments. Titles of credit. Effets
Documents of title. Warrants -- Continued

2413 Récépissé-warrants (Table K11)
Class here works on negotiable instruments in the form of warehouse receipts (récépissé d'entrepôt) for goods stored and warrants on the goods
Including bill of lading (connaissement)

Domiciled documents of title. Warrants à domicile
Class here works on promissory notes guaranteed by non-possessory liens on goods

2414 General (Table K11)

Warrants agricoles see KJV5727

Warrant industriel
Class here works on negotiable instruments incorporating nonpossessory liens of industrial stock

2415 General (Table K11)

Warrant petrolier see KJV5876

Bills of lading see KJV2815+

Banking. Operations de banque
Including public-law aspects of banking, and including works on both banking and stock-exchange transactions

2420 General (Table K11)

2420.3 Banking secret. Confidential communication (Table K11)

2421 Bank liability (General). Responsabilité des banques (Table K11)

2424 State supervision. Contrôle des banques et la direction du crédit

Banks of issue. Banques d'emission

2432 General (Table K11)

Banque de France

2433 General (Table K11)

2434 Shares of stock of the Bank of France. Actions de la Banque de France (Table K11)

2435 Saving banks. Caisses d'épargne (Table K11)

Bank deposits. Bank accounts. Dépôts en banque. Comptes de banque

2437 General (Table K11)

Current account. Compte courant
Including works on current accounts outside of banks

2439 General (Table K11)

2440 Attachment and garnishment of current accounts. Saisie-arrêt des comptes courants (Table K11)

Commercial law. Droit commercial
Commercial transactions and contracts. Actes de commerce. Contrats de commerce
Banking. Operations de banque
Bank deposits. Bank accounts. Depôts en banque. Comptes de banque
Current account. Compte courant -- Continued
Security for current account. Garantie d'un compte courant
2442 General (Table K11)
2443 Mortgage lodged for security of current account. Affectation hypothécaire à la garantie d'un compte courant (Table K11)
2445 Deposit of securities in bank. Dépôt de titres en banque (Table K11)
2447 Bank liability regarding deposits. Responsabilité du banquier en matière de dépôt (Table K11)
Bank credit. Bank loan. Crédit bancaire. Prêt de banque
2456 General (Table K11)
2457 Discount. Escompte (Table K11)
2458 Interest. Intérêt (Table K11)
2459 Bank suretyship. Caution bancaire (Table K11)
2459.5 Consumer credit. Small loans (Table K11)
Documentary credit. Advances on commercial documents. Crédit documentaire
For works on both documentary credit and C.I.F. clause see KJV2321
2460 General (Table K11)
2462 Letters of credit. Accréditifs (Table K11)
2464 Advances on goods. Avances sur marchandises (Table K11)
2465 Noncash funds transfer (Table K11)
Including electronic funds transfer
2466 Bankruptcy of banks. Faillite des banques (Table K11)
Commercial pledges and liens. Gages commerciaux
2470 General (Table K11)
Commercial possessory pledges and liens. Gages commerciaux avec dépossession
For works on possessory liens relating to a particular trade or industry, see the trade or the industry
2478 General (Table K11)
Warrants on merchandise stored in bonded warehouses see KJV2413
Pledges on public contracts see KJV4732
Commercial nonpossessory pledges and liens. Gages commerciaux sans dépossession

Commercial law. Droit commercial
Commercial transactions and contracts. Actes de commerce. Contrats de commerce
Commercial pledges and liens. Gages commerciaux
Commercial nonpossessory pledges and liens. Gages commerciaux sans dépossession -- Continued

2480 General (Table K11)
Hypothecation of aircraft see KJV2696.3
Hypothecation of ships see KJV2859
Domiciled documents of title see KJV2414+
Warrant industriel see KJV2415+

Marketing of securities. Stock exchange transactions. Ecoulement de valeurs. Operations de bourse
Including works on public law aspects

2491-2495.8 General (Table K10)
2497.A-Z Particular stock exchanges, A-Z
Subarrange each by Table K12
2497.P37 Paris (Table K12)

Investment of securities. Placement de titres
Including works on both investment and issuance of securities

2502 General (Table K11)
2504 Civil liability of banks in investment and issuance of securities. Responsabilité civile des banques dans le placement et l'émission de titres (Table K11)
2506 Settlement market. Marché à terme (Table K11)
Including works limited to an individual stock exchange
2510 Trading on stock exchange with partly paid stock or bonds. Exécution en bourse des actions ou des obligations non libérées (Table K11)
2512 Stockbrokers. Agents de change (Table K11)

Investment companies. Sociétés d'investissement

2514 General (Table K11)
2516 Investment trust companies. Sociétés de gerance (Table K11)
2520 Investment companies with a floating capital stock. Sociétés d'investissement à capital variable (Table K11)
2530 Criminal provisions

Contracts of carriage of goods and passengers. Contrats de transport des marchandises et des voyageurs
Cf. KJV6690+ Transportation

2541-2549 General (Table K9b)
Transport insurance see KJV2915+
2555 Travel agencies. Agences de voyages (Table K11)
Traveler's insurance see KJV2897.T73

Commercial law. Droit commercial
Commercial transactions and contracts. Actes de commerce. Contrats de commerce
Contracts of carriage of goods and passengers. Contrats de transport des marchandises et des voyageurs -- Continued
Civil liability. Responsabilité civile
For works limited to a particular mode of transportation or to a particular type of carrier, see the mode of transportation or the type of carrier
2580 General (Table K11)
Agreements on civil liability. Conventions de responsabilité civile
2584 General (Table K11)
2586 In contracts of adhesion. Dans les contrats d'adhesion (Table K11)
2588 Negligence and non-liability clauses. Négligence et les clauses de non-responsabilité (Table K11)
2590.A-Z Liabilities, A-Z
Subarrange each by Table K12
2590.L85 Luggage (Table K12)
Types of carriers. Transporteurs
2641-2645.8 General (Table K10)
Motor vehicles. Truck lines. Véhicules a moteurs
2650 General (Table K11)
Insurance see KJV2915+
Railroads. Chemins de fer
2661-2665.8 General (Table K10)
Carriage of goods. Transport des marchandises
2667 General (Table K11)
2668 Shipping documents. Titres de transport (Table K11)
2670 Carriage of passengers. Transport des voyageurs
Liability of railway companies. Responsabilité des companies de chemin de fer
2672 General (Table K11)
2673 Liability for cause of delay. Responsabilité pour cause de retard (Table K11)
2675 Combined carriage by rail and road. Transports mixtes rail-route (Table K11)
Water carrier. Transport par les eaux
For carriage by sea see KJV2774+
2681-2685.8 General (Table K10)
Jurisdictions
Including works on procedure, evidence, and arbitration and award
2690 General (Table K11)

Commercial law. Droit commercial
Commercial transactions and contracts. Actes de commerce. Contrats de commerce
Contracts of carriage of goods and passengers. Contrats de transport des marchandises et des voyageurs
Types of carriers. Transporteurs
Water carrier. Transport par les eaux
Jurisdictions -- Continued
Commercial maritime courts see KJV2791
Airlines. Services de transports aériens
2691-2695.8 General (Table K10)
2696 Aircraft ownership. Propriété des aéronefs (Table K11)
2696.3 Airline creditors. Hypothecation of aircraft. Credit tiré d'aéronef. Hypotheque des aéronefs (Table K11)
2697 Aircraft operator. Exploitant d'aéronefs (Table K11)
2698 Liability. Responsabilité (Table K11)
For liability insurance see KJV2720
2702 Air way bill (Table K11)
2704 Liability in carriage of goods by air. Responsabilité dans le transport aérien des marchandises (Table K11)
Carriage of passengers. Transport des voyageurs
2710 General (Table K11)
Liability in carriage of passengers by air. Responsabilité dans le transport aérien des voyageurs
2712 General (Table K11)
2714 Redress for injuries caused to passengers. Réparation des dommages causés aux voyageurs (Table K11)
2720 Aviation insurance. Assurances aériennes (Table K11)
Maritime law. Droit commercial maritime
For both maritime law and regulatory aspects of water transportation see KJV6035+
2774 History
2781-2789 General (Table K9b)
2791 Commercial maritime courts. Tribunaux de commerce maritime (Table K11)
Including works on procedure
For admiralty see KJV6130+
Maritime vessels see KJV6048.A+
2792 Ship ownership. Propriété du navire (Table K11)
Shipowner's liability. Responsabilité du proprietaire de navire
2793 General (Table K11)

Commercial law. Droit commercial
Maritime law. Droit commercial maritime
Shipowner's liability. Responsabilité du proprietaire de navire
Liability of shipowner-operator see KJV2795
2793.4 Limitations of liability. Restrictions à la responsabilité (Table K11)
Including limitation of shipowner's vicarious liability for crew members
Shipmasters see KJV6050+
Commissioning, fitting out and employment of the ship. Armament et exploitation du navire
2794 General (Table K11)
2795 Ship operator. Armateur (Table K11)
Including shipowner-operator (Armateur-propriétaire)
Vessel's crew see KJV6062
Agents ashore. Agents terrestres
2797 General (Table K11)
2797.2 Stevedore. Aconier (Table K11)
Including works on lighterage
2797.4 Ship brokers. Courtiers maritimes (Table K11)
For marine insurance brokers see KJV2863
2797.6 Transit agent. Transitaire (Table K11)
Contracts of affreightment. Carriage of goods by sea. Affrètements. Transports maritimes des marchandises
2801-2805.8 General (Table K10)
Charter party. Affrètement par charte-partie
For works on bill of lading as a charter-party document see KJV2815+
2812 General (Table K11)
2813 Net charter. Affrètement coque nue (Table K11)
Bills of lading. Connaissements
Including works on bill of lading as a charter-party document and including works on both bills of lading and consignment notes
2815 General (Table K11)
2816 Limitations of liability. Restrictions à la responsabilité (Table K11)
Inherent vice see KJV2839
Maritime transactions concerning the goods embarked on ship. Operations maritimes sur marchandises embarquées
2820 General (Table K11)
Maritime sales. Ventes maritimes
2830 General (Table K11)
C.I.F. clause see KJV2321

Commercial law. Droit commercial
Maritime law. Droit commercial maritime
Contracts of affreightment. Carriage of goods by sea. Affrètements. Transports maritimes des marchandises
Maritime transactions concerning the goods embarked on ship. Operations maritimes sur marchandises embarquées
2837 Documentary credit. Advances on bills of lading. Crédit documentaire (Table K11)
2838 Average. Avarie (Table K11)
2839 Inherent vice. Vice propre (Table K11)
2850 Carriage of passengers. Contrat de passage (Table K11)
2857 Towing. Remorquage (Table K11)
Assistance and salvage see KJV6128
Pilotage see KJV6090+
Protection of creditors. Protection des créanciers maritimes
2858 General (Table K11)
2859 Rights in ship as security for debts. Crédit tiré du navire
Including maritime liens and hypothecation of ship
2860 Arrest and judicial sale of a ship
2861 Bottomry and respondentia. Prêt à la grosse et la grosse sur facultés
Marine insurance. Assurances maritimes
Including works on both marine insurance and inland navigation insurance (assurances fluviales)
2862 General (Table K11)
2863 Marine insurance agents. Courtiers d'assurances maritimes (Table K11)
2864 Insurance on ship. Assurance maritime sur corps (Table K11)
2865 Insurance on cargo of a ship. Assurance maritime sur facultés (Table K11)
Liability. Responsabilité
2866 General (Table K11)
Shipowner's liability see KJV2793+
Shipmaster's liability see KJV6050+
Limitation of liability. Restrictions à la responsabilité
2867 General (Table K11)
2868 Negligence and non-liability clauses. Négligence et les clauses d'irresponsabilité (Table K11)
Limitation of liability in bills of lading see KJV2816
Vicarious liability. Responsabilité du fait d'autrui
Including vicarious liability action
2869 General (Table K11)
Inherent vice see KJV2839

Commercial law. Droit commercial
Maritime law. Droit commercial maritime
Liability. Responsabilité
Vicarious liability. Responsabilité du fait d'autrui -- Continued
Limitations of shipowner's vicarious liability for crew members see KJV2793.4
Insurance. Assurances
2871-2875.8 General (Table K10)
Insurance policies
2876 General (Table K11)
2877 Agreed valuation clause. Clause de valeur agréé (Table K11)
2878 Insurance policies signed on foreign currencies or on gold francs. Contrats d'assurance souscrits en monnaies étrangères ou en francs-or (Table K11)
For policies on particular lines of insurance, see the insurance, e.g. KJV2890 Life insurance policies
2878.2 Transfer of insurance policy. Transfert du contrat d'assurance (Table K11)
2879.A-Z Particular plans or modes of premium, A-Z
Subarrange each by Table K12
Friendly societies see KJV2879.M87
2879.G76 Group insurance. Assurance-group (Table K12)
2879.M87 Mutual insurance. Friendly societies. Assurances mutuelles. Sociétés de secours mutuels (Table K12)
2879.4 Insurance agents. Insurance brokers. Agents d'assurances. Courtiers d'assurances (Table K11)
Insurance companies. Sociétés d'assurance
2880 General (Table K11)
2880.2 Government control. Control français des assurances (Table K11)
2880.3 Finance. Capital (Table K11)
2881 Merger of insurance companies. Fusions de sociétés d'assurance (Table K11)
Including transfer of portfolio
Mutual insurance companies. Friendly societies see KJV2879.M87
Foreign insurance companies in France. Sociétés d'assurance étrangeres en France
2882 General (Table K11)
2883.A-Z By nationality, A-Z
Subarrange each by Table K12
Personal insurance. Assurances de personnes
2884 General (Table K11)
Life insurance. Assurances sur la vie
2885 General (Table K11)

Commercial law. Droit commercial
Insurance. Assurances
Personal insurance. Assurances de personnes
Life insurance. Assurances sur la vie -- Continued

2886 Life insurance companies. Sociétés d'assurance sur la vie (Table K11)
Including foreign life insurance companies in France

2887 Life insurance between husband and wife. Assurance sur la vie entre époux (Table K11)

Beneficiaries. Bénéficiaires

2888 General (Table K11)

2889 Third party beneficiary. Assurance au profit d'un tiers (Table K11)

2890 Life insurance policies signed on foreign currencies or on gold francs. Contrats d'assurance sur la vie souscrits en monnaies étrangères ou en francs-or (Table K11)

2891 Life insurance and risk of war. L'assurance-vie et le risque de guerre (Table K11)

2892 Health insurance. Medical care insurance. Assurance contre la maladie (Table K11)

Accident insurance. Assurance contre les accidents
Including personal accidents (accidents corporels)

2895 General (Table K11)

2897.A-Z Special topics, A-Z
Subarrange each by Table K12

Automobile insurance see KJV2928+
Aviation insurance see KJV2720
Marine insurance see KJV2862+
Transport insurance see KJV2915+

2897.T73 Travel insurance. Assurances au voyage
Including insurance of nonpaying passengers (assurance des personnes transportees a titre gratuit)

2898 Business insurance (Table K11)

Property insurance. Damage insurance. Assurances de dommages

2900 General (Table K11)

2905 Insurer's recourse against the perpetrator of the damage. Recours de l'assureur contre l'auteur d'un dommage (Table K11)

2908 Multiple line insurance. Assurances multiples (Table K11)

Transport insurance. Assurances de transports

2915 General (Table K11)

2919 Average. Régle proportionnelle (Table K11)
For average in shipping law see KJV2838

Commercial law. Droit commercial
Insurance. Assurances
Property insurance. Damage insurance. Assurances de dommages
Transport insurance. Assurances de transports -- Continued
2922 Average in overland insurance. Régle proportionnelle dans les assurances terrestres (Table K11)
2924 Insurance on account of a third party. Assurance pour le compte d'autrui (Table K11)
Particular hazards
Automobile insurance. Assurances automobile
Class here works on all motor vehicles used on land
2928 General (Table K11)
2930 Mandatory automobile insurance. Assurance automobile obligatoire (Table K11)
2940 Burglary insurance. Assurance-vol (Table K11)
2950 Fire insurance. Assurance contre l'incendie (Table K11)
2955 Water damage insurance (Table K11)
Liability insurance. Assurance de responsabilité civile
Including both statutory and private insurance
2957 General (Table K11)
2958 Direct action against the insurer. Action directe de la victime d'un dommage contre l'assureur (Table K11)
2959 Professional-liability insurance. Assurances de responsabilité professionnelle (Table K11)
Insurance and war. Assurances et la guerre
Class here war insurance, insurance during the war, and impact of war on insurance
2962 General (Table K11)
Life insurance and risk of war see KJV2891
2965 Reinsurance. Réassurance (Table K11)
Business associations. Sociétés commerciales
2985 History
2991-2999 General (Table K9b)
Employee ownership see KJV3454
Employee profit-sharing see KJV3453
3001 Syndic (Table K11)
Nationality. Nationalité
3002 General (Table K11)
Foreign companies see KJV3185+
Formation
3003 General (Table K11)

Commercial law. Droit commercial
Business associations. Sociétés commerciales
Formation -- Continued

3004 Articles of association. Contract. Memorandum. Statuts (Table K11)
For articles of association of a particular type of company, see the type

Registration. Register of commercial companies. Enregistrement. Registre du commerce des sociétés
3005 General (Table K11)
Changes of organizational status of companies, dissolution or bankruptcy see KJV3018+
3005.5 Publicity. Publicité (Table K11)
Cf. KJV316 Legal advertising

Managers and directors. Gérants et administrateurs
3006 General (Table K11)
Employees' representation in management see KJV3423.5+
Liability. Responsabilité
3008 General (Table K11)
3009.A-Z Particular acts or transactions, A-Z
Subarrange each by Table K12
Bankruptcy of a company see KJV3032
3009.B74 Breach of trust. Abus de confiance (Table K12)
Fraudulent conversion of funds see KJV3009.B74

Finance. Accounting. Auditing. Comptabilité. Vérification
3010 General (Table K11)
Assets brought into a company. Apport en société
3011 General (Table K11)
Partners' shares see KJV3035+
Founder's shares see KJV3120+
3012 Reserves (Table K11)
3013 Supervisory auditors. Commissaires aux comptes (Table K11)
Including liability

Corporate reorganization. Transformation des sociétés
3018 General (Table K11)
Registration see KJV3005+
Merger and split. Fusions et scissions
3020 General (Table K11)
Mergers and splits of stock companies see KJV3146
Winding up, dissolution or bankruptcy. Liquidation, dissolution ou faillite
For stock companies see KJV3148
3024 General (Table K11)
Registration see KJV3005+

Commercial law. Droit commercial
Business associations. Sociétés commerciales
Corporate reorganization. Transformation des sociétés
Winding up, dissolution or bankruptcy. Liquidation, dissolution ou faillite -- Continued
3026 Winding up out of court. Liquidation amiable (Table K11)
Dissolution of companies. Dissolution de sociétés
3028 General (Table K11)
3028.2 Creditors' rights. Droits des créanciers (Table K11)
Bankruptcy. Faillite
3030 General (Table K11)
3032 Effects in relation to managers. Effets à l'égard des gérants et administrateurs (Table K11)
Partnerships. Sociétés par intérêts
3033 General (Table K11)
3034 Inheritance of partner's rights. Succession de l'associé décedé (Table K11)
Partners' shares. Parts d'intérêt
Including works on partners' shares in civil companies
3035 General (Table K11)
3035.2 Attachment and execution sale of partners' shares. Saisie et vente forcée des parts d'intérêt (Table K11)
3036 Silent partners. Association en participation (Table K11)
3037 General partnership. Société en nom collectif (Table K11)
3038 Limited partnership. Société en commandite simple (Table K11)
Stock partnership see KJV3155
Private company. Société à responsabilité limitée
3039 General (Table K11)
3039.2 Partners. Associés (Table K11)
3039.4 Managers. Gérants (Table K11)
3039.5 Liability (Table K11)
Joint stock companies. Sociétés par actions
3040 General (Table K11)
3040.3 Joint stock company with a floating capital stock. Société par actions à capital variable (Table K11)
Incorporation and promoters
3042 General (Table K11)
3042.5 Articles of incorporation. Statuts (Table K11)
Registration see KJV3005+
Founders. Promoters. Fondateurs
3043 General (Table K11)
Issuing company see KJV3085+
Founder's share see KJV3120

Commercial law. Droit commercial
Business associations. Sociétés commerciales
Joint stock companies. Sociétés par actions
Incorporation and promoters
Founders. Promoters. Fondateurs -- Continued
3044 Liability. Responsabilité (Table K11)
Organs. Organes
Including works on organs of sociétés anonymes
3046 General (Table K11)
Stockholders' meeting. Assemblée générale
3047 General (Table K11)
3048 Attendance list. Feuille de présence (Table K11)
Information of stockholders see KJV3136
Voting rights see KJV3130+
Executives and supervisors. Management. Dirigeants
Including works on sociétés anonymes
3049 General (Table K11)
Employees' representation in management see KJV3423.5+
3050 Remuneration of executives. Rémunérations des dirigeants (Table K11)
3051 Directors or board of directors. Administrateurs. Conseil d'administration (Table K11)
3052 Board of supervision. Conseil de surveillance
Including the chairman (président) and chairman of the board and president of the corporation in personal union (président directeur général)
Managers. Directeurs. Gérants
3057 General (Table K11)
President of the corporation. Directeur général
3058 General (Table K11)
Président directeur général see KJV3052
3059 Managing committee. Sole general manager. Directoire. Directeur général unique (Table K11)
Liability. Responsabilité
Including works on both liability of founders and liability of organs
3061 General (Table K11)
3061.4 Qualification shares. Actions de garantie (Table K11)
3061.6 Vicarious liability actions against directors and managers. Actions en responsabilité contre les administrateurs et directuers (Table K11)
Labor-management councils see KJV3427
Finance. Capital
3066 General (Table K11)

Commercial law. Droit commercial
Business associations. Sociétés commerciales
Joint stock companies. Sociétés par actions
Finance. Capital -- Continued
Accounting. Auditing. Comptabilité. Vérification
Cf. KJV6864 Tax accounting
3068 General (Table K11)
Financial statement. Balance sheet. Bilan
3069 General (Table K11)
Offenses committed in connection with drawing up balance sheets see KJV3169
3071 Valuation of joint stock companies. Evaluation des sociétés par actions (Table K11)
Including works on valuation or revaluation of securities (actions; valeurs) of joint stock company
3076 Supervisory auditors. Commissaires aux comptes (Table K11)
Capital
3080 General (Table K11)
Reduction of capital. Réduction du capital
Including loss of capital (déperdition de capital), and dwindling assets (déperissement de capital)
For reduction of nominal and share capital see KJV3096
3082 General (Table K11)
3082.4 Fall of net assets below one fourth of the nominal capital. Perte des trois quarts du capital social (Table K11)
3082.6 Acquisition of its own shares by the issuing company. Acquisition de ses propres actions ou parts sociales par la société émetrice (Table K11)
Nominal capital. Capital social
3083 General (Table K11)
Issuance of securities. Emission de titres
Including works on subscription (souscription) and application money (versement)
3085 General (Table K11)
Issuance of securities in France by foreign companies see KJV3188
Issuance of shares of stock and bonds. Emissions d'actions et d'obligation
3086 General (Table K11)
Partly paid shares and bonds see KJV3098+
Premium on shares see KJV3129
Founder's shares see KJV3120+

Commercial law. Droit commercial
Business associations. Sociétés commerciales
Joint stock companies. Sociétés par actions
Finance. Capital
Capital
Nominal capital. Capital social
Issuance of securities. emission de titres
Issuance of shares of stock and bonds. Emissions d'actions et d'obligation

3087 Issuance of new shares. Emission d'actions nouvelles (Table K11)

Issuance of bonds convertible into shares of stock see KJV3125

Pre-emptive rights see KJV3143

Share capital. Capital-actions

3089 General (Table K11)

Shares of stock see KJV3106

Loan capital. Capital d'emprunt

3092 General (Table K11)

Bonds see KJV3106

Increase of nominal capital. Augmentation du capital social

For issuance of new shares and bonds see KJV3087

3094 General (Table K11)

3094.4 Increase by inclusion of reserves. Augmentation par incorporation des reserves (Table K11)

3096 Reduction of nominal capital. Réduction du capital social (Table K11)

Including reduction of share capital

Capital partly paid up. Capital non libéré

Including partly paid shares and partly paid bonds

3098 General (Table K11)

Trading on stock exchange with partly paid shares and bonds see KJV2510

Revaluation see KJV3071

Cash capital. Capital en numéraire

3099 General (Table K11)

3099.4 Increase of cash capital. Augmentation de capital en numéraire (Table K11)

For issuance of securities see KJV3085+

Decrease of cash capital see KJV3082+

Reserves

Including works on commercial-law aspects and tax-law aspects of reserves

3100 General (Table K11)

Commercial law. Droit commercial
Business associations. Sociétés commerciales
Joint stock companies. Sociétés par actions
Finance. Capital
Capital
Reserves -- Continued

3102 Distribution of reserves. Distribution de réserves (Table K11)
For use of reserves for dividends see KJV3127

Shares of stock and bonds. Stockholders' and bondholders' rights. Actionnaires et obligataires
For works on securities as authorized capital of the joint stock company see KJV3083+
Cf. KJV6528 Rentes sur l'Etat

3106 General (Table K11)

Transfer of shares of stock and of bonds. Transferts d'action et d'obligations
Including transfer of registered stocks and bonds of stock, and transfer of non-stock shares

3110 General (Table K11)

Non-possessory liens of industrial stock see KJV2415+

3115 Attachment of shares of stock and bonds. Saisie d'actions et d'obligations (Table K11)

3117.A-Z Other title claims to stocks and bonds, A-Z
Subarrange each by Table K12

Partly paid shares and bonds see KJV3098+

Unequal voting shares. Actions à droit de vote inégal
Cf. KJV3130 Voting rights

3118 General (Table K11)

3119 Multiple shares. Actions à vote privilégié (Table K11)
For founder's shares see KJV3120+

Actions de garantie see KJV3061.4

Founder's shares. Actions d'apport
Including works on both commercial-law aspects and tax-law aspects of founder's shares

3120 General (Table K11)

3122 Negotiability of founder's shares. Négotiabilité des actions d'apport (Table K11)

3124 Staff shares. Actions de travail (Table K11)

3125 Convertible bonds. Bonds convertible into shares of stock. Obligations convertibles (Table K11)

Dividends

3126 General (Table K11)

3127 Illegal dividends. Dividendes fictives (Table K11)
Including use of reserves for dividends

Extraordinary profits. Profits exceptionnels

Commercial law. Droit commercial
Business associations. Sociétés commerciales
Joint stock companies. Sociétés par actions
Shares of stock and bonds. Stockholders' and bondholders' rights. Actionnaires et obligataires
Dividends
Extraordinary profits. Profits exceptionnels -- Continued
3128 General (Table K11)
3129 Premium on shares. Primes d'emission (Table K11)
Distribution of reserves see KJV3102
Voting rights. Droits de vote
3130 General (Table K11)
Inequality of voting rights see KJV3118+
Pre-emptive rights see KJV3143
3132 Rights of minority stockholders. Droits de la minorité (Table K11)
3134 Conflict between the powers of stockholders' meeting and the individual rights of a stockholder. Conflit entre les pouvoirs de l'assemblée générale et les droits individuels de la'actionnaire (Table K11)
3136 Information of stockholders. Information des actionnaires (Table K11)
3138 Mortgage bonds. Obligations hypothécaires (Table K11)
3139 Interest on bonds. Intérets des obligations (Table K11)
3140 Groups of bondholders. Groupements d'obligataires (Table K11)
3141 Bondholders' meetings. Assemblées d'obligataires (Table K11)
3143 Pre-emptive rights. Droit de préférence (Table K11)
Usufruct of shares and of bonds. Usufruit des actions et des obligations
3144 General (Table K11)
Dividends see KJV3126+
Extraordinary profits (on shares) see KJV3128+
3145 Usufructuary's right in management of the company. Droits de l'usufruitier dans la gestion de la société (Table K11)
3146 Merger and split. Fusions et scissions (Table K11)
Winding up, dissolution or bankruptcy. Liquidation, dissolution ou faillite'
Including works limited to sociétés anonymes
3147 General (Table K11)

Commercial law. Droit commercial
Business associations. Sociétés commerciales
Joint stock companies. Sociétés par actions
Shares of stock and bonds. Stockholders' and bondholders' rights. Actionnaires et obligataires
Winding up, dissolution or bankruptcy. Liquidation, dissolution ou faillite' -- Continued
3148 Bondholders in case of liquidation or bankruptcy of a debtor company. Obligataires en case de liquidation ou de faillite (Table K11)
Bankruptcy, judicial liquidation or judicial administration. Faillite, liquidations judiciaire ou réglement judiciaire
3150 General (Table K11)
Fall of net assets below one fourth of the nominal capital see KJV3082.4
3155 Stock partnership. Société en commandité par actions (Table K11)
Sociétés anonymes
3160 General (Table K11)
Employees participation in management see KJV3423.5+
Staff shares see KJV3124
3168 Liability. Responsabilité (Table K11)
For criminal liability see KJV3169
3169 Criminal provisions regarding joint stock companies. Droit penal des sociétés par actions (Table K11)
Including sociétés anonymes
Companies regulated by special legislation. Sociétés spécialement reglementées
Cf. KJV1905+ Specially regulated associations
3171 General (Table K11)
3172 Commercial companies with civil purpose. Sociétés à objet civil et à forme commerciale (Table K11)
Cf. KJV1910+ Civil companies
3173 Companies with a floating capital stock. Sociétés à capital variable (Table K11)
For particular types of companies, see the subject
Cooperative societies. Sociétés cooperatives
Including cooperative societies with a floating capital stock (société à capital variable)
3174 General (Table K11)
3175 Consumers' cooperatives. Sociétés cooperatives de consommation (Table K11)
3176 Producers' cooperatives. Sociétés cooperatives ouvrières de production (Table K11)
For farmers' cooperatives see KJV5756

Commercial law. Droit commercial
Business associations. Sociétés commerciales
Companies regulated by special legislation. Sociétés spécialement reglementées
Cooperative societies. Sociétés cooperatives -- Continued
Mutual loan companies. Sociétés de crédit mutuel
3177 General (Table K11)
Investment companies with floating capital stock see KJV2520
Companies subject to government control
For a particular category of companies, see the category, e.g. insurance companies
3180 General (Table K11)
Government companies. Companies partly owned by government see KJV5592+
Sociétés conventionnés see KJV5564+
Foreign commercial companies. Sociétés commerciales étrangères
Including personal company and joint stock company
3185 General (Table K11)
Foreign insurance companies in France see KJV2882+
3188 Issuance of securities in France by foreign commercial companies. Emission de titres en France par des sociétés de commerce étrangères (Table K11)
Groupings for economic advantage. Groupements d'intéret économique
3190 General (Table K11)
Export syndicates see KJV5634
Combinations. Industrial trusts
3192 General (Table K11)
Cartels see KJV5598+
3192.2 Subsidiary and parent company. Société filiale. Société mere (Table K11)
3194 Criminal provisions (Table K11)
Insolvency
Including general works on merchants' and non-merchants' insolvency
For works limited to non-merchants see KJV4002
History
3195 General (Table K11)
3196 Judicial liquidation. Liquidation judiciaire (Table K11)
For composition see KJV3223+
3201-3205.8 General (Table K10)
3212 Stoppage of payments. Insolvency. Cessation des paiements (Table K11)

Commercial law. Droit commercial
Insolvency -- Continued
3213 Juge commissaire (judge appointed by the commercial court to supervise bankruptcy or judicial administration) (Table K11)
Creditors. Créanciers
Including judicial administration and bankruptcy
3214 General (Table K11)
3216 Priority of claims. Collocation des créanciers (Table K11)
Secured creditors see KJV2111+
Unsecured creditors. Créanciers chirographaires
3217 General (Table K11)
3218 Principle of equality between unsecured creditors. Le principe de l'égalité entre les créanciers chirographaires (Table K11)
Judicial administration of the insolvent's business. Règlement judiciaire
3220 General (Table K11)
3222 Judicial administrator. Administrateur judiciaire (Table K11)
Composition. Concordat
3223 General (Table K11)
3223.2 Composition approved by court. Concordat judiciaire (Table K11)
Bankruptcy. Faillite et banqueroute
3230 General (Table K11)
3232 Receiver in bankruptcy. Syndic (Table K11)
3236 Criminal bankruptcy. Fraudulent conveyances. Banqueroute (Table K11)
3237 Criminal provisions. Droit pénal des affaires (Table K11)
For criminal provisions regarding a particular subject, see the subject, e.g. KJV3194 Business associations
Intellectual and industrial property. Proprieté intellectuelle et industrielle
3248 General (Table K11)
Principles
3249 Intangible property (Table K11)
3250 Moral rights. Droit moral de l'auteur ou de l'artiste
3252-3252.92 Copyright in general. Droit d'auteur (Table KJV-KJW3)
Class here general works on copyright and works on two or more branches of copyright
For works limited to a particular branch of copyright, see the branch

Intellectual and industrial property. Proprieté intellectuelle et industrielle -- Continued
Copyright contracts. Contrats relatifs aux droits d'auteur
For works limited to a particular branch of copyright, see the branch
For works limited to reproduction rights or to performing rights, see KJV3252.62 and KJV3252.82
3260 General (Table K11)
3262 Transfer of copyright. Cession de droit d'auteur (Table K11)
Contracts of usage of copyright. Contrats d'exploitation du droit d'auteur
3264 General (Table K11)
3266 Public policy. Ordre public (Table K11)
The publishing contract see KJV3318+
Branches of copyright
3270-3270.92 Literary copyright. Propriété littéraire (Table KJV-KJW3)
For works on both literary copyright and legal status of writers see KJV6415+
3273-3273.92 Private correspondence. Letters (Table KJV-KJW3)
3275-3275.92 Scientific works. Oeuvres de caractère scientifique (Table KJV-KJW3)
3277.A-Z Special topics, A-Z
Subarrange each by Table K12
3280-3280.92 Computer programs (Table KJV-KJW3)
3282.A-Z Special topics, A-Z
Subarrange each by Table K12
3290.A-Z Special topics, A-Z
Subarrange each by Table K12
Literary and dramatic criticism see KJV6264
3290.P83 Public lectures. Lectures publiques (Table K12)
Musical and theatrical works. Oeuvres musicales et théatrales
3292 General (Table K11)
3295-3295.92 Musical copyright (Table KJV-KJW3)
For publishing contract see KJV3318+
3297.A-Z Special topics, A-Z
Subarrange each by Table K12
Theatrical works. Oeuvres théatrales
3298 General (Table K11)
3299-3299.92 Plays. Pièces de théâtre (Table KJV-KJW3)
3300-3300.92 Shows. Spectacles (Table KJV-KJW3)
Works of figurative arts and photography. Oeuvres des arts figuratifs et photographie
Motion pictures and television shows see KJV3316+
Violations of rights on one's own picture see KJV2093.5

Intellectual and industrial property. Proprieté intellectuelle et industrielle
Branches of copyright
Works of figurative arts and photography. Oeuvres des arts figuratifs et photographie -- Continued
3312-3312.92 Designs and models. Dessins et modèles (Table KJV-KJW3)
3313-3313.92 Prints and labels (Table KJV-KJW3)
Including works of commercial art, catalogs, etc.
3316-3316.92 Motion pictures and television shows. Oeuvres cinématographiques et télévision (Table KJV-KJW3)
3317.A-Z Special topics, A-Z
Subarrange each by Table K12
Recordings
see KJV3252.63
Author and publisher. Publishing contract. L'auteur et l'éditeur. Contrat d'edition
3318 General (Table K11)
3319.A-Z Special topics, A-Z
Subarrange each by Table K12
Designs and models see KJV3312+
International copyright see KJV1411
Patent law. Loi sur les brevets d'invention
3331-3335.8 General (Table K10)
3336 Scope of protection. Etendue du protection (Table K11)
Invention
3338 General (Table K11)
3339 Legal status of inventors. Community of inventors (Table K11)
3340 Employees' inventions (Table K11)
Patent practice and procedure
Class here works on issuance, recording and revocation of patents
3342 General (Table K11)
3343 Lapse and nullity of patents. Déchéance de brevets (Table K11)
3344 Duration and renewal (Table K11)
3345.A-Z Patented products, process, and engineering methods, A-Z
Subarrange each by Table K12
3345.B56 Biotechnology
Military armaments see KJV3345.W42
3345.W42 Weapons. Military armaments
Know-how (secret en matière d'inventions) see KJV3347+
Licenses
Class here contractual use of patents and contractual sharing of know-how
3347 General (Table K11)

Intellectual and industrial property. Proprieté intellectuelle et industrielle
Patent law. Loi sur les brevets d'invention
Licenses -- Continued
3348 Foreign licensing agreements (Table K11)
3349 Patent litigations (Table K11)
Designs and models see KJV3312+
Distinctive marks. Signes distinctifs
For works limited to a particular product, see the product
3352 General (Table K11)
Trademarks. Marques de commerce
3353 General (Table K11)
3354.A-Z Types of trademarks, A-Z
Subarrange each by Table K12
3354.M37 Marks of origin. Appellations d'origine (Table K12)
3355 Scope of protection. Etendue de protection (Table K11)
3356 Practice and procedure (Table K11)
3358 Licenses (Table K11)
3360 Infringement. Contrefaçon
Social legislation. Droit social
Including comprehensive works on both social legislation and family law, or social legislation and law on public health; and including both labor law and social security (législation industrielle)
3371-3379 General (Table K9b)
Administration
3382 General (Table K11)
3383 Ministry of Social Affairs. Ministère des affaires sociales (Table K11)
Labor law. Droit du travail
3384 History
3391-3399 General (Table K9b)
3403 Right to labor. Droit au travail (Table K11)
Free choice of employment. Liberté du travail
3404 General (Table K11)
3405 Infringement upon free choice of employment. Atteinte à la liberté du travail (Table K11)
Central administration and national advisory organs. Administration centrale et organes consultatives nationaux
3406 General (Table K11)
3407 Direction du travail et de l'emploi (Labor and Employment Board) (Table K11)
3408 Conseil National du Travail (National Council of Labor) (Table K11)
Superior Collective Agreements Board see KJV3437

Social legislation. Droit social
Labor law. Droit du travail -- Continued
3409 Conflict of laws (Table K11)
Labor contract. Contrat de travail
For labor contract limited to particular types of employment or groups of people see KJV3475.A+
3410 General (Table K11)
3410.5 Constitutional rights in employment (Table K11)
Freedom of association and liberty of contract see KJV3433
Collective labor agreements see KJV3436+
3411 Temporary work. Travail temporaire (Table K11)
3411.5 Supplementary employment
3412 Non-competition clause. Clause de non concurrence (Table K11)
Labor standards see KJV3445+
3413 Breach of contract. Rupture du contrat (Table K11)
Notice. Dismissal. Délai-congé. Licenciement
3414 General (Table K11)
3415 Dismissal wage. Indemnité de licenciement (Table K11)
3418 Transfers of enterprises and protection of workers. Mutations d'enterprises et protection des travailleurs (Table K11)
Management-labor relations. Relations du travail
3420 General (Table K11)
Management-labor relations at a plant or company level
3423 General (Table K11)
Employees' participation in management
3423.5 General (Table K11)
3424 Shop stewards. Délegués du personnel (Table K11)
Including works on regional or national conferences of shop stewards
3425 Delegates of labor unions. Délégués syndicaux (Table K11)
3427 Labor-management councils. Comités d'entreprise (Table K11)
Trade and professional associations. Syndicats professionnels
For works limited to a particular industry, see the industry
3429 General (Table K11)
3430 Legal capacity. Personnalité civile (Table K11)
Juristic personality. Freedom of association. Liberté syndicale. Capacité
3432 General (Table K11)

Social legislation. Droit social
Labor law. Droit du travail
Management-labor relations. Relations du travail
Trade and professional associations. Syndicats professionnels
Juristic personality. Freedom of association. Liberté syndicale. Capacité -- Continued
3433 Freedom of association and liberty of contract. Liberté syndicale et liberté contractuelle (Table K11)
Labor unions. Syndicats des salariés
3434 General (Table K11)
At a plant or company level see KJV3425
3435 Employers' unions. Syndicats d'employeurs (Table K11)
Collective bargaining and labor agreements. Conventions collectives
3436 General (Table K11)
3437 Commission superieure des conventions collectives (Superior Collective Agreements Board) (Table K11)
Labor standards see KJV3445+
3438.A-Z By industry or occupation, A-Z
Including national and regional collective labor agreements for a particular industry or occupation
3438.A37 Agriculture. Food industries. Industries agricoles et alimentaires (Table K12)
3438.C65 Construction industry (Table K12)
Food industries see KJV3438.A37
3438.L38 Lawyers. Avocats (Table K12)
Labor disputes. Conflits du travail
3439 General (Table K11)
Labor courts see KJV3485+
Strikes and lockouts. Greves
3440 General (Table K11)
Public services see KJV5008+
Arbitration. Arbitrage
3441 General (Table K11)
Cour supérieure d'arbitrage see KJV3486
Conciliation Boards. Conseils de prud'hommes see KJV3488
3443.A-Z By industry or occupation, A-Z
Subarrange each by Table K12
Labor standards
3445 General (Table K11)
Non-competition clause see KJV3412
Preferential employment. Emploi réservé

Social legislation. Droit social
Labor law. Droit du travail
Labor standards
Preferential employment. Emploi réservé -- Continued
3446 General (Table K11)
3447 Veterans and war victims (Table K11)
Wages and supplements. Remunérations du travail
3448 General (Table K11)
3449 Minimum and maximum wage. Salaire minimum et salaire maximum (Table K11)
Dismissal wage see KJV3415
3450 Family supplements. Sursalaires familiaux (Table K11)
For both family supplements as wage supplements and family allowances as social security benefits see KJV3567+
3452 Housing allowances. Allocation de logement (Table K11)
3453 Employee profit sharing. Participation aux bénéfices (Table K11)
3454 Employee ownership. Investment wages (Table K11)
Cf. KJV3124 Staff shares
3455.A-Z Special topics, A-Z
Subarrange each by Table K12
3455.A88 Attachment and garnishment of wages. Saisie-arrêt des rémunerations du travail (Table K12)
3455.E66 Employee dwellings (Table K12)
3455.P75 Privileges for wages, salaries and related debts. Privilèges des salaires et créances accessoires (Table K12)
3456 Labor discipline. Work rules. Règlement intérieur d'entreprise (Table K11)
Labor supply. Manpower controls. Marché du travail
3457 General (Table K11)
3458 Alien labor (Table K11)
3459.A-Z Group of employees or industries, A-Z
Subarrange each by Table K12
3459.D66 Domestics. Gens de maison (Table K12)
3459.H66 Home labor. Industrie à domicile (Table K12)
Protection of labor
For works limited to a particular industry or type of labor see KJV3475.A+
3460 General (Table K11)
Freedom of association see KJV3432+
Hours of labor
3462 General (Table K11)
3463.A-Z By industry or trade, A-Z
Subarrange each by Table K12

Social legislation. Droit social
Labor law. Droit du travail
Protection of labor -- Continued
Vacations. Holidays. Leave of absence. Congés
3464 General (Table K11)
3465.A-Z By industry or type of labor, A-Z
Subarrange each by Table K12
Highway transport workers see KJV3465.T73
3465.T73 Transport workers. Routiers (Table K12)
3466 Youth labor (Table K11)
Womens' labor see KJV3617+
Home labor see KJV3475.H66
Labor hygiene and safety. Hygiene et securité des travailleurs
Including safety regulation (accident prevention) for equipment and hazardous substance and factory inspection
For occupational diseases see KJV3550+
3467 General (Table K11)
3468.A-Z By industry or type of labor, A-Z
Subarrange each by Table K12
3469.A-Z By machinery, equipment, etc., A-Z
3469.E54 Electric equipment (Table K12)
3469.E56 Elevators. Hoisting machinery. Ascenseurs. Appareils de levage (Table K12)
3469.G37 Gas manufacture equipment (Table K12)
Hoisting machinery. Appareils de levege see KJV3469.E56
3469.W66 Woodworking machinery. Machines-outils pour le travail du bois (Table K12)
3475.A-Z Labor law for particular industries or occupations, A-Z
Subarrange each by Table K12
Including works on both labor law and social security
3475.A38 Actors (Table K12)
Agricultural laborers see KJV5812+
3475.A78 Artisans (Table K12)
3475.A79 Artists (Table K12)
3475.B35 Bank employees. Employés de banque (Table K12)
3475.B88 Businessmen. Commercants et industriels (Table K12)
Civil servants see KJV5032+
3475.C65 Computer industry (Table K12)
3475.D66 Domestics. Gens de maison (Table K12)
3475.E57 Entertainers. Performing artists (Table K12)
3475.E94 Executives. Cadres (Table K12)
3475.G68 Government business enterprises. Entreprises publiques (Table K12)

Social legislation. Droit social
Labor law. Droit du travail
Labor law for particular industries or occupations, A-Z -- Continued
3475.H66 Home labor of women. Travail des femmes à domicile (Table K12)
3475.H67 Home laborers. Industrie à domicile (Table K12)
Hotel workers. Employés d'industrie hotelière see KJV3475.I55
3475.I55 Inn-keeping personnel. Employés d'industrie hotelière (Table K12)
3475.I67 Insurance company employees. Employés des assurances (Table K12)
3475.L66 Longshoremen. Ouvriers aux docks (Table K12)
3475.L86 Lumbermen. Employés d'exploitation forrestière (Table K12)
3475.M47 Merchant's clerks. Employés de commerce (Table K12)
Military. Militaires see KJV7418+
Miners see KJV5850+
3475.M68 Motor vehicle drivers (Table K12)
3475.M69 Movie actors. Acteurs cinématographiques (Table K12)
3475.N38 Nationalized enterprise employees. Employés des entreprises nationalisées (Table K12)
3475.N66 Non-supervisory employees. Salariés non cadres (Table K12)
Performing artists see KJV3475.E57
Railway employees. Employés de chemins de fer see KJV6016
3475.S24 Salaried employees (Table K12)
3475.S45 Self-employed. Non salariés (Table K12)
3475.S89 Students. Etudiants (Table K12)
3477.A-Z Labor law for particular groups, A-Z
Subarrange each by Table K12
3477.A55 Aliens. Etrangers (Table K12)
3477.W66 Women. Femmes (Table K12)
For material welfare see KJV3617+
3480 Criminal provisions. Penalties. Sanctions pénales (Table K11)
Labor courts. Tribunaux du travail
3485 General (Table K11)
3486 Cour supérieure d'arbitrage (Table K11)
Cf. KJV3441+ Arbitration
3488 Conciliation Boards. Conseils de prud'hommes (Table K11)
Social insurance. Social security. Assurances sociales. Sécurité sociale
Legislation industrielle see KJV3371+

Social legislation. Droit social
Social insurance. Social security. Assurances sociales. Sécurité sociale -- Continued

3511-3515.8 General (Table K10)

Evidence. Preuve

3520 General (Table K11)

3522 Expert medical evidence. Expertise médicale (Table K11)

Liability. Responsabilité

3524 General (Table K11)

3525 Unwarranted negligence. Faute inexcusable (Table K11)

3530 Contentious jurisdiction in social security. Contentieux de la sécurité sociale (Table K11)

Organization and administration

3532 General (Table K11)

Direction generale de la securité sociale (General Directorate of Social Security)

3534 General (Table K11)

3536 Conseil supérieur de la sécurité sociale (Senior Council on Social Security) (Table K11)

High Commission for Family Allowances see KJV3567+

3538 Caisses de sécurité sociale de la sécurité sociale (Social Security Funds) (Table K11)

3540 Féderation nationale des organismes de sécurité sociale (National Federation of Social Security Organizations) (Table K11)

3542 Employees. Personnel (Table K11)

Contributions. Contribution au titre de la sécurité sociale

Including social security taxes (cotisations au titre de la sécurité sociale)

3544 General (Table K11)

Workers' compensation taxes see KJV3554

3545.A-Z Particular industries, occupations, and groups of employees, A-Z

Subarrange each by Table K12

3545.A34 Agricultural laborers (Table K12)

3545.A76 Authors (Table K12)

Health and maternity insurance. Assurance maladie et maternité

For private health insurance see KJV2892

3546 General (Table K11)

Workers' compensation see KJV3550+

Housing allowances see KJV3569

Workers' compensation. Réparation des accidents de travail et maladies professionnelles

Including accidents at work and occupational diseases

Social legislation. Droit social
Social insurance. Social security. Assurances sociales. Sécurité sociale
Workers' compensation. Réparation des accidents de travail et maladies professionnelles -- Continued
3550 General (Table K11)
3552 Disability evaluation. Evaluation d l'incapacité (Table K11)
Cf. KJV5334 Medical law
Permanent disability pensions see KJV3560+
3554 Workers' compensation taxes. Cotisations d'accidents du travail et de maladies professionnelles (Table K11)
Life annuities. Disability pensions. Rentes viagères. Pensions d'invalidité
3556 General (Table K11)
3558 Retirement pensions. Pensions de retraite (Table K11)
Permanent disability pensions
3560 General (Table K11)
3562 Disability evaluation. Evaluation de l'incapacité (Table K11)
3564.A-Z By industry or group of workers, A-Z
Subarrange each by Table K12
Family allowances. Prestations familiales
3567 General (Table K11)
3569 Housing allowances. Allocation de logement (Table K11)
3572.A-Z Beneficiaries, A-Z
Subarrange each by Table K12
3572.R44 Refugees (Table K12)
3572.W38 War victims, Civilian. Victimes civiles de la guerre (Table K12)
Social services. Public welfare. Assistance sociale
3601-3609 General (Table K9b)
3613 Social work. Social workers. Travail social. Travailleurs sociaux (Table K11)
Protection of families. Protection sociale de la famille
Including works on both social and private law aspects
3615 General (Table K11)
Family allowances see KJV3567+
Maternal and child welfare. Protection sociale de la maternité et de l'enfance
Including works on widowed mothers
3617 General (Table K11)
Child welfare. Protection de l'enfance
For protection of youth labor see KJV3466
For works on juvenile delinquency see KJV8840+
3620 General (Table K11)

Social legislation. Droit social
Social services. Public welfare. Assistance sociale
Protection of families. Protection sociale de la famille
Maternal and child welfare. Protection sociale de la maternité et de l'enfance
Child welfare. Protection de l'enfance -- Continued
War orphans. Orphelins de la guerre
3624 General (Table K11)
3626 Office national des pupilles de la nation (National bureau of wards of France) (Table K11)
Orphans of soldiers killed in action see KJV3680
3632 Homeless children as wards of public assistance. Enfants assistés (Table K11)
Including vagrancy of children (vagabondage des mineurs)
3635 Juvenile courts. Tribunaux pour enfants (Table K11)
For juvenile criminal courts see KJV8840+
People with disabilities. Handicapés. Invalides
3640 General (Table K11)
Disabled service personnel see KJV3670+
3642 Blind. Aveugles (Table K11)
Disability evaluation see KJV5334
3643 Vocational rehabilitation. Reclassement professionel (Table K11)
Birth control. Family planning. Limitation des naissances. Conception dirigée
3646 General (Table K11)
Abortion. Avortement
3648 General (Table K11)
Criminal aspects see KJV8188
3650 Repression of begging and vagrancy. Répression de la mendicité et du vagabondage (Table K11)
For criminal aspects of vagrancy and begging see KJV8384
Charitable institutions and organizations. Etablissements de bienfaisance
3660 General (Table K11)
3664 Public institutions of relief. Etablissements publics d'assistance (Table K11)
3666 Housing aid. Aide au logement (Table K11)
Veterans and war victims. Anciens combattants et victimes de guerre
3670 General (Table K11)
3672 Coverage and benefits (Table K11)
Preferential employment see KJV3447

Social legislation. Droit social

Social services. Public welfare. Assistance sociale

Veterans and war victims. Anciens combattants et victimes de guerre -- Continued

3674 Veterans of World War II underground movements. Anciens combattants de la Résistance (Table K11)

Including déportés, internés, etc.

3680 Widows and orphans of soldiers killed in action. Veuves et orphelins des militaires tués a l'ennemi (Table K11)

Repatriates. Refugees. French dispossessed abroad. Rapatriés. Réfugiés. Français déposs é dés outre-mer

Including works on indemnification by government

3690 General (Table K11)

3692 Coverage and benefits (Table K11)

Courts and procedure

Administration of justice. Administration de la justice

For administration of criminal justice see KJV7981.2+

3721 General (Table K11)

Ministère de la justice (Department of Justice)

3730 General (Table K11)

Ministère public see KJV3845+

Courts. Cours

Class here works on courts of several jurisdictions

For courts (several or individual) of an individual jurisdiction, see the jurisdiction

History

Including works on procedure

3745 General (Table K11)

3747 Parlement de Paris (Sovereign Court of Paris)

Including works on the court before it assumed the role of a supreme court for most of France

3749 Court de pairs. Court of peers

3752 Cour du roi. Court of the king

3754 Parlements. Provincial Sovereign Courts (Table K11)

For courts (several or individual) of an individual province or region see the province or region

3758 Justices seigneuriales. Manorial courts (Table K11)

For courts (several or individual) of an individual region or place, see the region or place

3760 Tribunaux révolutionnaires (Revolutionary courts)

3771-3775.8 General (Table K10)

Including procedure

Supreme courts

For works on supreme courts of special jurisdiction, see the subject, e.g. KJV2218+, Commercial court

3790 General (Table K11)

Cour de cassation (Court of Cassation)

Courts and procedure
Courts. Cours
Supreme courts
Cour de cassation (Court of Cassation) -- Continued

3792 General (Table K11)

3793 Chambre de requêtes. Division of Preliminary Examination (Table K11)

Chambres civiles. Civil divisions

For criminal division see KJV8440

3795 General (Table K11)

Procedure

3796 General (Table K11)

3797.A-Z Special topics, A-Z

Subarrange each by Table K12

Ministère Public à la Cour de Cassation (Public Ministry at the Court of Cassation)

Class here works on officials appointed by the Government to the Court of Cassation to represent the public interest

For Public Ministry in general see KJV3845+

3798 General (Table K11)

3799 Procureur Général à la Cour de Cassation (Head of the Ministère Public at the Court of Cassation) (Table K11)

3802 Cours d'appel (Regional courts of appeal) (Table K11)

For courts (several or individual) of an individual region, see the region

Tribunaux de grande instance

3804 General (Table K11, modified)

History

3804.A8 General

Bailliages. Seneschals see KJV3838.A8

3804.A82 Tribunaux d'arrondissement

3806-3806.22 Procureurs de la République

3806 General (Table K11)

Procurator of the king see KJV3845.A8

Public prosecution see KJV8516+

Tribunaux civils (Civil courts)

3808 General (Table K11)

Jurisdiction

Including competence in subject matter (Civil and commercial) and venue

3810 General (Table K11)

Tribunaux correctionnels (Criminal courts) see KJV8460

Tribunaux de commerce (Commercial courts) see KJV2218+

Courts and procedure
Courts. Cours -- Continued
Tribunaux d'instance
3812 General (Table K11, modified)
History
3812.A8 General
Prévôts see KJV3838+
Viguiers see KJV3838+
3813 Justice of the peace. Cantonal courts. Tribunaux de paix. Tribunaux cantonaux
Tribunaux de simple police (Magistrate courts) see KJV8464
3814 Costs. Frais de justice (Table K11)
Procedure
3815 General (Table K11)
Summary proceedings see KJV3968+
3817.A-Z Special topics, A-Z
Subarrange each by Table K12
Courts of special jurisdiction. Tribunaux d'exception
3819 General (Table K11)
Joint rural lease commissions (Tribunaux paritaires de baux ruraux) see KJV5719
Juvenile courts (Tribunaux pour enfants) see KJV8858+
Rent courts (Juges des loyers) see KJV1827.2
3820 Competence conflict courts. Tribunal des conflits (Table K11)
Other courts of special jurisdictions
see the subject
Judicial personnel. Magistracy. Corps judiciaires. Magistrature
For legal profession in general see KJV170+
3831-3835.8 General (Table K10)
Admission to the profession see KJV172
3836 Court dress. Costumes du magistrat (Table K11)
Judges. The bench. Juges. Magistrat du siège
For works on judges of a particular court, see the court
3838 General (Table K11, modified)
3838.A8 History
Including officials as prévôte de l'hotel, baillis, sénéchaux, viguiers, etc.
Appointment. Tenure. Retirement
3840 General (Table K11)
3842 Permanent tenure of judges. Inamovibilité des magistrats (Table K11)
3843 Civil liability of judges. Responsabilité civile des juges (Table K11)

Courts and procedure
Courts. Cours
Judicial personnel. Magistracy. Corps judiciaires.
Magistrature -- Continued
Ministère public (Public Ministry). Officials prosecuting crimes and representing the public interest in civil procedure
For Public Ministry at a particular court, see the appropriate court
3845 General (Table K11, modified)
3845.A8 History
Including Procurators and Attorneys of the king (Procureurs et Avocats du roi)
3847 Competence in civil matters. Compétence civile (Table K11)
3848 Procureurs Généraux (Heads of Public Ministries attached to courts of appeal) (Table K11)
For Procureur Général at the Court of Cassation see KJV3797.A+
Procureurs de la République see KJV3806+
3850 Avocats Généraux (Advocates General) (Table K11)
3852 Assistants (Table K11)
3853 Huissiers (Table K11)
3855 Fees and honoraria. Frais et honoraires (Table K11)
For works on fees limited to a particular office of the Public Ministry, see the office
3859 Court clerks. Administrative offices. Secretaries. Greffiers. Greffes. Secrétaires (Table K11)
3862 Liability of members of magistracy. Responsabilité des magistrats (Table K11)
Including liability of members of the Public Ministry
For liability of judges see KJV3843
Procedure in general
3865 General (Table K11)
Jurisdiction
Including competence in subject matter and venue (juridiction territoriale)
3869 General (Table K11)
Conflits d'attribution (competence conflicts between administration and judiciary) see KJV4687
Actions and defenses. Actions et défenses
3872 General (Table K11)
3874 Actions directes. Actions against a third party (having assumed the debtor's rights and obligations) (Table K11)
Cf. KJV1640+ Successors of the debtor
Indirect action see KJV1616

Courts and procedure
Procedure in general
Actions and defenses. Actions et défenses -- Continued
3876 Preventive actions. Actions préventives (Table K11)
Exceptions see KJV3970
Parties
For parties in a particular type of procedure, see the procedure
3878 General (Table K11)
Foreign states as parties to actions see KJV410
Trial. Procès
3880 General (Table K11)
Evidence in court. Preuve judiciaire
For evidence in general see KJV525+
3882 General (Table K11)
Admissibility of records of criminal proceedings in civil and commercial courts see KJV3950
Evidence by witnesses. Preuve par témoins
3886 General (Table K11)
3888 Children as witnesses
3890 Documentary evidence. Preuve littérale (Table K11)
Expert testimony. Expertise
3892 General (Table K11)
3894 Court ordered appraisal. Expertise judiciaire (Table K11)
3895 Medical expert testimony (Table K11)
Cf. RA1001+ Forensic medicine
Judicial decisions. Décisions judiciaires
3898 General (Table K11)
Injunctions see KJV3987
Judgment. Jugement
3902 General (Table K11)
3904.A-Z Types of judgments, A-Z
Subarrange each by Table K12
Appealable judgments see KJV3914.A77
3904.D43 Declaratory judgments. Jugements déclaratoires (Table K12)
3906 Advisory opinions. Avis (Table K11)
3910 Mistrial. Erreur judiciaire (Table K11)
Cf. KJV3843 Civil liability of judges
3911 Res judicata. Chose jugée (Table K11)
Legal remedies. Appellate procedure. Procédure de recours
3912 General (Table K11)
3914.A-Z Special topics, A-Z
Subarrange each by Table K12

Courts and procedure
Procedure in general
Legal remedies. Appellate procedure. Procédure de recours
Special topics, A-Z -- Continued
3914.A77 Appealable judgments. Jugements susceptibles d'appeal (Table K12)
Civil procedure. Procédure civile
Including comprehensive works on both civil procedure and commercial procedure
History
3920 General
3923 Civil jury. Jury civil
3931-3935.8 General (Table K10)
Jurisdiction
Including competences in subject matter and venue (juridiction territoriale)
For works limited to a particular court, see the court
3936 General (Table K11)
3937 Forum rei sitae (Table K11)
3938 Clause d'attribution de compétence territoriale (Table K11)
3939 Conflict of jurisdictions. Conflits de juridictions (Table K11)
Cf. KJV3820 Competence conflict courts
Actions and defenses
3942 General (Table K11)
3943 Civil actions before criminal courts (Table K11)
3944 Limitation of actions. Prescription d'action (Table K11)
Parties
3946 General (Table K11)
Foreign states as parties to actions see KJV410
3947 Intervention. Opposition by a third party. Tierce opposition (Table K11)
Trial. Procédure au contentieux judiciaire
3948 General (Table K11)
Evidence in court. Preuve judiciaire
3949 General (Table K11)
3950 Admissibility of records of criminal proceedings. La production et la force probante des pièces d'une procédure pénale (Table K11)
For effect of criminal res judicata on civil judgment see KJV3962
3952 Evidence by witnesses. Preuve par témoins (Table K11)
Documentary evidence. Preuve littérale
3953 General (Table K11)

Courts and procedure
Civil procedure. Procédure civile
Trial. Procédure au contentieux judiciaire
Evidence in court. Preuve judiciaire
Documentary evidence. Preuve littérale -- Continued
3954.A-Z Special topics, A-Z
Subarrange each by Table K12
Expert testimony. Expertise
3955 General (Table K11)
3956 Court ordered appraisal. Expertise judiciaire (Table K11)
3957 Medical expert testimony. Expertise médicale (Table K11)
Cf. RA1001+ Forensic medicine
Judicial decisions. Décisions judiciaires
3959 General (Table K11)
Judgment. Jugement
3960 General (Table K11)
3962 Effect of criminal res judicata on civil judgment. Autorité de la chose jugée au criminel sur le civil (Table K11)
3964 Contracts of record. Contrats judiciaires (Table K11)
3965 Res judicata. Chose jugée (Table K11)
Special procedures. Procédures exceptionnelles
3967 General (Table K11)
Summary proceedings. Procedure in chambers. Injunctio. Procedure d'urgence. Juridiction des référés. Ordonnance de référé
3968 General (Table K11)
Astreinte see KJV3980
Arbitration and award see KJV4000
3970 Interlocutory proceedings. Incidents de la procédure (Table K11)
Including exceptions
Remedies. Appellate procedure. Procédure de recours
3972 General (Table K11)
3974.A-Z Special topics, A-Z
Subarrange each by Table K12
3976 Costs. Frais (Table K11)
Enforcement of judgment. Exécution d'un jugement
Including procedures for distribution
3978 General (Table K11)
3980 Astreinte (fine for debtor's delay) (Table K11)
Execution against debtor's property. Exécution sur les biens des débiteurs
3982 General (Table K11)

Courts and procedure
Civil procedure. Procédure civile
Enforcement of judgment. Exécution d'un jugement
Execution against debtor's property. Exécution sur les biens des débiteurs -- Continued
Attachment and garnishment of current accounts see KJV2440
3984 Attachment of real property. Saisie immobilière (Table K11)
Attachment and garnishment of wages see KJV3455.A88
Judicial sale see KJV3989+
3985 Detention of debtor. Contrainte par corps (Table K11)
3987 Injunctions. Exécution provisoire (Table K11)
Judicial sale. Foreclosure sale. Vente judiciaire
3989 General (Table K11)
3990 Court-ordered licitation. Licitation judiciaire (Table K11)
Non-contentious jurisdiction. Ex parte jurisdiction. Juridiction gracieuse
3992 General (Table K11)
3993 Aboard sea vessels (Table K11)
3994 Aboard aircraft (Table K11)
Notarial acts see KJV189+
Registration, recording see KJV527
Negotiated settlement. Réglement à amiable
3996 General (Table K11)
3998 Compromise. Transaction (Table K11)
Cf. KJV3223+ Composition (Commercial law)
4000 Arbitration clause. Arbitration and award. Compromis. Arbitrage (Table K11)
4002 Non-merchant's insolvency. Déconfiture (Table K11)
For works on merchant's insolvency see KJV3195+
Costs. Frais de justice
4010 General (Table K11)
4012 Courts (Table K11)
Including witnesses and expert witnesses
Costs in special proceedings or special courts see the subject
4015 Execution. Enforcement (Table K11)
Public law. Droit public
Class here works on all aspects of public law, including early works
For civics see KJV235
4050 General (Table K11)
4051 Corporate bodies of public law. Personnes morales de droit public (Table K11)

Public law. Droit public -- Continued
The State. L'Etat
Including philosophy and theory of the state
4052 General (Table K11)
Law and the state see KJV287+
Church and state see KJV4240
4054.A-Z Special topics, A-Z
Subarrange each by Table K12
Principles of natural justice and equity see KJV287+
Constitutional law. Droit constitutionnel
History see KJV4080.5+
4056 Constitutional reform. Criticism (Table K11)
For works on a particular constitution, see the constitution
4071.2 Bibliography
Including bibliography of constitutional history, and including bibliography of sources
Sources
Including 18th and 19th century constitutions and related material, beginning with the constitution of 1791
4073.6 Collections. Compilations
Constitutions
Collections see KJV4073.6
Individual constitutions
4074.51791 Constitution of September 3, 1791. Constitution du 3 septembre 1791 (Table K17)
4074.51793 Constitution of June 24, 1793. Constitution du 24 juin 1793 (Table K17)
4074.51795 Constitution of August 22, 1795. Constitution du 5 fructidor an III (Table K17)
4074.51799 Constitution of December 15, 1799. Constitution du 22 frimaire an VIII (Table K17)
4074.51802 Senatus consultum of August 4, 1802. Sénatus-consulte du 16 thermidor an X (Table K17)
4074.51804 Organic senatus consultum, of May 18, 1804. Sénatus-consulte organique de 18 floréal an XII (Table K17 modified)
4074.51804.Z8 Act of 1815
4074.51814 Constitutional Charter, June 4, 1814. Charte constitutionnelle, 4 juin 1814 (Table K17)
4074.51830 Constitutional Charter, August 13, 1830. Charte constitutionnelle, 13 août 1830 (Table K17)
4074.51848 Republican constitution, November 4, 1848. Constitution républicaine, 4 novembre 1848 (Table K17)
4074.51852 Constitution of January 14, 1852. Constitution du 14 janvier 1852 (Table K17 modified)

Constitutional law. Droit constitutionnel
Sources
Constituitons
Individual constitutions
Constitution of January 14, 1852. Constitution du 14 janvier 1852 -- Continued
4074.51852.Z8 Senatus consultum of November 7, 1852. Sénatus-consulte du 7 novembre 1852
4074.51870 Constitution of May 1870. Constitution de mai 1870 (Table K17)
4074.51946 Constitution of October 27, 1946. Constitution du 27 octobre 1946 (Table K17)
4074.51958 Constitution of October 4, 1958. Constitution du 4 octobre 1958 (Table K17)
Sources other than constitutions
Collections see KJV4073.6
4074.55 Declaration of the rights of man and of the citizen. La Declaration des droits de l'homme et du citoyen, August 26, 1789
Constitutional laws. Lois constitutionnelles
Collections see KJV4073.6
4074.6[date] Individual laws
e.g.
4074.6194 Constitutional law of July 10, 1940. Loi constitutionelle du 10 juillet 1940
4074.61945 Law of November 2, 1945. La loi du 2 novembre 1945
4074.61958 Constitutional law of June 3, 1958. La loi constitutionelle du 3 juin 1958
Referenda see KJV4287+
Court decisions. Reports
4075.5 Indexes and tables. Digests
4075.8 Serials
4076 Monographs. By date
4077.2 Dictionaries. Encyclopedias
4078 Conferences. Symposia
Collected works (nonserial) see KJV4079
4079 General works. Treatises
Constitutional history
For non-legal works on constitutional history see JN2301+
For sources (constitutions and related material, and other documents) see KJV4073.6+
4080.5 General works
By period

Constitutional law. Droit constitutionnel
Constitutional history
By period -- Continued
Ancien Régime (to 1789)
For early (Germanic) and Frankish period to ca. 900, see KJ

4081 General works
The crown. La couronne
4082 General works
Crown property see KJV5094+
Regalia see KJV5095
4083 Succession to the throne. Monarchial legitimacy. Succession au trône. Légitimité monarchique
Including works on dynastic rights to the French throne
4084 Sovereign's rights. Royal power. Droits du souvereign. Pouvoir royal
4084.2 King's Council. Conseil du roy
4084.3 Royal chancellery. Chancellerie royale
Quasi-representative institutions
4085 General works
Estates-General. Etats généraux
4086 General works
4087 Electoral system for the General Estates. Régime électoral des États généraux
Assembly of Notables. Assemblée des notables
4088 General works
Prévôts see KJV3838.A8
Baillis. Sénéchaux see KJV3838.A8
Judiciary parliaments
see KJV3747 and KJV3754
Social orders. Les Ordres
Cf. KJV4086+ The General Estates
4089 General works
The clergy. Le clergé
4089.2 General works
Seigneurial rights see KJV4096
The nobility. La noblesse
Including works on nobility in the 19th century
4090 General works
Titles of nobility. Titres de noblesse
4091 General works
4091.2 Seigniorial honorific rights of churchmen
4092 The Third Estate. Le Tiers-Etat
4093 Foreign relations
Feudal system. Seigniorial rights. Régime féodal. Droits seigneuriaux
For regalia see KJV5095

Constitutional law. Droit constitutionnel
Constitutional history
By period
Ancien Régime (to 1789)
Feudal system. Seigniorial rights. Régime féodal. Droits seigneuriaux -- Continued

4094 General works

Feudal tenure. Fief see KJV1177+

4095 Serfdom. Servage

4096 Seignioirial rights in the ecclesiastical area. Droits seigneuriaux dans les églises
Including temporalities, tithes regalia, etc.
For benefices of the clergy see KJV1177+
For seigniorial honorific rights of churchmen see KJV4091.2

Seigniorial administration of justice (Justice de seigneur) see KJV3758

4097 Abolition of feudal system. Liquidation du régime féodal

1789-

4100 General works

Revolution, 1789-1792

4101 General works

Declaration of the rights of man and of the citizen, August 26, 1789 see KJV4074.55

4102.A-Z Special topics, A-Z

First Republic and Consulate. La Première République et le Consulat, 1792-1804

4104 General works

4106 Convention, September 22, 1792-October 1795

4108 Directory. Directoire, October 1795-9 November 1799

Consulate, 1799-1804

4110 General works

4112 Life Consulate. Consulate à vie, 1802-1804

4114.A-Z Special topics, A-Z

4116-4118 First Empire. Premier Empire, 1804-1815

4116 General works

The nobility see KJV4090+

4118.A-Z Special topics, A-Z

Restoration. Restauration, 1814-1830

4120 General works

The nobility see KJV4090+

4122.A-Z Special topics, A-Z
Subarrange each by Table K12

4122.C46 Chambre des pairs (Table K12)

July monarchy. Monarchie de Juillet, 1830-1848

Constitutional law. Droit constitutionnel
Constitutional history
By period
1789-
July monarchy. Monarchie de Juillet, 1830-1848 -- Continued
4124 General works
The nobility see KJV4090+
4126.A-Z Special topics, A-Z
e. g.
4126.A23 Abdication
Cf. DC267.8 History
Second Republic. La Seconde République, 1848-1851
4128 General works
4129.A-Z Special topics, A-Z
e. g.
4129.P76 Provisional government
Cf. DC272.7 History
Second Empire. Empire deuxième, 1852-1870
4130 General works
The nobility see KJV4090+
4132.A-Z Special topics, A-Z
Third Republic. La Troisieme République, 1871-1940
4134 General works
4136.A-Z Special topics, A-Z
The French State from 1940-1946
4138 General works
France under German occupation. Militärbefehlshaber in Frankreich, 1940-1944
4139 General (Table K22)
Pétain régime, 1940
4140 General works
4142 Legality of the Vichy Government
4144.A-Z Special topics, A-Z
Constitutional movement of the Liberation of France. Mouvement constitutionnel de la Libération, 1940-1946
4146 General works
4148 Chief of Free Frenchmen (De Gaulle). Chef des Français libres, June 1940-September 1941
4150 French National Committee in London. Le Comité National Français de Londres, September 1941-June 1943
4152 Chief Civil and Military Command (Giraud), Algiers. Commandement en chef civil et militaire, Alger, November 1942-June 1943

Constitutional law. Droit constitutionnel
Constitutional history
By period
1789-
The French State from 1940-1946
Constitutional movement of the Liberation of France. Mouvement constitutionnel de la Libération, 1940-1946 -- Continued
4154 French Committee of National Liberation. le Comité Français de la Libération Nationale, June 1943-April 1944
4156 Provisional Governments of the Republic. Gouvernements provisoires de la République, 24 April 1944-December 1946
For referenda see KJV4287+
Fourth Republic. La Quatrième République, 1946-1958
4158 General works
French Union (L'Union Française) see KJV4646+
4160 Fifth Republic. La Cinquième République, 1958-
4162 Interpretation and construction (Table K11)
4164 Revision and amending process. Procédure de révision de la constitution. Droit d'amendement dans la constitution (Table K11)
For a particular amendment, see the appropriate constitution
Constitutional principles. Principes constitutionnels
4166 General (Table K11)
4166.2 Rule of law (Table K11)
4167 Legality (Table K11)
4168 Republicanism. Principes républicains (Table K11)
Separation of powers. Séparation des pouvoirs
4170 General (Table K11)
4172 Competence conflicts between the administration and the judiciary. Conflits d'attribution (Table K11)
For competence conflict courts (Tribunaux des conflits) see KJV3820
4173 Intervention of the legislature in the administration of justice. Interventions du législateur dans le fonctionnement de la justice (Table K11)
4174 Conflict of interests. Incompatibility of offices. Ethics in government (Table K11)
War and emergency powers see KJV7184
International law and municipal law see KJV304+
4177 Constitutional aspects of international cooperation, membership in supranational organizations, etc. (Table K11)
4178 Foreign relations. Affaires étrangères (Table K11)

Constitutional law. Droit constitutionnel -- Continued
Public policy and police power. Order public et pouvoir de police
4180 General (Table K11)
Censorship see KJV4216
Individual and state
4182 General (Table K11)
Nationality and citizenship
4184 General (Table K11)
Acquisition and loss
4186 General (Table K11)
Immigration. Naturalization
Cf. KJV376+ Private international law
4187 General (Table K11)
4188.A-Z By country, A-Z
Subarrange each by Table K12
e.g.
4188.A54 Algeria (Table K12)
4189 Right of asylum. Droit d'asile (Table K11)
4190 Emigration (Table K11)
Repatriation
4192 General (Table K11)
4193.A-Z By region or country, A-Z
Subarrange each by Table K12
4193.O94 Overseas. Outre-mer (Table K12)
4194 Expatriation (Table K11)
Control of individuals
4196 General (Table K11)
4197 Passports. Identification. Registration (Table K11)
4198.A-Z Particular groups, A-Z
Subarrange each by Table K12
4198.A55 Aliens. Etrangères (Table K12)
Including expulsion and deportation
4198.G96 Gypsies. Romanies. Gitanes (Table K12)
4198.J49 Jews. Juifs (Table K12)
Romanies see KJV4198.G96
Internal security. Control of subversive activities. Sûreté de l'Etat
4200 General (Table K11)
Security police see KJV5252.A34
Censorship see KJV4216
Processions and manifestations see KJV5285
4202.A-Z Groups or parties, A-Z
Subarrange each by Table K12
Civil and political rights. Droits civiques et libertés publiques
4204 General (Table K11)

Constitutional law. Droit constitutionnel
Individual and state
Civil and political rights. Droits civiques et libertés publiques -- Continued
The declaration of the Rights of Man and of the Citizen, August 26, 1789 see KJV4074.55
Equality before the law (Antidiscrimination in general). Egalité en droit
4206 General (Table K11)
4207.A-Z Particular groups, A-Z
Subarrange each by Table K12
4207.F74 French political émigrés, 1792-1830 (Table K12)
Including works on property of French political refugees
4207.G96 Gypsies. Romanies. Nomades (Table K12)
4207.H85 Huguenots (Table K12)
4207.J49 Jews. Juifs (Table K12)
4207.M56 Minorities (Table K12)
Romanies see KJV4207.G96
4207.W65 Women (Table K12)
4208 Right to life (Table K11)
Freedom of thought. Freedom of expression. Liberté de la pensée. Liberté d'opinion
4210 General (Table K11)
4212 Freedom of religion. Liberté religieuse (Table K11)
4216 Freedom of education. Liberté de l'enseignement (Table K11)
Freedom of information and censorship
4220 General (Table K11)
Censorship of the theater see KJV5489
Censorship of motion pictures see KJV5500+
Censorship of the press see KJV6258
Processions. Manifestations see KJV5285
Freedom of assembly and association. Liberté de réunion et d'association
4224 General (Table K11)
Processions. Manifestations see KJV5285
Personal liberty. Liberté individuelle
4226 General (Table K11)
Freedom of movement. Liberté de circulation
4227 General (Table K11)
Free choice of domicile (Liberté de domicile) see KJV578
4228 Right to habeas corpus. Interdiction de toute arrestation et détention arbitrale (Table K11)
Free choice of employment see KJV3404+
Right to vote see KJV4298+
Right to run for public office see KJV4305+

Constitutional law. Droit constitutionnel
Individual and state -- Continued
4230 Political parties. Partis politiques (Table K11)
Secular ecclesiastical law. Droit ecclésiastique français
Class here works on the relationship of church and state, regardless of denomination
Concordats. Treaties between church and state
Including related material such as court decisions, official reports, memoranda, etc.
For treaties relating to a particular region or province, see the region or province
For treaties on a particular subject matter, see the subject
For treaties in general, see KZ
4234 Collections. Compilations
4235 Individual concordats. By date
4237 General (Table K11)
Separation of church and state. Séparation des églises et de l'état
4239 General (Table K11)
4240 State and church jurisdiction. Policymaking (Table K11)
Religious corporations, societies, and congregations
4244 General (Table K11)
4246 Legal status. Corporations of public law. Juristic personality (Table K11)
4248 Religious congregations unauthorized by the State. Congrégations religieuses non autorisées dans l'État (Table K11)
Church autonomy and state supervision
History
4250 General works
4252 King's authority. Autorité royale
Clergy as a social order see KJV4089.2+
4256 General (Table K11)
Jurisdiction of secular courts over church matters and the clergy
4262 General (Table K11)
4263 Appeal as from abuse. Appel comme d'abus (Table K11)
4264 Criminal jurisdiction (Table K11)
4268 Education and training of the clergy. Degrees (Table K11)
4275 Church property. Administration and maintenance of church property (Table K11)
Organs of government. Autorités gouvernementales
4280 General (Table K11)
The people. Le peuple
4282 General (Table K11)

Constitutional law. Droit constitutionnel
Organs of government. Autorités gouvernementales
The people. Le peuple -- Continued
Referendum. Plebiscite
Collections. Compilations
4287 Serials
4289 Monographs. By date
4292 Individual referenda. By date of adoption
Including official editions with or without annotations, and related works
4293 General works
Election law. Droit électoral
4295 General (Table K11)
Right to vote. Suffrage (Active and passive). Droit de vote
4298 General (Table K11)
4300.A-Z Groups of voters, A-Z
Subarrange each by Table K12
4300.W66 Women. Femmes (Table K12)
4301 Campaign financing. Comptes des campagnes (Table K11)
Election to particular offices
4305 President of the Republic. Président de la République (Table K11)
The legislature. Corps législatif
4307 General (Table K11)
4309 Senat (Table K11)
4311 National Assembly. Assemblée nationale (Table K11)
4313 Voting registers. Listes électorales (Table K11)
Verification of elections. Contrôle de la régularité des élections
4315 General (Table K11)
4317 Election contest. Contentieux des élections (Table K11)
Corrupt practices in elections see KJV8302
4319 Campaign funds and expenditures. Financement des campagnes électorales
The legislature. Legislative power. Corps législatif. Pouvoir législatif
4321 General (Table K11)
Legislative initiative. Initiative législative
Including works on legislative initiative of the head of the State or of the executive
4324 General (Table K11)
Parliamentary initiative in financial matters see KJV6454

Constitutional law. Droit constitutionnel
Organs of government. Autorités gouvernementales
The legislature. Legislative power. Corps législatif. Pouvoir législatif -- Continued
Rules and practice. Règlements
4326 General (Table K11)
4327 Interpellation (Table K11)
Parliamentary investigations. Enquêtes parlementaires
4329 General (Table K11)
4330 Parliamentary commissions of inquiry. Commissions d'enquête parlementaire (Table K11)
Legislators
4332 General (Table K11)
4334 Parliamentary immunity. Inviolabilité parlementaire (Table K11)
Senat
Including works on the Council of the (4th) Republic (Conseil de la République)
4336 General (Table K11)
4338 Membership (Table K11)
Election see KJV4309
4340 Rules and practice. Réglement (Table K11)
For interpellation see KJV4327
For commission of inquiry see KJV4330
Assemblée nationale (National Assembly)
4342 General (Table K11)
4344 Membership (Table K11)
Election see KJV4311
4346 Rules and practice. Règlement (Table K11)
For interpellation see KJV4327
For commissions of inquiry see KJV4330
Head of State. President of the Republic. Chef d'Etat. Président de la République
4350 General (Table K11)
Election see KJV4305+
Powers and duties
4355 General (Table K11)
4357 President's power to issue decrees. Pouvoir réglementaire de Président (Table K11)
War and emergency powers see KJV7184
The executive. Executive power. Le gouvernement. Pouvoir exécutif
4360 General (Table K11)
Conseil des ministres (Council of Ministers)
4362 General (Table K11)
4365 Président du Conseil des ministres (Prime Minister) (Table K11)

Constitutional law. Droit constitutionnel
Organs of government. Autorités gouvernementales
The executive. Executive power. Le gouvernement. Pouvoir exécutif -- Continued
Ministerial responsibility. Responsabilité des ministres
4367 General (Table K11)
4369 Criminal liability of ministers. Responsabilité pénale des ministres (Table K11)
4372 Ministerial power to issue administrative orders and regulations. Pouvoir réglementaire des ministres (Table K11)
Ministères (National departments)
Class here works on several departments not related to a particular branch of law or subject
For works on several departments related to a branch of law or subject, as well as an individual department or its regulatory agencies, see the branch of law or the subject
4375 General (Table K11)
Ministère des affaires étrangères (Ministry of Foreign Affairs)
4377 General (Table K11)
Personnel
Cf. KJV5030+ Civil service
4380 General (Table K11)
4382 Legal status (Table K11)
Including salaries, allowances, pensions, etc.
Conseil d'Etat (Council of State)
4385 General (Table K11)
4387 Judicial Section. Section du contentieux (Table K11)
4388 Commissaire de gouvernement (Table K11)
Conseil constitutionnel (Constitutional Council)
4390 General (Table K11)
4392 Judicial review. Contrôle de la constitutionnalité des lois (Table K11)
Verification of elections. Contrôle des élections see KJV4315+
Overseas France. Overseas territories see KJV4530+
4500 National emblem. Flag. Seal. National anthem (Table K11)
4502 Political oath (Table K11)
4504 Patriotic customs and observances (Table K11)
Decorations of honor. Awards of honor. Dignities
4507 General (Table K11 modified)
History
4507.A8 General
4507.A82 Honorary seigniorial rights of churchmen. Droits honorifiques des seigneurs dans les églises

Constitutional law. Droit constitutionnel
Decorations of honor. Awards of honor. Dignities -- Continued
Civilian
4509 General (Table K11)
4512 Legion of honor. Légion d'honneur (Table K11)
Military see KJV7476
4515.A-Z Other, A-Z
Subarrange each by Table K12
Economic constitution see KJV5547
Overseas France. France d'outre-mer
Class here works on several French overseas departments, French overseas territories, and the French Community as a whole
For works on an individual overseas department, territory, or group of departments and territories in a particular region, see the department, the territory or the group
For works on an individual overseas state, or group of states in a particular region associated with France, see the state or the group
History
4530 General
Colonies
4533 General
4534 Code noir. Laws regarding the black populace
Including legal status
French Union see KJV4646+
4535-4540.8 General (Table K10)
Private international law. Conflict of laws. Droit international privé. Conflits de lois
Including works on colonial law
4541 General (Table K11)
4542.A-Z Special topics, A-Z
Subarrange each by Table K12
French nationality see KJV4542.N38
4542.N38 Nationality (Table K12)
Private law. Droit privé
4544 General (Table K11)
4545 Persons. Personnes (Table K11)
For nationality see KJV4542.N38
Property. Ownership and possession. Biens. Propriété et possession
4546 General (Table K11)
Real property. Immeubles
4548 General (Table K11)

Overseas France. France d'outre-mer
Private law. Droit privé
Property. Ownership and possession. Biens. Propriété et possession
Real property. Immeubles -- Continued

4550 Land tenure. Régime foncière (Table K11)
Including works on eminent domain (privation de la propriété foncière au profit de personnes morales publiques)

4552 Succession upon death. Successions (Table K11)

Choses in action. Obligations. Contracts

4554 General (Table K11)

Associations and companies. Sociétés

4556 General (Table K11)

4557.A-Z Special topics, A-Z
Subarrange each by Table K12

Business associations see KJV4562

Commercial law. Droit commercial

4560 General (Table K11)

4562 Business associations. Sociétés commerciales (Table K11)

Social legislation. Droit social
For works on a particular industry, see the industry

4566 General (Table K11)

Labor law. Droit du travail

4568 General (Table K11)

4570 Management-labor relations. Relations du travail (Table K11)

4572 Trade and professional associations. Syndicats professionnels (Table K11)

Public law. Droit public

4576 General (Table K11)

4578 Law making. Régime legislatif (Table K11)

Administrative law. Droit administratif

4580 General (Table K11)

Administration of colonies see KJV4640

4583 Public contracts. Marchés publics (Table K11)
Including colonial law or the French Community

4584 Local government (Table K11)

Civil service. Fonction publique
Including colonial law or the French Community

4585 General (Table K11)

4586.A-Z Special topics, A-Z
Subarrange each by Table K12

Allowances see KJV4586.S35

Colonial administrators see KJV4640

Pays see KJV4586.S35

Overseas France. France d'outre-mer
Administrative law. Droit administratif
Civil service. Fonction publique
Special topics, A-Z -- Continued
4586.R47 Retirement system. Régime des retraites (Table K12)
4586.S35 Salaries. Pays. Allowances. Traitements. Soldes. Indemnités (Table K12)
Government liability
4590 General (Table K11)
Indemnification to Frenchmen evicted overseas see KJV3721+
Rural law. Droit rural
Including colonial law or the French Community
4594 General (Table K11)
4599.A-Z Particular, A-Z
Subarrange each by Table K12
4602 Mining. Exploitation minière (Table K11)
Particular industrial and trade lines. Branches de l'industrie et du commerce
Including private and public law aspects
4608 General (Table K11)
Food processing industries. Produits alimentaires
Sugar. Sucre
4614 General (Table K11)
Alcohol distilling see KJV4618
Beverages. Boissons
4616 General (Table K11)
4618 Alcoholic beverages. Liquor law. Boissons alcooliques. Régime des alcools (Table K11)
4620-4622 Import trade. Export trade. Commerce d'importation. Commerce d'exportation
4620 General (Table K11)
4622.A-Z Special topics, A-Z
Subarrange each by Table K12
Public finance. Finances publiques
4624 General (Table K11)
4626 Public accounts. Comptabilité publique (Table K11)
Including auditing (vérification des comptes)
4630 Taxation and customs. Régime fiscal. Régime douanier (Table K11)
4635 Criminal law and procedure. Droit penal. Procédure criminelle

Overseas France. France d'outre-mer -- Continued
Colonial law. Droit colonial
Including French protectorates (protectorats) and mandated territories (pays sous mandat)
For a particular colony, protectorate, mandated territory or a regional grouping, see the colony, the protectorate, the mandated territory or regional grouping
4638 General (Table K11)
Code noir see KJV4534
4640 Administration of colonies (Table K11)
Including status of colonial administrators
Legislative power see KJV4578
Public finance see KJV4624+
Criminal law see KJV4635
French Community. La Communauté
History
4644 General (Table K11)
French Union. Union française
Cf. KJV4074.51946 Constitution of October 27, 1946
4646 General
4648 Supreme Council of French Union. Le Haut-Conseil de l'Union française
4650.A-Z Special topics, A-Z
4650.C57 Citizenship of French Union. Citoyenneté de l'Union française
4652 General (Table K11)
Administrative law. Droit administratif
4656 History
4661-4669 General (Table K9b)
4675 Public interest. Utilité publique (Table K11)
Public policy (Ordre public) see KJV4180+
4680 Renunciation. Renonciation (Table K11)
4682 Abuse of one's right. Abus de droit (Table K11)
For abuse of administrative power see KJV4745+
The judiciary and administration
4685 General (Table K11)
4687 Conflits d'attribution (Table K11)
Judicial review see KJV4840
4690 Control of private institutions and establishments by the state. Contrôle de l'État sur les organismes privés (Table K11)
Cf. KJV5541+ Public economic law
Administrative process
4692 General (Table K11)
4693 Governmental investigations. Enquêtes publiques (Table K11)
Administrative acts. Actes administratifs

Administrative law. Droit administratif
Administrative process
Administrative acts. Actes administratifs -- Continued
4695 General (Table K11)
4697 Hierarchy of administrative acts. Hiérarchie des acts administratifs (Table K11)
Cf. KJV4890+ Hierarchic authority
Administrative discretion. Pouvoir discrétionnaire de l'administration
4700 General (Table K11)
Judicial review see KJV4840
Abuse of administrative power see KJV4745+
Acts of the executive. Actes de gouvernement
4707 General (Table K11)
Exercise of the power of pardon see KJV8080
Carrying out of international treaties see KJV304+
Wartime and emergency measures see KJV7186
Administrative ordinances. Réglements d'administration
4709 General (Table K11)
Judicial review of administrative ordinances see KJV4830
Unilateral administrative acts. Actes administratifs unilatéraux
4711 General (Table K11)
Requirements for validity see KJV4743+
Administrative permits. Autorisations administratifs
4715 General (Table K11)
4717 Licenses (Table K11)
4719 Concessions (Table K11)
Administrative contracts. Public contracts. Contrats administratifs. Marchés publics
Cf. KJV5240+ Public works contracts
4722 General (Table K11)
Application of private law. Application du droit privé
4724 General (Table K11)
Requirements for validity see KJV4743+
4726 Intention. Declaration of intention. Volonté. Declaration de volonté (Table K11)
4730 Financing. Financement (Table K11)
4732 Pledges on public contracts. Nantissements sur marchés public (Table K11)
Wartime and emergency measures see KJV7180+
4735 Conclusion. Passation (Table K11)
4737 Breach of contract. Rupture du contrat (Table K11)
4739.A-Z Particular contracts, A-Z
Subarrange each by Table K12
Defense contracts see KJV7484

Administrative law. Droit administratif
Administrative process
Administrative contracts. Public contracts. Contrats administratifs. Marchés publics
Particular contracts, A-Z -- Continued
Development contracts see KJV4739.R48
Public works contracts see KJV5240+
4739.R48 Research and development contracts (Table K12)
Requirements for validity. Nullity and ineffectiveness. Conditions de validité. Nullité et inefficacité
4743 General (Table K11)
Abuse of administrative power. Détournement du pouvoir
4745 General (Table K11)
4747 Unlawful interference. Voies de fait (Table K11)
4749 Plea of illegality. Exception d'illégalité (Table K11)
Including works on either noncontentious administrative matters or on contentious administrative matters
4750 Revocation (Table K11)
4752 Res judicata. Chose jugée (Table K11)
Remedies. Recours
For works limited to court procedure see KJV4870
4755 General (Table K11)
4757 Petitions to administrative authority for change of decision. Recours gracieux (Table K11)
Appeals through official channels see KJV4892
Enforcement. Administrative sanctions. Exécution
4762 General (Table K11)
4764 Stay of execution of administrative decisions. Sursis à exécution des décisions administratives (Table K11)
4765 Ombudsman. Control over abuse of administrative power (Table K11)
Administrative courts and procedure. Cours administratives et controle juridictionnel de l'administration
History
4766 General
4768 High Constable's Court. Tribunal de la connétablie
4770 Conseils de préfecture
Class here former country councils with regional jurisdiction
4781-4789 General (Table K9b)
Council of State see KJV4385+
4793 Appelate administrative courts. Cours administratives d'appel (Table K11)
4795 Regional administrative courts. Tribunaux administratifs (Table K11)
Procedural principles
4800 Constitutional aspects (Table K11)

Administrative law. Droit administratif
Administrative courts and procedure. Cours administratives et controle juridictionnel de l'administration
Procedural principles -- Continued
4802 Authorizations to plead in court. Autorisations pour plaider en justice (Table K11)
Judicial competence. Jurisdiction. Competence judiciaire
4810 General (Table K11)
Tribunal des conflits see KJV3820
4820 Competence of courts of general jurisdiction to adjudicate in administrative matters. Competence des tribunaux judiciaires en matière administrative (Table K11)
4830 Judicial review of administrative ordinances. Contrôle juridictionnel des règlements d'administration (Table K11)
4840 Judicial review of administrative acts. Contrôle juridictionnel de l'administration (Table K11)
4850 Evidence in administrative courts. Preuve devant la juridiction administrative (Table K11)
4853 Summary proceedings. Procedure in chambers. Procédure d'urgence. Juridiction des referés (Table K11)
Court decisions. Décisions des juridictions administratives
4860 General (Table K11)
Stay of execution of administrative decisions see KJV4764
4865 Res judicata. Chose jugée (Table K11)
4868 Opposition by a third party. Tierce-opposition (Table K11)
4870 Remedies. Recours (Table K11)
For works on both remedies in contentious administrative matters and administrative remedies see KJV4755+
4875 Arbitration. Arbitrage (Table K11)
Administrative organization. Administrative power. Structure de l'administration. Pouvoir administratif
4880 General (Table K11)
4882 Centralization and decentralization (Table K11)
4884 Separation of administrative courts from active administration. Séparation de la juridiction administrative et de l'administration active (Table K11)
Pouvoir de gestion
4886 General (Table K11)
Liability see KJV5080+
Abuse of administrative power see KJV4745+
Hierarchic authority. Pouvoir hierarchique
4890 General (Table K11)

Administrative law. Droit administratif
Administrative organization. Administrative power. Structure de l'administration. Pouvoir administratif
Hierarchic authority. Pouvoir hierarchique -- Continued
4892 Official channels. Voie hiérarchique
Including works on appeals through official channels (recours hiérarchiques)
Juristic persons of public law. Personnes morales de droit public
4895 General (Table K11)
4897 Juristic personality (Capacity). Personnalité civile (Table K11)
4899 Independent regulatory agencies. Autorités administratives Indépendantes (Table K11)
Central administrative institutions (Institutions centrales d'administration) see KJV4350+
Local administrative institutions see KJV4910+
4902 Government business enterprises (Table K11)
For particular government enterprises, see the subject
4904 Executive advisory bodies. Administration consultative (Table K11)
Local government. Administrative departments and divisions of the state. Collectivités locales
4910 General (Table K11)
4912 Déconcentration (Table K11)
Class here works on delegation of powers by the central authority to regions or other local jurisdictions
Public contracts made by local government. Marchés des collectivités locales
4914 General (Table K11)
4916 Real estate transactions by local government. Opérations inmobilières des collectivités locales (Table K11)
Local civil service see KJV5070+
Local police. Police locale
4920 General (Table K11)
Rural police see KJV5820+
Regions
Organization and administration
4922 General (Table K11)
4924 Regional prefect. Préfet régional (Table K11)
Departments. Départements
Organization and administration
4926 General (Table K11)
Prefecture. Prefect. Préfet
4928 General (Table K11)

Administrative law. Droit administratif
Administrative organization. Administrative power. Structure de l'administration. Pouvoir administratif
Local government. Administrative departments and divisions of the state. Collectivités locales
Departments. Départements
Organization and administration
Prefecture. Prefect. Préfet -- Continued
County council. Conseil général
Including works on both county councils and district councils (conseils d'arrondissement)
4930 General (Table K11)
Conseil de préfecture see KJV4770
4933 Police power of prefects. Pouvoir de police des préfets (Table K11)
4936 Judicial power of prefects. Pouvoir judiciaire des préfets (Table K11)
Finance see KJV7040+
Districts. Arrondissements
Organization and administration
4940 General (Table K11)
4942 District council. Conseil d'arrondissement (Table K11)
4944 Sub-prefects. Sous-préfets (Table K11)
Cantons
4946 General (Table K11)
4948 Cantonal delegate. Délégué cantonal (Table K11)
4950 Syndicate de communes (Table K11)
Municipal government. The community. La commune
4953 General (Table K11)
4955 Municipal reform (Table K11)
4957 Autonomy and rulemaking power (Table K11)
4959 Municipal territory (Table K11)
Including boundaries, incorporation and merger of communities
Constitution and organization of municipal government
4963 General (Table K11)
4965 Councils and civic associations. Conseil municipal (Table K11)
Officers and employees
For general works on municipal civil service see KJV5070+
4967 General (Table K11)
Municipal elections. Elections municipales
4970 General (Table K11)

Administrative law. Droit administratif
Administrative organization. Administrative power. Structure de l'administration. Pouvoir administratif
Municipal government. The community. La commune
Constitution and organization of municipal government
Officers and employees
Municipal elections. Elections municipales -- Continued
4973 Verification of elections. Contrôle de la régularité des élections (Table K11)
Including contested elections (contentieux)
4980 Mayor. Maire (Table K11)
Including mayor's police power
4982 Municipal police. Police municipale (Table K11)
Municipal economy
4985 General (Table K11)
Municipal ownership. Régies municipales
4987 General (Table K11)
4990 Alienable and prescriptible communal property. Domaine privé de la commune (Table K11)
4992 Municipal business enterprises. Entreprises économiques des municipalités (Table K11)
Budget see KJV7049+
Public contracts. Contrats des communes
4994 General (Table K11)
4996 Communal public works. Travaux publics (Table K11)
4998 Concessions (Table K11)
5000 Municipal markets. Crées municipales (Table K11)
Supra-municipal corporations and cooperation
5004 General (Table K11)
Syndicat de communes see KJV4950
Fusion et regroupements des communes see KJV4959
Public services. Services publics
Including works on both public services and government business enterprises
5008 General (Table K11)
5010 Concession of public service. Concession de service public (Table K11)
Public utilities. Entreprises de service public
5012 General (Table K11)
Electricity. Gas see KJV5947+
5014 Public services under private management. Services publics à gestion privée (Table K11)
Public offices. Offices
5020 General (Table K11)
Venality of offices. Venalité des offices
5022 General (Table K11)

Administrative law. Droit administratif
Administrative organization. Administrative power. Structure de l'administration. Pouvoir administratif
Public services. Services publics
Public offices. Offices
Venality of offices. Venalité des offices -- Continued
5024 Lien on the price of transfer. Privilege sur le prix de cession (Table K11)
Private assistance to public administration. Collaboration des particuliers avec l'administration
5026 General (Table K11)
Chambers of commerce see KJV2228+
Foundations see KJV1486
Trade and professional associations see KJV3429+
Civil service. Fonction publique
5030 General (Table K11)
Appointment. Nominations
5032 General (Table K11)
5035 Illegal appointment. Nominations illégales (Table K11)
5038 Discipline (Table K11)
Types and modes of employment
5040 People with disabilities. Personnes handicapées (Table K11)
Rights and duties of civil servants. Droits et obligations des fontionnaires
5042 General (Table K11)
Civil and political rights. Droits civiques et libertés publiques
5045 General (Table K11)
5046 Liberty of opinion. Liberté d'opinion (Table K11)
Freedom of assembly and association. Liberté de réunion et d'association
5048 General (Table K11)
5050 Legality of trade unions of civil servants. Legalité des syndicats de fontionnaires (Table K11)
5052 Right to strike. Droit de grève (Table K11)
5056 Liability. Responsabilité des agents publics
Including civil liability of civil servants
For criminal liability see KJV8322+
5058 Transfer. Déplacement
Salaries. Pays. Traitements. Soldes
5060 General (Table K11)
Allowances. Indemnités
5062 General (Table K11)
5064 Travel expenses. Moving expenses. Indemnité de voyage. Frais de déplacement (Table K11)
5066 Retirement pensions. Retraite. Pensions (Table K11)

Administrative law. Droit administratif
Civil service. Fonction publique -- Continued
Military pensions see KJV7456+
Local civil service. Agents des collectivités locales
For works on civil service of a particular jurisdiction, see the jurisdiction
5070 General (Table K11)
Retirement pensions. Retraite. Pensions
5072 General (Table K11)
5074 National pension fund for employees of local government. La caisse nationale de retraites des agents des collectivités locales (Table K11)
Government liability. Responsabilité publique
5080 General (Table K11)
Indemnity to repatriates, refugees and to French dispossessed abroad. Indemnisation des repatriés, réfugiés et des Français dépossé dés outre-mer see KJV3690+
Contractual liability of the State see KJV4737
Government tortious liability. Responsabilité delictuelle ou quasi delictuelle de la puissance publique
5082 General (Table K11)
Strict liability. Liability without fault. Responsabilité sans faute
Including presumption of fault (présomption de faute)
5083 General (Table K11)
5084 Accidents and damage caused by public works. Accidents et dommages causés par les travaux publics (Table K11)
Including moral and personal injuries, and including damage to private property
Government vicarious liability for its agents. Responsabilité de la puissance publique à raison defautes de ses agents
5085 General (Table K11)
5086 State's liability for losses caused by the Armed Forces. Responsabilité de l'État pour les dommages causés par l'Armée (Table K11)
5087 Government liability for losses caused by riots. Responsabilité de la puissance publique à raison des dommages occassionnés par les émeutes (Table K11)
War damage compensation see KJV7191+
Public property. Public restraints on private property. Propriété publique
History
5090 General

Public property. Public restraints on private property. Propriété publique

History -- Continued

Crown property. Domaine de la couronne

5094 General

5095 Regalia. Régales

5101-5109 General (Table K9b)

Government property

5111 General (Table K11)

5111.5 Records management. Access to public records (Table K11)

Right of ownership and police power. Le droit de propriété et le pouvoir de police

5112 General (Table K11)

Eminent domain. Privations de la propriété au profit de personnes morales publiques see KJV5190+

5114 Use of private real property for public purposes. Emprises administratives sur les propriétés privées (Table K11)

Including works on competence of administrative courts in such matters

Public domain. Domaine public

5116 General (Table K11)

Acquisition and transfer see KJV5123

Eminent domain see KJV5190+

Conservation of public natural resources see KJV5410

5118 Thoroughfare permits. Permis de voirie (Table K11)

Police of the public domain. Police du domaine public

5119 General (Table K11)

5120 Game police. Police de la chasse (Table K11)

Water police see KJV5187

Maritime public domain see KJV5152+

Alienable and prescriptible public property. Domaine privé de la propriété publique

5122 General (Table K11)

5123 Acquisition and transfer. Acquisition et alienation (Table K11)

Public land law

5125 General (Table K11)

National preserves. Recreation grounds

5127 General (Table K11)

Wildlife conservation see KJV5802

Public servitudes. Servitudes de droit public

5129 General (Table K11)

5130 Servitudes concerning roads and waterways. Servitudes de voire (Table K11)

Public property. Public restraints on private property. Propriété publique

Public servitudes. Servitudes de droit public -- Continued

5132 Servitudes established for places of war activities and for the frontier zone. Servitudes établies pour des places de guerre et de la zone des frontières (Table K11)

Roads and highways. Chemins

5134 General (Table K11)

Construction and maintenance

Including bridges, and including regional planning

5136 General (Table K11)

5137 Public contracts. Marchés publics (Table K11)

Including contractors

Highway transport workers see KJV6010

Local roads. By-roads. Chemins communaux. Chemins vicinaux

5139 General (Table K11)

5140 Urban streets. Voirie urbaine (Table K11)

5141 Rural roads. Rural pathways. Sentiers d'exploitation rurale. Chemins ruraux (Table K11)

Including rural right of way

5142.A-Z Other, A-Z

Subarrange each by Table K12

5142.P75 Private roads. Chemins privés (Table K12)

Abutting property

5146 General (Table K11)

Servitudes see KJV5129+

Water resources. Regime des eaux

Including works limited to private law

5148 General (Table K11)

Inalienable and imprescriptible public water resources. Eaux domaniales

5150 General (Table K11)

Public maritime resources. Domaine public maritime

5152 General (Table K11)

Offshore structures see KJV5844

Coastal zones. Rivage

5154 General (Table K11)

Sea ports. Ports maritimes

5156 General (Table K11)

5157 Anchorage. Ancrage (Table K11)

Protection of biological resources of the sea see KJV5184+

Public inalienable and imprescriptible navigable inland waters. Eaux intérieures domaniales

For works on land water navigation see KJV6096+

5159 General (Table K11)

Public property. Public restraints in private property. Propriété publique
Water resources. Regime des eaux
Inalienable and imprescriptible public water resources. Eaux domaniales
Public inalienable and imprescriptible navigable inland waters. Eaux intérieures domaniales
Channels see KJV5167
5162 Eaux non domaniales
Running waters. Rivers. Watersheds. Rivières. Fleuves. Eaux courantes
Including navigable and non-navigable rivers
5164 General (Table K11)
5166 Water rights. Droits des riverains
Cf. KJV1231.5 Adjoining landowners
5167 Channels (Table K11)
5168 Springs. Eaux de sources (Table K11)
Waterfalls. Chutes d'eau
5170 General (Table K11)
5172 Concession of a waterfall. Concession de chute d'eau (Table K11)
Development and conservation of water resources
5174 General (Table K11)
Industrial utilization of water. Utilisation industrielle de l'eau
5176 General (Table K11)
Water power. Force hydraulique
5177 General (Table K11)
Water-power electric plants see KJV5956
Fishing see KJV5822+
Water supply. Provision d'eau
5179 General (Table K11)
5180 Aqueduct. Aqueduc (Table K11)
5182 Drinking water. Eau potable (Table K11)
For drinking water standards see KJV5304
5183 Irrigation. Drainage (Table K11)
Protection of biological resources of waters. Protection des resources biologiques des eaux
Including inland waters and the sea
5184 General (Table K11)
Fisheries and fishing see KJV5822+
5186 Flood control (Table K11)
Water pollution see KJV5416+
5187 Water police. Police des eaux (Table K11)
Government-owned industry see KJV5590+
Eminent domain. Privation de la propriété au profit de personnes morales publiques

Public property. Public restraints on private property. Propriété publique

Eminent domain. Privation de la propriété au profit de personnes morales publiques -- Continued

5190 General (Table K11)

5192 Expropriation (Table K11)

Requisitions

5194 General (Table K11)

5195 Civil requisitions. Requisitions civiles (Table K11)

Military requisitions see KJV7191+

5198 Nationalization (Table K11)

Confiscations

5199 General (Table K11)

Confiscation of illicit profits see KJV6777

Regional planning. Aménagement du territoire

5200 General (Table K11)

Ecological aspects

5204 General (Table K11)

5206.A-Z Special topics, A-Z

Subarrange each by Table K12

5206.B55 Billboards. Placarding. Affichage (Table K12)

5208 Land subdivisions. Lotissements (Table K11)

Road and bridge construction. Road maintenance see KJV5136+

City planning and redevelopment. Urbanisme

5210 General (Table K11)

Land subdivisions see KJV5208

5212 Sanitation (Table K11)

5214 Charges on private property in the interest of urban planning and redevelopment. Charges d'urbanisme (Table K11)

Cf. KJV5190+ Eminent domain

Housing. Logements

5218 General (Table K11)

5220 Public housing agencies. Services du logement (Table K11)

Housing projects. Home construction program. Projets d'immeubles d'habitation. Programme de construction d'habitation

5222 General (Table K11)

Dwelling for employees see KJV3455.E66

Co-ownership of building see KJV1236+

Housing allowances see KJV3452

Housing aid see KJV3666

Building and construction. Legislation du batiment

For building industry see KJV5892+

5226 General (Table K11)

Regional planning. Aménagement du territoire
Building and construction. Legislation du batiment -- Continued
5228 Building permits. Permis de construction (Table K11)
Including demolition and renovation permits
5229 Building materials. Matériaux de construction (Table K11)
5230 Safety (Table K11)
Including liability
Home construction program. Housing project see KJV5222+
5232.A-Z Buildings and structures, A-Z
Subarrange each by Table K12
5232.E37 Earthworks. Terrassements (Table K12)
5232.I54 Industrial buildings (Table K12)
Road and bridge construction see KJV5136+
5232.R87 Rural buildings (Table K12)
Public works. Travaux publics
5238 General (Table K11)
Public works contracts. Marchés de travaux publics
Cf. KJV4722+ Public contracts
5240 General (Table K11)
5242 General clauses and conditions imposed on contractors. Clauses et conditions générales imposées aux entrepreneurs (Table K11)
5243 Public construction contracts. Marchés de travaux publics de bâtiment (Table K11)
Road and bridge building see KJV5136+
5245 Liability for damage caused by public works. Dommages causés par les travaux publics (Table K11)
Police and public safety. Police et maintien de l'ordre public
5246 General (Table K11)
5247 Organization and administration (Table K11)
Police courts (Tribunaux de simple police) see KJV8464
Police measures
5249 General (Table K11)
5250 Judicial review of acts of police (Table K11)
5252.A-Z Police forces, A-Z
Subarrange each by Table K12
5252.A34 Administrative police (Table K12)
5252.C75 Criminal police. Police criminelle (Table K12)
Local police see KJV4920+
Military police see KJV7500
Municipal police see KJV4982
Police of the public domain see KJV5119+
Rural police. Gendarmerie rurale see KJV5820+
Traffic police. Police de la circulation see KJV6002+
Public safety. Securité publique

Police and public safety. Police et maintien de l'ordre public
Public safety. Securité publique -- Continued
5255 General (Table K11)
5257 Weapons. Explosives. Explosifs (Table K11)
Including manufacturing, import, and trade of firearms and ammunition
Hazardous articles and processes
Including transportation by land
For transportation by sea see KJV6042+
5259 General (Table K11)
5260 Etablissements dangereux, incommodes et insalubres (Table K11)
5262 Radioactive substances. Nuclear power (Table K11)
Including nuclear waste disposal, and including works on use of radioactive substances in medicine
Poisons and toxic substances. Substances vénéneuses
5264 General (Table K11)
5265.A-Z Particular, A-Z
Subarrange each by Table K12
Herbicides see KJV5265.P47
5265.P47 Pesticides. Herbicides (Table K12)
5265.R33 Radon (Table K12)
Accident control
5267 General (Table K11)
Accidents at work see KJV3467+
5269 Accidents caused by electric current. Accidents provoqués par le courant électrique (Table K11)
Including electric installations and engineering
5270 Accidents caused by elevators. Accidents d'ascenseurs (Table K11)
5272.A-Z Other, A-Z
Subarrange each by Table K12
Fire prevention and control. Prévention de l'incendie. Securité contre l'incendie
5274 General (Table K11)
5275 Firefighters. Fire departments. Sapeurs-pompiers. Corps de sapeurs-pompiers (Table K11)
Including voluntary firefighters
Flood control see KJV5186
Control of social activities
5280 General (Table K11)
Fairs. Exhibitions. Foires. Salons. Expositions
5282 General (Table K11)
5284.A-Z Particular fairs and expositions, A-Z
Subarrange each by Table K12
5284.P37 Paris exposition of 1878. Exposition universelle internationale, 1878

Police and public safety. Police et maintien de l'ordre public
Control of social activities -- Continued
5285 Assembly. Processions and manifestations. Réunions. Cortèges et manifestations (Table K11)
Sports. Tourism. Recreation
Including recreation areas
5286 General (Table K11)
5287 Holiday camps. Colonies de vacances (Table K11)
Including holiday camps run by the State of local communities
Winter resorts. Stations d'hiver
5288 General (Table K11)
Winter sports resorts see KJV5292.S55
Sport activities
Cf. KJV5464+ Physical education
5290 General (Table K11)
5292.A-Z Sports, A-Z
Subarrange each by Table K12
5292.B85 Bullfights. Corridas (Table K12)
Corridas see KJV5292.B85
Football (Soccer) see KJV5292.S62
5292.M68 Moutaineering. Sports de montagne (Table K12)
5292.S55 Skiing. Winter sports resorts. Stations de sports d'hiver (Table K12)
5292.S62 Soccer. Football (Table K12)
5294 Criminal aspects (Table K11)
Lotteries. Games of chance. Jeux de hasard
5296 General (Table K11)
5297 Casinos (Table K11)
5300 Disaster control. Disaster relief (Table K11)
Public health. Santé publique
5302 General (Table K11)
Maternal and child welfare see KJV3617+
Food laws see KJV5900+
Water supply see KJV5179+
5304 Drinking water standards. Fluoridation (Table K11)
5306 Refuse disposal. Enlèvement des ordures (Table K11)
Including urban waste (déchets urbains) or industrial waste (déchets industriels)
For environmental pollution see KJV5412+
Burial and cemetery laws. Législation de la sépulture
Including dead bodies and death (déces; mort)
5310 General (Table K11)
5312 Concession of a burial place. Concession de sépulture (Table K11)
Transplantation of human organs, tissues, etc. see KJV5372

Public health. Santé publique -- Continued
Contagious and infectious diseases. Maladies contagieuses et infectueuses
5314 General (Table K11)
5316.A-Z Diseases, A-Z
5316.A53 AIDS. SIDA (Table K12)
SIDA see KJV5316.A53
Mental health. Santé mentale
5318 General (Table K11)
The mentally ill. Malades mentaux
Cf. KJV995+ Civil law
5320 General (Table K11)
Institutions for the mentally ill see KJV5360
5324 Drug addiction. Toxicomania (Table K11)
Including works on narcotics and toxic substances (substances vénéuses) and including works on social legislation relating to drug addiction
5326 Alcoholism. Dipsomania (Table K11)
Cf. KJV5929+ Alcoholic beverages industry
Narcotics see KJV5380
Poisons. Toxic substances see KJV5264+
Tobacco smoking see KJV5421
Medical law. Droit medical
5328 General (Table K11)
Certificats médicaux
5330 General (Table K11)
5332 Appraisal of personal injury. Appréciation du dommage corporel (Table K11)
5334 Disability evaluation. Evaluation de l'incapacité (Table K11)
5336 Medical social legislation (General). Médicine légale sociale (Table K11)
For labor hygiene and safety see KJV3467+
For health insurance see KJV3545.A+
For occupational diseases see KJV3560+
For birth control and family planning see KJV3646+
The health professions. Professions medicales
5338 General (Table K11)
Individual professions
Class here works on education, licensing, professional representation, ethics, fees, and liability
For malpractice see KJV2088.2.M44
5340 Physicians. Médecins
5342 Dentists. Dental hygienists, etc.
5345 Radiologists
5347.A-Z Other, A-Z
5347.A53 Anaesthetists. Anésthesistes

Medical law. Droit medical
The health professions. Professions medicales
Individual professions
Other, A-Z -- Continued
5347.P89 Psychiatrists. Psychologists
For forensic psychiatry and psychology see RA1001+
5347.S87 Surgeons. Chirurgiens
Auxiliary medical professions. Paramedical professions. Auxiliaires medicaux
5349 General (Table K11)
5352 Nurses and nursing. Infirmiers et infirmières (Table K11)
5353 Midwives. Accoucheuses (Table K11)
5354 Physical therapists. Thérapeutes (Table K11)
5355 Laboratory assistants (Table K11)
Hospitals and other medical institutions or services. Hôpitaux et établissements de cure et de prevention
Including public and private hospitals and institutions
5357 General (Table K11)
5358 Organization and administration (Table K11)
5360 Institutions for the mentally ill. Malades mentaux (Table K11)
Personnel
5362 General (Table K11)
5364 Physicians. Médécins (Table K11)
5365.A-Z Other, A-Z
Subarrange each by Table K12
5367.A-Z Other health organizations, institutions, or services, A-Z
5367.B56 Blood banks (Table K12)
Including blood donations
5367.D39 Day care centers for infants and children (Table K12)
5367.E43 Emergency medical services. Ambulance service. Service d'assistance médicale d'urgence (Table K12)
Nursing homes see KJV5367.O42
5367.O42 Old age homes. Nursing homes (Table K12)
Biomedical engineering. Medical technology
Including human experimentation in medicine
5369 General (Table K11)
5370 Genetic engineering (Table K11)
For artificial insemination (human reproductive technology) see KJV5374
5372 Transplantation of organs, tissues, etc. Greffes, transplantation et autres actes de disposition concernant le corps humain (Table K11)
Including donation of organs, tissues, etc.
5374 Human reproductive technology (Table K11)
Including artificial insemination, fertilization in vitro, etc.

Medical law. Droit medical -- Continued
(5375) Medical experiments with humans
see KJV5369+
Pharmaceutical law. Droit pharmaceutique
5376 General (Table K11)
Drugs. Médicaments
5377 General (Table K11)
Distribution of drugs. Délivrance des médicaments
5378 General (Table K11)
5379 Licensing of drugs for distribution. New drugs. Visa des spécialités pharmaceutiques. Nouveaux médicaments (Table K11)
Including works on registration (enregistrement) of new drugs
5380 Narcotics. Stupéfiants (Table K11)
Poisons and toxic substances see KJV5264+
Pharmaceutical industry see KJV5878
5386 Pharmacists and pharmacies (Table K11)
5388 Cosmetics (Table K11)
Medical jurisprudence. Médecine légale
For forensic medicine see RA1001+
5390 General (Table K11)
Certificate médicaux see KJV5330+
5394 Establishment of viability of a new-born child. Etablissement de la viabilité chez les nouveau-nés (Table K11)
Cf. KJV556+ Natural persons (Civil law)
Expert testimony see KJV3892+
Veterinary medicine and hygiene. Veterinary public health. Législation vétérinaire
5396 General (Table K11)
5398 Veterinarians. Vétérinaires (Table K11)
Sanitary provisions. Législation sanitaire
5400 General (Table K11)
Control and inspection of meat, meat animals and slaughterhouses see KJV5912
Contagious diseases. Maladies contagieuses
5402 General (Table K11)
5404 Animal tuberculosis. Tuberculose animale (Table K11)
Environmental law. Droit de la protection de l'environment
5406 General (Table K11)
5408 Organization and administration (Table K11)

Environmental law. Droit de la protection de l'environment -- Continued

5410 Environmental planning. Conservation of environmental resources (Table K11)

For conservation of water resources see KJV5174+

For ecological aspects of regional planning see KJV5204+

For wildlife conservation see KJV5802

Environmental pollution. Pollutions de l'environnement

5412 General (Table K11)

Water and groundwater pollution. Pollution des eaux

5416 General (Table K11)

5418.A-Z Pollutants, A-Z

Subarrange each by Table K12

5418.R33 Radioactive substances (Table K12)

Air pollution. Pollution atmospherique

Including control of noxious gases, automobile emissions, etc.

5420 General (Table K11)

5421 Tobacco smoking. Tabagisme (Table K11)

5422 Noise control. Lutte contre le bruit (Table K11)

Including traffic noise

Ecological damage. Dommage écologique

5424 General (Table K11)

5425 Redress. Réparation (Table K11)

5425.5 Wilderness preservation. Droit de la protection de la nature (Table K11)

Cultural affairs. L'action culturelle des pouvoirs publics

5426 General (Table K11)

5428 Cultural policy (Table K11)

5430 Organization and administration (Table K11)

5432 Language (Table K11)

Including regulation of use, purity, etc.

Education

5434 General (Table K11)

Freedom of education see KJV4216

Organization and administration

5436 General (Table K11)

5437 Decentralization of national educational administration. Déconcentration administrative a l'éducation nationale (Table K11)

Teachers. Enseignants

5439 General (Table K11)

5440 Teacher training. Formation des maitres (Table K11)

Elementary school teachers see KJV5446

Secondary school teachers see KJV5450

Physical education teachers see KJV5466+

Cultural affairs. L'action culturelle des pouvoirs publics
Education -- Continued
5442 School liability. School and playground accidents. Accidents dans les établissements d'enseignement public (Table K11)
Elementary education. Enseignement primaire
Including pre-elementary education (enseignement préélémentaire)
5444 General (Table K11)
5446 Elementary school teachers. Instituteurs (Table K11)
Secondary education. Enseignement secondaire
5448 General (Table K11)
5450 Secondary school teachers. Fonctionnaires de l'enseignement secondaire (Table K11)
5452 Academic secondary schools. Collèges d'enseignement général (Table K11)
5453 Vocational secondary schools. Collèges d'enseignement professionnel (Table K11)
5455 Education of students with disabilities. Handicapés. Les inadaptés (Table K11)
Including students with social, physical, and mental disabilities
Higher education. Enseignement supérieur
For works on legal education see KJV150+
5456 General (Table K11)
Universities. Universités
5457 General (Table K11)
Faculties. Institutes
For law schools see KJV156+
5458 General (Table K11)
5460.A-Z Particular. By place, A-Z
Subarrange each by Table K12
5461.A-Z Particular schools of higher learning. By place or name, A-Z
Subarrange each by Table K12
e.g.
5461.G74 U.E.R. Grenoble (Table K12)
5461.3 Private schools (Table K11)
Curricula. Course of instruction
For works limited to a particular school, see the school
5462 General (Table K11)
5463 Technical education. Enseignement technique (Table K11)
Vocational education. Formation professionnelle
5464 General (Table K11)
Vocational secondary schools see KJV5453

Cultural affairs. L'action culturelle des pouvoirs publics
Education
Curricula. Course of instruction -- Continued
Physical education. Education physique
Cf. KJV5290+ Sports
5465 General (Table K11)
Physical education teachers. Maîtres d'éducation physique
5466 General (Table K11)
5467 Qualifications. Training. Formation (Table K11)
5468 Social advancement. Promotion sociale (Table K11)
Science and the arts. Recherche
5470 General (Table K11)
5472 Public policies in research (Table K11)
Including research in higher education
Public institutions
5474 General (Table K11)
5475.A-Z Academies. By name, A-Z
Subarrange each by Table K12
5476.A-Z Research institutes. By name, A-Z
Subarrange each by Table K12
5476.C46 Centre national de la recherche scientifique (Table K12)
5477.A-Z Branches and subjects, A-Z
Subarrange each by Table K12
The arts. Les arts
5479 General (Table K11)
5483 Fine arts. Arts figuratives (Table K11)
Performing arts. Représentations artistiques
5485 General (Table K11)
5486 Music. Musicians (Table K11)
Including musicians'contracts
Theatre. Théâtre
Including opera
For copyright see KJV3298+
5487 General (Table K11)
5489 The state and the theatre (Table K11)
Including censorship
5492 Playwrights. Contract. L'auteur et contrat (Table K11)
5494 Personnel (Table K11)
Including managerial, performing, and technical staff
For labor contracts and collective labor agreements see KJV3475.A38
5496.A-Z Individual theatres, A-Z
Subarrange each by Table K12
5496.C65 Comedie française (Table K12)

Cultural affairs. L'action culturelle des pouvoirs publics
Science and the arts. Recherche
The arts. Les arts
Theatre. Théâtre -- Continued
5498.A-Z Special topics, A-Z
Subarrange each by Table K12
Dramatic criticism see KJV6264
Motion pictures. Films de cinéma
Copyright see KJV3316+
Motion picture industry. Industrie cinématographique
Including regulation of trade practice and censorship
5500 General (Table K11)
5502 Lease of motion pictures. Location des films cinématographiques (Table K11)
5505 Professional organization of the motion picture industry. Organisation professionnelle de la cinématographie (Table K11)
5507 Personnel (Table K11)
Including managerial, performing, and technical staff
For labor contracts and collective labor agreements see KJV3475.M69
5510 Screen writers. Contracts (Table K11)
5512 Criminal aspects (Table K11)
Public collections
5514 General (Table K11)
5516 Archives. Historic and scientific documents (Table K11)
Libraries. Bibliothèques
5518 General (Table K11)
5520.A-Z Particular types of libraries, A-Z
Subarrange each by Table K12
5520.P83 Public libraries. Bibliothèques publiques (Table K12)
5522.A-Z Special topics, A-Z
Subarrange each by Table K12
5524 Museums and galleries (Table K11)
Historic buildings and monuments. Architectural landmarks. Monuments historiques et sites
Including vessels, battleships, archaeological sites, etc.
5526 General (Table K11)
5528.A-Z By department, A-Z
Subarrange each by Table K12
5530 Educational, scientific, and cultural exchange (Table K11)
Economic law. Droit économique
5541-5545.8 General (Table K10)
5547 Economic constitution. Droit constitutionnel économique. Ordre public économique (Table K11)

Economic law. Droit économique -- Continued
5549 Theory and principles. Principes fondamentaux du droit public économique (Table K11)
Including free enterprise system (liberté du commerce et de l'industrie), économic dirigée, interventionnisme, etc.)
Organization and administration
Class here works on central organs and organizations, or central and regional organs and organizations
5552 General (Table K11)
5554 Ministère de l'Economie et des Finances (Department of Economy and Finance) (Table K11)
5556.A-Z Other, A-Z
Subarrange each by Table K12
Including public, semi-private, and private organs of economic intervention
5556.C66 Conseil économique et social actuel
Government control and policy
5560 General (Table K11)
National planning. Planification économique
5562 General (Table K11)
Sociétés conventionnées (commercial companies following the government's directives for national economic planning)
5564 General (Table K11)
Economic assistance to sociétés conventionnées
5565 General (Table K11)
5566 Subsidies. Contrats d'aide financière (Table K11)
5568 Tax incentive contracts. Contrats fiscaux (Table K11)
5570 Distribution. Droit de la distribution (Table K11)
Including circuits de la distribution
5572 Investments. Investissements (Table K11)
Including foreign investments
Foreign exchange control see KJV6510+
State control of banks and coordination of credits see KJV2424
5574.A-Z Special topics, A-Z
Subarrange each by Table K12
Prices and price control. Controle des prix
5575 General (Table K11)
Index adjustment forms regarding contracts see KJV1553.3
5580 Price fixing. Fixation des prix (Table K11)
5582 Forced price boost. Hausse illicite des prix (Table K11)
Price delicts and sanctions. Sanctions pénales
5584 General (Table K11)
5586 Seizure and confiscation. Saisie et confiscation (Table K11)

Economic law. Droit économique
Government control and policy -- Continued
Government-owned industry. Secteur public industriel
Including semi-public enterprises (entreprises semi-publiques)
For a particular category of companies, see the category, e.g. insurance companies
5590 General (Table K11)
Government companies. Companies partly owned by government. Sociétés d'economie mixte
5592 General (Table K11)
5594 Nationalized enterprises. Entreprises nationalisées (Table K11)
Cf. KJV5198 Public property
Sociétés conventionnés see KJV5564+
Public utilities see KJV5012+
Competition rules. Restraint of trade control. Concurrence. Entraves au commerce
5595 General (Table K11)
Horizontal and vertical combinations
5596 General (Table K11)
5597 Corporate consolidation, merger, etc. (Table K11)
Cartels
5598 General (Table K11)
5600.A-Z Types of cartels, A-Z
Subarrange each by Table K12
5602.A-Z Industries, occupations, etc., A-Z
Subarrange each by Table K12
Monopolies. Monopoles
5604 General (Table K11)
5606 State monopolies. Regie monopole d'etat (Table K11)
Exclusive privileges
5608 General (Table K11)
Concessions see KJV4719
Unfair competition. Concurrence déloyale
5610 General (Table K11)
5614 Standards. Norms. Quality control (Table K11)
For standards, grading, and quality control of agricultural products or consumer products, see the product
Money, currency and foreign exchange control see KJV6496+
Regulation of industry and trade. Code industriel
5620 General (Table K11)
5622 Comsumer protection. Protection des consommateurs (Table K11)

Economic law. Droit économique
Regulation of industry and trade. Code industriel -- Continued
Advertising. Réclame
For works limited to a particular industrial or trade line, see the industrial or trade line
5624 General (Table K11)
Bill posting see KJV5206.B55
5626 Advertising contract. Contrat de publicité (Table K11)
State control of banks and coordination of credits see KJV2424
Foreign trade. Commerce extérieur
Including foreign trade practice and procedure
5630 General (Table K11)
Export and import controls. Exportations. Importations
5632 General (Table K11)
Tariffs. Customs see KJV7012+
Foreign exchange regulations see KJV6520+
Foreign investments see KJV5572
Payment in foreign currency see KJV1554+
5634 Export syndicates. Syndicats d'exportation (Table K11)
Domestic trade
5638 General (Table K11)
5640 Wholesale trade. Commerce de gros (Table K11)
Retail trade. Commerce en détail
5642 General (Table K11)
Conditions of trading
5646 Sunday legislation
Special modes of trading
5648 Markets. Fairs. Marchés. Foires (Table K11)
5650 Peddling. Canvassing. Colportage. Sollicitation de commandes (Table K11)
5652 Mail-order business. Maisons de commandes par correspondance (Table K11)
Department stores. Magasins généraux
5654 General (Table K11)
5655 Credit to customers. Crédit sur marchandises (Table K11)
5657 Vending machines. Distributeurs automatiques (Table K11)
Secondhand trade. Brocantage
5659 General (Table K11)
5662 Pawnbroking. Prêt sur gage (Table K11)
Service trades
5664 General (Table K11)
Hotels. Restaurants. Hotellerie
5666 General (Table K11)

Economic law. Droit économique
Regulation of industry and trade. Code industriel
Domestic trade
Service trades
Hotels. Restaurants. Hotellerie -- Continued
5667 Promissory notes guaranteed by liens on furniture and equipment of hotel. Warrant hôtelier (Table K11)
5669 Innkeepers' liability (Table K11)
5670 Innkeepers' personnel. Employés d'industrie hôtelière (Table K11)
5672 Real estate investment companies. Sociétés civiles immobilières de capitaux (Table K11)
5674 Real estate agencies. Real estate agents. Agences immobilières. Courtiers en immeubles (Table K11)
Filling stations. Service stations. Postes d'essence. Garages
5676 General (Table K11)
5678 Vending machines for gasoline. Distributeurs automatiques d'essence (Table K11)
5680 Garages. Car repair stations. Garages de réparation (Table K11)
5682 Auctioneers. Commissaires-priseurs (Table K11)
5683.A-Z Other service trades, A-Z
5683.P47 Photographers. Photographs (Table K12)
5685 Criminal provisions. Législation pénale (Table K11)
For criminal provisions limited to a particular branch of economic law or subject, see the subject, e.g. KJV5584+ , Price delicts
Primary production. Production primaire
Agricultural law. Rural law. Droit agraire. Droit rural
5687 General (Table K11)
Land reform and agrarian land policy legislation. Réforme agraire. Politique agricole
5690 General (Table K11)
Farmland ownership and possession. Farmland tenure. Propriété et possession foncières en agriculture. Régime foncier en agriculture
5692 General (Table K11)
Feudal tenure see KJV1185
5694 Commonage and pasture. Vaine pâture (Table K11)
5696 Consolidation of land holdings. Remembrement rural (Table K11)
Inheritance of farm land see KJV5702+
Agricultural credits see KJV5722+
Organization and administration
5698 General (Table K11)

Primary production. Production primaire
Agricultural law. Rural law. Droit agraire. Droit rural
Organization and administration -- Continued
5700 Office national interprofessionnel du blé (Table K11)
Inheritance of farms. Dévolution successorale des exploitations agricoles
Including rural succession upon death (succession rurales)
5702 General (Table K11)
5704 Family farm. Bien de famille paysanne (Table K11)
Entail. Entailed estate. Substitution of heirs see KJV1359
Agricultural contracts
5708 General (Table K11)
Farming lease. Farm rent. Bail à ferme. Fermage
Including lease of rural property (bail rural)
5710 General (Table K11)
5712 Metayer system. Bail à métaire (Table K11)
5713 Emphyteusis. Emphytéose (Table K11)
5714 Lease of livestock. Bail à cheptel (Table K11)
5715 Farm equipment leasing (Table K11)
Lease of hunting and fishing grounds see KJV5797
5717 Lessors liens. Privilèges du bailleur (Table K11)
5719 Tribunaux paritaires de baux ruraux (rural lease commissions having jurisdiction over disputes between lessors and lessees of rural properties) (Table K11)
Agricultural credit. Crédit agricole
Including rural credit (crédit rural)
5722 General (Table K11)
5724 Farmers' loan associations. Sociétés de crédit agricole (Table K11)
Farming credit on personal property. Crédit agricole mobilier
5726 General (Table K11)
5727 Promissory notes guaranteed by nonpossessory liens on farm goods. Warrants agricoles (Table K11)
Including warrants vincoles
5729 Marketing orders (Table K11)
5730 Standards and grading (Table K11)
Livestock industry and trade. Cheptels
For meat and meat products see KJV5912
5732 General (Table K11)
Lease of livestock see KJV5714
Livestock insurance see KJV5744.L58
5734.A-Z Particular, A-Z
Subarrange each by Table K12
5734.C38 Cattle (Table K12)

Primary production. Production primaire
Agricultural law. Rural law. Droit agraire. Droit rural
Livestock industry and trade. Cheptels
Particular, A-Z -- Continued
5734.S85 Swine (Table K12)
5736 Milk production. Dairy farming (Table K12)
For dairy products see KJV5918+
5738.A-Z Agricultural commodities, A-Z
Subarrange each by Table K12
5738.C47 Cereals and grain. Céréales et blés (Table K12)
5738.F78 Fruits and vegetables. Fruit et légumes (Table K12)
Grain see KJV5738.C47
5738.S44 Seeds (Table K12)
5738.T63 Tobacco. Tabac (Table K12)
Vegetables see KJV5738.F78
5740 Agricultural disasters. Calamités agricoles (Table K11)
Agricultural insurance. Assurances agricoles
5742 General (Table K11)
5744.A-Z Particular lines or risks, A-Z
Subarrange each by Table K12
5744.A33 Accident insurance. Casualty insurance (Table K12)
5744.F57 Fire. Assurance incendie (Table K12)
5744.H35 Hail storms. Assurance contre la grêle (Table K12)
5744.L58 Livestock. Assurance du bétail (Table K12)
Social insurance see KJV5816+
5746 Farmers' mutual insurance companies. Mutuelles agricoles (Table K11)
Corporate representation. Agricultural organization
5750 General (Table K11)
5752 Chambers of agriculture. Chambres d'agriculture (Table K11)
5754 Nonprofit associations of landowners for common interest projects. Associations syndicales des propriétaires (Table K11)
5756 Farmers cooperatives. Coopératives agricoles (Table K11)
Farmers' loan associations see KJV5724
Viticulture
5760 General (Table K11)
5762.A-Z Special topics, A-Z
Subarrange each by Table K12
5770 Apiculture (Table K11)
5775 Horticulture (Table K11)
Forestry. Droit forestier
Including works on both forestry law and water resources
5780 General (Table K11)

Primary production. Production primaire
Agricultural law. Rural law. Droit agraire. Droit rural
Forestry. Droit forestier -- Continued
Forest rangers. Gardes forestiers
Cf. KJV5820+ Rural police
5782 General (Table K11)
Game keepers see KJV5799
Lumbering. Sylviculture. Exploitation forestière
5786 General (Table K11)
5788 Timber trade. Commerce des bois (Table K11)
5790 Sale of standing wood. Vente des coupes de bois (Table K11)
Game laws. Wildlife. Droit de chasse. Animaux sauvage
5795 General (Table K11)
5797 Lease of hunting grounds. Bail de chasse (Table K11)
Including works on fishwater lease (bail de pêche)
5799 Game keepers. Garde-chasse (Table K11)
5802 Wildlife conservation (Table K11)
5804 Hunting accidents. Accidents de chasse (Table K11)
Social legislation. Droit social
Including horticulture, viticulture, and forestry
5810 General (Table K11)
Labor law for agricultural workers. Ouvriers agricoles
5812 General (Table K11)
5814.A-Z Special topics, A-Z
Subarrange each by Table K12
Social insurance. Assurances sociales
Including all branches of social insurance
5816 General (Table K11)
5818.A-Z Special topics, A-Z
Rural police. Gendarmerie rurale
5820 General (Table K11)
Forest rangers see KJV5782+
Game keepers see KJV5799
Fisheries and fishing. Pêche
Cf. KJV5176+ Industrial utilization of waters
5822 General (Table K11)
5824 Sea fisheries and fishing. Pêche maritime (Table K11)
Cf. KJV5184+ Protection of biological resources of the sea
Freshwater fisheries and fishing. Pêche en eau douce
5826 General (Table K11)
5828 Lease of fishing waters (Table K11)
Mining. Quarrying. Exploitation minière. Industries extractives
Including metallurgy (industries métallurgiques)

Primary production. Production primaire
Mining. Quarrying. Exploitation minière. Industries extractives -- Continued
5830 General (Table K11)
Ownership and possession of mines. Propriété et possession des mines
5832 General (Table K11)
5833 Ownership of mines in relation to surface ownership. Propriété des mines et ses rapports avec la superficie (Table K11)
Mines covered by concession. Mines concédés
5835 General (Table K11)
5836 Subsoil royalty. Redevance tréfonçiere (Table K11)
Ownership and possession of coal mines. propriété et possession des houillères
5840 General (Table K11)
5842 Nationalization of coal mines. Nationalisation des houillères (Table K11)
5844 Continental shelf (Table K11)
Including offshore structures
5846 Miners. Ouvriers mineurs (Table K11)
Social legislation. Droit social
5848 General (Table K11)
Labor law
5850 General (Table K11)
5852.A-Z Special topics, A-Z
Subarrange each by Table K12
5854 Mine safety and sanitation. Rescue work. Sécurité et hygiène dans les mines
Including rescue equipment
5856 Social insurance
Including all branches of social insurance
5858 Land reclamation. Environmental law. Responsabilité des mines a l'occasion des affaissements de la surface du sol (Table K11)
Cf. KJV5424+ Environmental law
5860.A-Z Resources, A-Z
Subarrange each by Table K12
5860.H94 Hydrocarbons. Hydrocarbures (Table K12)
5860.S65 Solid universal fuels. Combustibles solides (Table K12)
Particular industrial and trade lines. Branches de l'industrie et du commerce
Manufacturing industries. Industries manufacturieres
Including heavy and light industries
5862 General (Table K11)
5864 Automobile industry (Table K11)
Chemical industries. Industries chimiques

Particular industrial and trade lines. Branches de l'industrie et du commerce
Manufacturing industries. Industries manufacturieres
Chemical industries. Industries chimiques -- Continued
5866 General (Table K11)
5868 Alcohol. Alcool (Table K11)
Including distilleries
For alcoholic beverages see KJV5929+
5870 Fertilizers. Engrais (Table K11)
Petroleum. Oil. Pétrole. Huile
For works on extraction and pipelines of crude oil or natural gas see KJV5860.A+
5872 General (Table K11)
5874 Refineries. Raffineries (Table K11)
Pipelines see KJV6029
Filling stations see KJV5676+
5876 Negotiable instruments incorporating non-possessory liens of an oil company stock. Warrant pétrolier (Table K11)
5878 Pharmaceutical industry. Industrie pharmaceutique (Table K11)
5880 Plastics industry. Production et transformation des matières plastiques (Table K11)
Clothing industry and trade. Industries de l'habillement
5882 General (Table K11)
5884 Fashion. Modes (Table K11)
For copyright see KJV3312+
5886 Furniture industry and trade. Ameublement (Table K11)
5890 Jewelry. Watchmaking. Bijouterie. Horlogerie (Table K11)
Building and construction industry. Industrie de construction
5892 General (Table K11)
Building partnerships. Sociétés de construction
5893 General (Table K11)
5894 Promoters. Promoteurs (Table K11)
5895 Contractors (Table K11)
Public construction contracts see KJV5240+
5897 Contracts and specifications
Including liability of architects and building contractors
Labor hygiene and safety see KJV3467+
5899 Criminal provisions (Table K11)
Food processing industries. Food products. Industrie alimentaire. Denrées destinees à l'alimentation humaine
5900 General (Table K11)
5902 Labeling (Table K11)
5904 Purity (Table K11)
Including regulation of adulteration and additives (addsitifs alimentaires)

Particular industrial and trade lines. Branches de l'industrie et du commerce

Food processing industries. Food products. Industrie alimentaire. Denrées destinees à l'alimentation humaine

5906 Cereal products. Céréales (Table KJV-KJW4)

5908 Fruits and vegetables. Fruit et légumes (Table KJV-KJW4)

5910 Confectionary. Confiserie (Table KJV-KJW4)

5912 Meat. Viandes (Table KJV-KJW4)

Including meat animals and slaughter houses (animaux de boucherie et tueries)

5914 Poultry products. Volaille (Table KJV-KJW4)

5916 Egg products. Oeufs (Table KJV-KJW4)

Dairy products. Produits laitiers

5918 General (Table KJV-KJW4)

Milk see KJV5736

5920 Cheese. Fromage (Table KJV-KJW4)

Butter see KJV5922

5922 Oils and fats. Matières grasses (Table KJV-KJW4)

Including animal and vegetable oils and fats, essential oils, margarine, etc.

5924 Fishery products. Seafood. Produits de la pêche (Table KJV-KJW4)

Beverages. Boissons

5926 General (Table KJV-KJW4)

5927 Mineral waters. Eaux minerales (Table KJV-KJW4)

For drinking water see KJV5182

Alcoholic beverages. Boissons alcooliques

5929 General (Table KJV-KJW4)

5932 Wine and wine making. Vin (Table KJV-KJW4)

5934 Beer and brewing. Biere. Brasserie (Table KJV-KJW4)

5936 Brandy. Distilleries. Eau-de-vie. Bouilleries (Table KJV-KJW4)

5938.A-Z Related industries and products, A-Z

Subarrange each by Table K12

5938.C35 Canning industry. Industrie de la conserve (Table K12)

Power production and supply. Energy policy

Cf. KJV5012+ Public utilities. Entreprises de service public

5941-5945.8 General (Table K10)

Electricity and gas. Electricité et gaz

5947 General (Table K11)

5948 Nationalization. Nationalisation (Table K11)

Including indemnification

5949 Price regulation. Réglementation des prix (Table K11)

Public works for production and distribution of electric power. Travaux publics pour la production et la distribution d'énergie électrique

Particular industrial and trade lines. Branches de l'industrie et du commerce
Power production and supply. Energy policy
Electricity and gas. Electricité et gaz
Public works for production and distribution of electric power. Travaux publics pour la production et la distribution d'énergie électrique -- Continued
5950 General (Table K11)
5952 Restraint on private property. Atteintes à la propriété privée (Table K11)
5954 Geothermal power plants. Centrales thermiques (Table K11)
5956 Hydroelectric plants. Usines hydroélectriques (Table K11)
5958 Nuclear-power plants. Centrales nucléo-électriques (Table K11)
Distribution and conveyance of electric power. Distribution et transport de l'énergie électrique
5960 General (Table K11)
5962 Distribution in rural areas. Rural electrification. Distribution de l'énergie électrique. Electrification rurale (Table K11)
5964 Statutory servitudes related to distribution and conveyance of electric power. Servitudes légales en matière de distribution et de transport de l'énergie électrique (Table K11)
5966 Liability. Responsabilité (Table K11)
5968 High voltage lines. Lignes à haute tension (Table K11)
5970 Gas. Gas companies. Gaz. Entreprises gazières
Nuclear energy. Energie atomique
5972 General (Table K11)
Nuclear power plants see KJV5958
Publishing. Printing. Book trade. Edition. Imprimieries. Librairie
5973 General (Table K11)
Author and publisher. Publishing contract see KJV3318+
Printing industry. Imprimeries et industries graphiques
Cf. KJV6251+ Press law. Droit de la presse
5974 General (Table K11)
National collective labor agreement see KJV5980
5977 Book trade. Librairie (Table K11)
For censorship (livres interdits) see KJV6258
Social legislation. Droit social
5978 General (Table K11)
Collective labor agreements. Conventions collectives de travail
5979 General (Table K11)

Particular industrial and trade lines. Branches de l'industrie et du commerce
Publishing. Printing. Book trade. Edition. Imprimieries. Librairie
Social legislation. Droit social
Collective labor agreements. Conventions collectives de travail -- Continued
5980 National collective labor agreements. Conventions collectives nationales de travail. By date of publication
Class here works on collective labor agreements vested by government with the force of public law
Including national collective labor agreements for the printing industry
Transportation. Transports
For works on commercial law of transportation see KJV2541+
5981-5989 General (Table K9b)
Surface transportation. Transport en surface
5995 General (Table K11)
Transport by land. Road transport. Transports terrestres. Transports routiers
Including carriage of passengers and goods
5997 General (Table K11)
Safety and sanitary regulations
5999 General (Table K11)
6000 Transport of dangerous goods. Transport des matières dangereuses (Table K11)
Traffic regulation and enforcement. Code de la route
6002 General (Table K11)
Traffic accidents. Accidents de la circulation
6005 General (Table K11)
Insurance see KJV2928+
Civil (tort) liability see KJV2100.A+
6009 Traffic violations. Contraventions de grande voirie
6010 Highway transport workers. Routiers
Railroads. Chemins de fer
6012 General (Table K11)
Operations of railroads
6014 General (Table K11)
6016 Officials and employees (Table K11)
Including salaries, pensions, social legislation, etc.
6020 Carriage of passengers and goods. Transport par chemin de fer (Table K11)
Liability see KJV2672+
6022.A-Z Particular railway companies or networks, A-Z
Subarrange each by Table K12

Transportation. Transports
Surface transportation. Transport en surface
Railroads. Chemins de fer -- Continued
6024 Kinds of railroads or railways, A-Z (Table K12)
6029 Pipelines (Table K11)
Water transportation. Administrative maritime law. Transports par eau. Droit administratif maritime
6035 General (Table K11)
Ships. Navires
Including ocean going vessels
6037 General (Table K11)
Nationality of ships. Nationalité des navires
6039 General (Table K11)
6040 Registry as a French ship and ship's papers. Franciscation (Table K11)
Safety and sanitary regulations
6042 General (Table K11)
6044.A-Z Types of cargo, A-Z
Subarrange each by Table K12
6044.D35 Dangerous goods. Matières dangereuses (Table K12)
6046 Floatability. Sea worthiness. Navigabilité (Table K11)
6048.A-Z Particular types of vessels, A-Z
Subarrange each by Table K12
6048.M47 Merchant vessels. Navires de commerce (Table K12)
6048.O23 Ocean-going vessels. Navires de haute mer (Table K12)
6048.P54 Pleasure boats. Bateaux de plaisance (Table K12)
Ship owners see KJV2985+
Ship creditors see KJV2859
Ship operators see KJV2795
Shipmaster. Le capitaine
6050 General (Table K11)
6052 Shipmaster's jurisdiction. Compétence du capitaine (Table K11)
For criminal jurisdiction see KJV6140
6056 Juristic acts aboard a vessel (Table K11)
Seamen. Marins
6060 General (Table K11)
6062 Vessels crew. L'équipage (Table K11)
Pilots see KJV6090+
Social legislation for seamen. Régime social des gens de mer
6070 General (Table K11)
Maritime labor law. Droit du travail maritime
Cf. KJV3475.L66 Longshoremen (Labor law)

Transportation. Transports
Surface transportation. Transport en surface
Water transportation. Administrative maritime law. Transports par eau. Droit administratif maritime
Seamen. Marins
Social legislation for seamen. Régime social des gens de mer
Maritime labor law. Droit du travail maritime -- Continued
6072 General (Table K11)
6074 Recruitment of seamen. Contract of employment. Recruitement des gens de mer. Contrat d'engagement (Table K11)
Social insurance of seamen. Régime d'assurance des gens de mer
6076 General (Table K11)
Health and maternity insurance. Assurance maladie et maternité
6078 General (Table K11)
Occupational diseases see KJV6086
Retirement pensions and benefits. Permanent-disability pensions. Régime des retraites
6080 General (Table K11)
6082 Seamen's retirement fund. Caisse de retraites des marines (Table K11)
6086 Workers' compensation. Réparation des accidents de travail et maladies professionnelles (Table K11)
Including accidents at work and occupational diseases
Disciplinary and penal rules see KJV6140
Navigation and pilotage
6090 General (Table K11)
6092 Coastwise and inland navigation (Table K11)
6094 Sea diving. Plongée sous marine (Table K11)
Inland water transportation. Navigation intérieure
6096 General (Table K11)
River traffic regulations. Code de la route fluviale
6098 General (Table K11)
6100.A-Z Particular waterways, A-Z
Subarrange each by Table K12
e.g.
6100.S45 Seine (Table K12)
Water police see KJV5187
Maritime contingencies. Evénements de mer
6114 General (Table K11)
Collision at sea. Abordage maritime

Transportation. Transports
Surface transportation. Transport en surface
Water transportation. Administrative maritime law. Transports par eau. Droit administratif maritime
Maritime contingencies. Evénements de mer
Collision at sea. Abordage maritime -- Continued
6118 General (Table K11)
6120 Jurisdiction in matters of collision at sea. Compétence judiciaire en matière d'abordage (Table K11)
6124 Abandonment of ship and freight. Delaissement du navire et du fret (Table K11)
6128 Wreckage and salvage. Naufrage. Assistance et sauvetage (Table K11)
Average see KJV2838
Marine insurance see KJV2862+
Admiralty. Juridictions maritimes
6130 General (Table K11)
6133 Maritime expert evidence. Expertise maritime (Table K11)
Commercial maritime courts see KJV2791
Prize courts see KZ6440+
6140 Disciplinary and penal rules. Régime disciplinaire et pénal (Table K11)
Including work on shipmaster's criminal jurisdiction and on shipmaster's criminal liability
Air law. Civil aviation. Droit aerien. Aviation civile
6145 General (Table K11)
Aircraft. Aéronef
6147 General (Table K11)
Nationality of aircraft
6149 General (Table K11)
6152 Registry and aircraft's papers (Table K11)
Aircraft ownership see KJV2696
Airline creditors see KJV2696.3
Safety and sanitary regulations
Including safety and sanitary conditions of aircraft
6160 General (Table K11)
6164 Transport of dangerous goods. Transport des matières dangereuses (Table K11)
6166 Faulty construction. Vices de construction (Table K11)
Aeronautics. Navigation aérienne
6168 General (Table K11)
6170 Aerial servitudes. Servitudes aériennes (Table K11)
Air traffic rules. Régles de la circulation
6172 General (Table K11)

Transportation. Transports
Air law. Civil aviation. Droit aerien. Aviation civile
Aeronautics. Navigation aérienne
Air traffic rules. Régles de la circulation -- Continued
6174.A-Z Particular air-control regions, A-Z
Subarrange each by Table K12
e.g.
6174.P37 Paris
Airports
6176 General (Table K11)
6178.A-Z Particular, A-Z
Subarrange each by Table K12
Air personnel. Personnel aérien
Including licensing, wages, etc.
6194 General (Table K11)
6196 Flight crew. L'équipage d'aéronef (Table K11)
6198 Aircraft commander. Commandant d'aéronef (Table K11)
6200 Air navigator. Navigateur aérien (Table K11)
6205 Disciplinary and penal rules. Régime disciplinaire et pénal (Table K11)
Communication. Mass media. Communications. Moyens de diffusion d'information
6220 General (Table K11)
Freedom of information and censorship (General) see KJV4220+
Freedom of the press see KJV6258
Postal, telegraph and telephone services. Postes, télégraphes, téléphones
6228 General (Table K11)
6230 Organization and administration (Table K11)
Postal service. Service postal
6238-6240 General (Table K11)
6240.A-Z Special topics, A-Z
Subarrange each by Table K12
Cheque de virement see KJV2399
Press law. Droit de la presse
For printing industry and book trade see KJV5974+
6251-6255.8 General (Table K10)
6258 Freedom of the press. Liberté de la presse (Table K11)
Copyright see KJV3270+
Right to information see KJV4220+
6264 Rights of literary and dramatic criticism. Droit du critique littéraire et dramatique (Table K11)
6270 Right to reply. Droit de réponse (Table K11)
Cf. KJV2090 Injury to reputation
Journalists. Journalistes

Communication. Mass media. Communications. Moyens de diffusion d'information
Press law. Droit de la presse
Journalists. Journalistes -- Continued
6275 General (Table K11)
Copyright of journalists see KJV3270+
6279 Liability. Responsabilité (Table K11)
Misinformation. Fausse information
6283 General (Table K11)
Right to reply see KJV6270
Radio and television communications
6290 General (Table K11)
6292 Organization and administration (Table K11)
Telecommunication lines. Lignes de télécommunication
6300 General (Table K11)
6302 Servitudes (Table K11)
Including servitudes to protect radio communication centers (centres radioélectriques)
Frequency bands. Television channels see KJV6310+
Cable media. Community antenna. Communication par fil au public. Antenne collective
6307 General (Table K11)
Intellectual property see KJV3248+
Frequency bands. Television channels. Bandes de fréquence. Chaînes de télévision
6310 General (Table K11)
6312 Radio interference. Perturbations radioélectriques (Table K11)
Broadcasting. Radiodiffusion
6315 General (Table K11)
6317 Listener's rights. Droits de l'auditeur (Table K11)
Programming
6320 General (Table K11)
6325.A-Z Particular programs, etc., A-Z
Subarrange each by Table K12
6328 Information services. Databases. Banques de donneés (Table K11)
Professions
Including liberal, e.g. independent artistic and intellectual, professions (professions libérales)
6330 General (Table K11)
Organization. Professional corporations. Ordres professionnels
Including professional monopoly
For particular professional associations, see the profession
6334 General (Table K11)
Trade and professional associations see KJV3429+

Professions -- Continued
Professional ethics. Déontologie professionnelle
For code of ethics of a particular profession, see the profession
6340 General (Table K11)
Professional misconduct. Faute professionnelle
6342 General (Table K11)
6346 Disclosure of confidential communication. Violation du secret professionnel (Table K11)
Including professional secrets (General)
6349 Practice. Clientele (Table K11)
Individual professions
Accountants. Auditors. Comptables. Vérificateurs des comptes
6352 General (Table KJV-KJW5)
6354 Chartered accountants. Commercial court accountants. Experts comptables. Comptables agrées (Table KJV-KJW5)
Auditors. Vérificateurs des comptes
6355 General (Table KJV-KJW5)
Supervisory auditors. Commissaires aux comptes
6357 General (Table KJV-KJW5)
Supervisory auditors in commercial companies see KJV3013
Actors see KJV5494
Architects. Architectes
6359 General (Table KJV-KJW5)
6362 Civil service architects. Architectes fontionnaires (Table KJV-KJW5)
6364.A-Z Special topics, A-Z
Subarrange each by Table K12
6364.W37 War damage. Dommage de guerre. Reconstruction (Table K12)
6370 Artisans (Table KJV-KJW5)
Including works on artisan enterprises
6375 Artists. Artistes (Table KJV-KJW5)
6377 Auctioneers (Table KJV-KJW5)
Bankers and financiers see KJV2420+
Barristers see KJV173+
6385 Commercial intelligencers. Informateurs de commerce (Table KJV-KJW5)
Including credit information bureaus
Health professions see KJV5338+
Lawyers see KJV218+
6390 Merchant's clerks. Employés de commerce (Table KJV-KJW5)
(6395) Musicians. Musiciens
see KJV5486

Professions
Individual professions -- Continued
6400 Painters. Peintres (Table KJV-KJW5)
Pharmacists see KJV5386
Trading agents. Agents de commerce
6410 General (Table KJV-KJW5)
VRP (voyager, représentant, placier) see KJV2315
Auctioneers see KJV6377
Veterinarians see KJV5398
Writers. Ecrivains
6415 General (Table KJV-KJW5)
Journalists see KJV6275+
Public finance. Finances publiques
6426 History
For regalia see KJV5095
Finance reform and policies
6430 General (Table K11)
Monetary policies see KJV6496+
6441-6449 General (Table K9b)
6454 Right of parliamentary initiative. Droit d'initiative parlementaire (Table K11)
Organization and administration
For works on tax administration or tax procedure see KJV6592+
6460 General (Table K11)
6462 Officers and personnel (Table K11)
Including tenure, salaries, pensions, etc.
Direction du trésor (The Treasury Division)
6465 General (Table K11)
6468 Litigation service. Service du contentieux (Table K11)
Including works on the Treasury's court representative (agent judiciaire du trésor public)
Field services. Services exterieurs
6470 General (Table K11)
6474 Personnel (Table K11)
Including tenure, salaries, pensions, etc.
State Audit Office see KJV6492+
6476 Inspection générale des finances (Inspectorate General of Finance)
Public accounts. Comptabilité publique
6480 General (Table K11)
Budget see KJV6520+
Auditing. Contrôlement des finances. Vérification des comptes
6486 General (Table K11)
Cour des comptes (State Audit Office)
Including procedure

Public finance. Finances publiques
Auditing. Contrôlement des finances. Vérification des comptes
Cour des comptes (State Audit Office) -- Continued
6492 General (Table K11)
6494 Registers. Registres (Table K11)
Money. Currency
6496 General (Table K11)
6500 Coinage. Mint regulations (Table K11)
6504 Bank notes. Billets de banque (Table K11)
Foreign exchange control. Contrôle des monnaie des changes
6510 General (Table K11)
Valuta clause see KJV1554.2
Budget. Government expenditures. Dépenses publiques
6520 General (Table K11)
Public debts. Dettes publiques
6526 General (Table K11)
6528 State bonds. Rentes sur l'Etat (Table K11)
Public claims. Créances publiques
6530 General (Table K11)
Collection. Recouvrement
6534 General (Table K11)
Treasury liens. Privilèges du trésor
6536 General (Table K11)
Treasury liens in regard to direct taxes see KJV6746
National revenue. Revenus publics
6539 History
6541-6545.8 General (Table K10)
Taxation
Criticism and reform see KJV6430+
6548 History
6551-6559 General (Table K9b)
6562 Constitutional aspects (Table K11)
6564 Taxing power. Pouvoir fiscal (Table K11)
6566 Interpretation (Table K11)
Double taxation. Double imposition
6568 General (Table K11)
6570 Domicile (Table K11)
6574.A-Z Special topics, A-Z
Subarrange each by Table K12
6574.F67 Foreign corporations, companies, etc. (Table K12)
6574.F68 Foreign states as taxpayers (Table K12)
6574.M85 Multi-national corporations (Table K12)
6574.S52 Shares of stocks. Bonds (Table K12)
Taxation and tax exemption as a measure of social and economic policy

Public finance. Finances publiques
National revenue. Revenus publics
Taxation
Taxation and tax exemption as a measure of social and economic policy -- Continued
6580 General (Table K11)
6582 Assistance to developing countries (Table K11)
Tax administration. Administration fiscale
6592 General (Table K11)
6594 Discretionary power. Pouvoir discrétionnaire (Table K11)
Tax rates (Tarif fiscale) see KJV6600+
Tax collection and enforcement. Recouvrement des impôts
6600 General (Table K11)
Tax tables see KJV6600+
Assessment. Calcul de l'impôt
6604 General (Table K11)
6608 Taxation at a flat rate. Taxation à forfait (Table K11)
6610.A-Z Special topics, A-Z
Subarrange each by Table K12
6610.S42 Search and seizure (Table K12)
Tax courts. Cours de droit fiscal
Including litigation procedures (Contentieux)
6614 General (Table K11)
Remedies. Recours
6616 General (Table K11)
Security. Sûrétés
6618 General (Table K11)
Treasury liens see KJV6746
6622 Tax appeals. Oppositions en matière fiscale
Classes of taxpayers
6630 General (Table K11)
6634 Head of household. Chef de famille (Table K11)
6637 Married couples. Families (Table K11)
6638 Divorced people
Juristic persons. Personnes morales
6640 General (Table K11)
Juristic persons of public law. Personnes morales de droit public
6644 General (Table K11)
Foreign states. Etats étrangers
6648 General (Table K11)
Double taxation see KJV6574.F68
Companies. Sociétés
For income tax see KJV6851+

Public finance. Finances publiques
National revenue. Revenus publics
Taxation
Classes of taxpayers
Juristic persons. Personnes morales
Companies. Sociétés -- Continued
6650 General (Table K11)
6652 Nonprofit associations, nonprofit corporations, foundation (endowments), and pension trust funds (Table K11)
6654 Government companies. Companies partly owned by government. Sociétés d'économie mixte (Table K11)
Sociétés conventionnées see KJV5568
6660 Private limited company. Société à responsabilité limitée
Including direct and income taxes
6665 Joint stock companies. Sociétés par actions
6670 Cooperative societies. Sociétés cooperatives (Table K11)
6680 Foreign companies active in France. Sociétés travaillant en France (Table K11)
For double taxation see KJV6574.F67
6685 Business enterprises Entreprises commerciales ou industrielles (Table K11)
Including direct taxes of business enterprises, and on taxation of businessmen
Agriculture. Horticulture
6690 General (Table K11)
6692 Farmers' cooperatives. Coopératives agricoles (Table K11)
Direct taxes in farming. Impôts directs en agriculture
6694 General (Table K11)
6696 Farm income tax. Impôts sur les bénéfices agricoles (Table K11)
Indirect taxes in farming. Impôts indirects en agriculture
6698 General (Table K11)
6700 Value-added tax in agriculture. Taxe sur la valeur ajoutée en agriculture (Table K11)
6704 Artisans
6706 Banking. Bankers. Opérations de banque. Banquiers
Including works on indirect taxes on banking and financial activities
6708 Barristers. Avocats
Businessmen see KJV6685
Company officers and directors see KJV6838+

Public finance. Finances publiques
National revenue. Revenus publics
Taxpayers
Classes of taxpayers
Farmers (Agriculteurs) see KJV6690+
6710 Liberal professions. Professions libérales (Table K11)
Real estate business
6714 General (Table K11)
6716 Real estate companies. Sociétés immobilières (Table K11)
Direct taxes. Impôts directs
History
6720 General
6722 Tallages. Tailles
6723 Tithes. Dîmes
6731-6735.8 General (Table K10)
Particular methods of assessment and collection
6740 General (Table K11)
6742 Payment at source. Withholding tax. Retenu à la source (Table K11)
6744 Tax assessment in lump-sum payment. Imposition forfaitaire (Table K11)
6746 Treasury liens. Privilèges du trésor (Table K11)
Income taxes. Impôts sur le revenu
History see KJV6720+
6751-6755.8 General (Table K10)
Tax rates and tables see KJV6751+
6760 Assessment (Table K11)
6764 Tax returns. Déclaration de revenu (Table K11)
Income. Revenu
6766 General (Table K11)
Classes of taxpayers see KJV6630+
6768.A-Z Special sources of income, A-Z
Gross income. Revenue global
6770 General (Table K11)
Deductions. Allowances. Déductions
6773 General (Table K11)
6774.A-Z Kinds of deductions and allowances, A-Z
Subarrange each by Table K12
Taxable income. Exemptions. Revenu imposable. Exonerations d'impôt
6775 General (Table K11)
6776.A-Z Profits and capital gains, A-Z
Subarrange each by Table K12
Capital income. Revenu du capital see KJV6787+
Excess profits see KJV6892+

Public finance. Finances publiques
National revenue. Revenus publics
Taxation
Direct taxes. Impôts directs
Income taxes. Impôts sur le revenu
Income. Revenu
Taxable income. Exemptions. Revenu imposable. Exonerations d'impôt -- Continued
War profits see KJV6895
6777 Confiscation of illicit profits. Confiscation des profits illicites (Table K11)
Non-commercial profits. Bénéfices non commerciaux
6778 General (Table K11)
Earnings of liberal professions see KJV6710
Industrial and intellectual property
6780 General (Table K11)
6782 Proceeds of inventions. Produits des inventions (Table K11)
6783 Copyright proceeds. Produits des droits d'auteur (Table K11)
Remunerations of company officers and directors see KJV6838+
6785 Proceeds of stock exchange transactions. Produits des operations de bourse (Table K11)
Capital income tax. Impôt sur le revenu de capital
6787 General (Table K11)
Fixed assets. Capitaux immobilisés
6789 General (Table K11)
6792 Revaluation. Réévaluation (Table K11)
6794 Depreciation. Amortissement (Table K11)
Income from real property see KJV6834
Capital gains on fixed assets. Plus-values des capitaux immobilisés
6800 General (Table K11)
6802 Appreciation of real property. Plus-values immobilières (Table K11)
Floating assets. Capitaux mobiliers
6804 General (Table K11)
Income from shares and stock. Revenus variables
6810 General (Table K11)
6812 Dividends. Dividendes (Table K11)
6814 Income from partners' shares. Revenus de parts d'intérêt (Table K11)

Public finance. Finances publiques
National revenue. Revenus publics
Taxation
Direct taxes. Impôts directs
Income taxes. Impôts sur le revenu
Capital income tax. Impôt sur le revenu de capital
Floating assets. Capitaux mobiliers -- Continued

6816 Income from bonds and other fixed-yield investments. Revenus fixes (Table K11)

Extraordinary profits. Profits exceptionnels

6820 General (Table K11)

6822 Capital gains on floating assets. Plus-values des valeurs mobilières (Table K11)

6826 Premium on shares. Primes d'émission (Table K11)

6828 Distribution of reserves. Distribution des réserves (Table K11)

6830 Interest on loans. Intérêts de créances (Table K11)

6834 Income from real property. Revenus fonciers

Wages and salaries. Revenu du travail

6838 General (Table K11)

Tax tables see KJV6838+

6840 Salaries of company officers and directors. Traitements des dirigeants de sociétés (Table K11)

6845 Pensions and annuities (Table K11)

6847.A-Z Other sources of income, A-Z

Subarrange each by Table K12

Corporation tax. Impôt sur les sociétés

Including unincorporated and incorporated associations and business associations

6851-6855.8 General (Table K10)

6857 Undistributed profits tax. Impôt des revenus non distribués (Table K11)

Government companies. Companies partly owned by the government see KJV6654

Private limited company see KJV6660

Joint stock companies. Sociétés par actions

6860 General (Table K11)

Tax tables see KJV6860

6864 Tax accounting. Comptabilité (Table K11)

6866 Assessment. Calcul de l'impôt (Table K11)

6870 Tax returns. Déclaration de revenu (Table K11)

6872 Taxable income. Revenu imposable (Table K11)

6873 Closing stock. Stock à l'inventaire (Table K11)

6875 Fixed assets. Capitaux mobiliers (Table K11)

Public finance. Finances publiques
National revenue. Revenus publics
Taxation
Direct taxes. Impôts directs
Income taxes. Impôts sur le revenu
Corporation tax. Impôt sur les sociétés
Joint stock companies. Sociétés par actions -- Continued
6877 Floating assets. Capitaux mobiliers (Table K11)
Cooperative societies. Sociétés cooperatives
6879 General (Table K11)
6882.A-Z Special topics, A-Z
Subarrange each by Table K12
6883 Business concern, holding company and industrial trust
Foreign companies active in France. Sociétés étrangères travaillant in France
6884 General (Table K11)
Double taxation see KJV6574.F67
Multi-national corporations
6886 General (Table K11)
Double taxation see KJV6574.M85
Surtaxes
6890 General (Table K11)
Excess profit tax. Contribution sur les bénéfices excesifs
6892 General (Table K11)
6895 War profit tax. Impôt sur les bénéfices de guerre (Table K11)
Property tax. Impôt sur la fortune
Including natural and juristic persons, and business enterprises
6900 General (Table K11)
Tax assessment. Imposition
6902 General (Table K11)
6904 Tax valuation. Détermination de la valeur vénale (Table K11)
6906 Depletion allowances. Déductions pour épuisement (Table K11)
Capital levy. Prélèvement sur le capital
6910 General (Table K11)
6912 Anti-inflationary measures (Table K11)
6914 Wartime and emergency measures. Measures exceptionnelle. Impôts de crise (Table K11)
Real property tax see KJV7068+
Transfer duties. Impôts de transmission
6920 General (Table K11)

Public finance. Finances publiques
National revenue. Revenus publics
Taxation
Transfer duties. Impôts de transmission -- Continued
Estate, inheritance and gift taxes. Impôt sur les successions et donations
6922 General (Table K11)
Estate and inheritance tax. Impôt sur les successions
Including works on déclaration des successions
6924 General (Table K11)
6930 Alien's estate or inheritance in France. Succession de l'étranger en France (Conflict of laws) (Table K11)
Gift taxes. Impôts sur les donations
6932 General (Table K11)
6934 Marriage portion. Dowry. Apport dotal (Table K11)
Indirect taxes. Impôts indirects
6940 General (Table K11)
Registration taxes and stamp duties. Impôts d'enregistrement et de timbre
6944 General (Table K11)
Commodity, services, or transactions see KJV6970+
6952 Registration tax on real property. Droit fiscal de publicité foncière (Table K11)
6956 Stamp duties. Impôts de timbre (Table K11)
Social security taxes see KJV3544+
Sales tax. Taxe sur le chiffre d'affaires
6960 General (Table K11)
Tax tables see KJV6960
6964 Sales tax on work and labor. Taxe sur les prestations de service (Table K11)
6966 Value-added tax. Taxe sur la valeur ajoutée (Table K11)
Taxation of particular commodities, services or transactions
For customs duties on particular commodities see KJV7026.A+
Domestic animals. Animaux domestiques
6970 General (Table K11)
6974 Dogs. Chiens (Table K11)
Horses. Chevaux see KJV6977
6977 Carriages and horses. Voitures et chevaux (Table K11)
6980 Entertainment. Spectacles, jeux et divertissements (Table K11)

Public finance. Finances publiques
National revenue. Revenus publics
Taxation
Taxation of particular commodities, services or transactions -- Continued
6990 Promises of contract. Promesses de contrat (Table K11)
Registration tax on real property see KJV6952
6995 Securities of foreign states. Fonds d'états étrangers (Table K11)
6998 Shares of stock and bonds. Valeurs mobilières (Table K11)
Including shares of stock and bonds of foreign companies active in France
For shares of stock and bonds of foreign states see KJV6995
7004 Stock exchange transactions (Table K11)
7008 Telegrams. Radiotelegrams (Table K11)
Customs. Tariffs. Droits de douane. Douanes
For foreign trade regulations see KJV5630+
7012 General (Table K11)
Lists of goods subjected to tariffs. Tables (Tarif douanier) see KJV7012
Customs organization and administration. Administration des douanes
7020 General (Table K11)
7022 Customs service. Service des douanes (Table K11)
7024 Practice and procedure (Table K11)
Including remedies and enforcement
Commodities and services, A-Z
Cereals see KJV7026.G73
7026.C67 Corn. Blé de Turquie
7026.G73 Grains. Cereals. Blés. Céréales
7030.A-Z Special topics, A-Z
Subarrange each by Table K12
Criminal provisions see KJV7140+
Departmental and communal finance. Finances départmentales et communales
For the public finance of an individual jurisdiction, see the jurisdiction
7040 General (Table K11)
Departmental finance. Finances départementales
7044 General (Table K11)
7046 Financial control of departments. Contrôlement des finances départementales (Table K11)
Including accounting and auditing
Taxes see KJV7060+

Public finance. Finances publiques
Departmental and communal finance. Finances départmentales et communales
Communal finance. Finances communales
For the public finance of an individual commune, see the commune
7049 General (Table K11)
7052 Financial control of communes. Contrôlement des finances communales (Table K11)
Including accounting and auditing
7054 Financing of urban planning and redevelopment. Fiscalité (Table K11)
Local taxes. Impôts locaux
Including departmental and communal taxes
7060 General (Table K11)
7064 Tax collector. Receveur (Table K11)
Real property tax. Impôt foncier
7068 General (Table K11)
7072 Property tax on undeveloped land. Taxe foncière sur les propriétés non bâties (Table K11)
7078 Property tax on developed land. Taxe foncière sur les propriétés bâties (Table K11)
7082 Tax on furnished accommodations. Taxe d'habitation
7100 Business tax. Impôt des patentes (Table K11)
7110 Payroll tax. Taxe sur les salaires (Table K11)
7120 Apprenticeship tax. Taxe d'apprentissage (Table K11)
Tax and customs crimes and delinquency
7140 General (Table K11)
7146 Tax evasion. Evasion fiscale (Table K11)
Violations of customs law. Infractions douanières
7150 General (Table K11)
7155 Smuggling. Contrebande (Table K11)
Government measures in time of war, national emergency, or economic crisis. Emergency and wartime legislation. Mesures exceptionnelles
7180 General (Table K11)
7184 Emergency powers. Pouvoirs exceptionnels (Table K11)
7186 Emergency police forces. Police de la sécurité (Table K11)
By period
7191-7210 1339-1453. The Hundred Years War (Table KJV-KJW6)
7221-7240 1870-1871. Franco-German War. Guerre franco-allemande (Table KJV-KJW6)
7251-7270 1914-1918. World War I. Première guerre mondiale (Table KJV-KJW6)
7281-7300 1919-1940. Reconstruction (Table KJV-KJW6)
7311-7330 1939-1945. World War II. Deuxième guerre mondiale (Table KJV-KJW6)

Government measures in time of war, national emergency, or economic crisis. Emergency and wartime legislation. Mesures exceptionnelles

By period -- Continued

7341-7360 1944- . Reconstruction (Table KJV-KJW6 modified)

7343 Confiscation of collaborator property. Compensation by collaborators to victims of occupation of France (Table K11)

7359.A-Z Particular victims, A-Z

Subarrange each by Table K12

Frenchmen dispossessed abroad see KJV3690+

Orphans and widows of soldiers killed in actions see KJV3680

Repatriated Frenchmen see KJV3690+

Veterans see KJV3670+

National defense. Military law. Defense nationale. Code militaire

History

7370 General

7375.A-Z Special topics, A-Z

Subarrange each by Table K12

7381-7389 General (Table K9b)

Organization and administration

7395 General (Table K11)

7397 Accounting. Comptabilité (Table K11)

Procurement see KJV7482+

Military districts. Circonscriptions territoriales militaires

7400 General (Table K11)

Commanding general of the district. Général commandant de la circonscription territoriale

7402 General (Table K11)

7404 Judicial powers. Pouvoirs judiciaire (Table K11)

Cf. KJV7540+ Military criminal law

The Armed Forces. Les Forces Armées

7408 General (Table K11)

Personnel

7410 General (Table K11)

7414 Civil and political rights. Droits civiques et libertés publiques (Table K11)

Soldiers. Militaires

7418 General (Table K11)

Civil status. Etat civil

7420 General (Table K11)

7422 Civil status of mobilized troops. Etat civil des mobilisés (Table K11)

Conscription. Draft. Contingent

7428 General (Table K11)

National defense. Military law. Defense nationale. Code militaire
The Armed Forces. Les Forces Armées
Personnel
Soldiers. Militaires
Conscription. Draft. Contingent -- Continued
Deferment. Suspension
Including disqualification and exemption
7430 General (Table K11)
7432.A-Z Particular groups, A-Z
Subarrange each by Table K12
7432.C65 Conscientious objectors. Objecteurs de conscience (Table K12)
7436 Mobilization. Mobilisation (Table K11)
Education. Training. Career
7440 General (Table K11)
7442 Academies. Schools, etc. (Table K11)
Officers. Career officers
7446 General (Table K11)
Courts of honor see KJV7472
Non-commissioned officers. Sous-officiers
7448 General (Table K11)
7450 Career non-commissioned officers. Sous-officiers de carrière (Table K11)
7452 Enlistment. Recruiting. Enrôlement. Recruitement (Table K11)
Pay, allowances, benefits. Solde
Including drafted and career military personnel of all services
7454 General (Table K11)
Military pensions. Pensions militaires
7456 General (Table K11)
7460 War pensions. Pensions de guerre (Table K11)
Military pensions of disability see KJV3670+
7462 Discharge. Désenrôlement (Table K11)
7470 Military discipline. Discipline militaire (Table K11)
7472 Courts of honor. Cours d'honneur (Table K11)
7476 Decorations (Table K11)
Equipment. Equipement
Including weapons, plants, and installations
7480 General (Table K11)
Supplies. Procurement. Fournitures. Approvisionnement
7482 General (Table K11)
7484 Contracts for supplies. Defense contracts. Marchés de fournitures. Marchés de la défense nationale (Table K11)

National defense. Military law. Defense nationale. Code militaire

The Armed Forces. Les Forces Armées -- Continued

Army. Armée de terre

7486 General (Table K11)

Pay, allowances, benefits see KJV7454+

7490 Artillery. Artillerie (Table K11)

7495 Cavalry. Cavalerie (Table K11)

7500 Military police. Gendarmerie (Table K11)

Army criminal law and procedure see KJV7546+

Trials see KJV7578+

Navy. Armée de mer

7510 General (Table K11)

Organization and administration

7512 General (Table K11)

7516 Corps du commissariat de la marine (Table K11)

7518 Corps de l'equipage de la flotte (Table K11)

Personnel

7520 General (Table K11)

Sailors. Marins

7524 General (Table K11)

7526 Enlistment. Recruiting. Enrôlement. Recruitement (Table K11)

Naval criminal law and procedure see KJV7550

Trials see KJV7578+

7530 Air Force. Armée de l'air (Table K11)

Military criminal law and procedure. Code de justice militaire pour l'armée de terre

7540 General (Table K11)

Army criminal law and procedure. Code de justice militaire pour l'armée de terre

7546 General (Table K11)

Trials see KJV7578+

7550 Naval criminal law and procedure. Code de la justice maritime (Table K11)

7558.A-Z Special topics, A-Z

Subarrange each by Table K12

7558.P43 Peacetime violation of common law by soldiers. Infractions de droit commun commises par les militaires (Table K12)

Courts and procedure

Including all branches of the armed forces

7565 General (Table K11)

Courts-martial. Courts of inquiry. Conseils de guerre. Conseils d'enquête

7568 General (Table K11)

National defense. Military law. Defense nationale. Code militaire
Military criminal law and procedure. Code de justice militaire
Courts and procedure
Courts-martial. Courts of inquiry. Conseils de guerre. Conseils d'enquête -- Continued
7570.A-Z Special topics, A-Z
Subarrange each by Table K12
7570.N49 Newspaper reporting (Table K12)
Trials. Procès
Including all branches of the Armed Forces
7578 Collections. Compilations
7580.A-Z Individual trials. By name of defendant, A-Z
7590 Civil defense. Protection civile. Défense passive. Défense aérienne (Table K11)
Criminal law. Droit penal
7962 History
7967 Reform of criminal law, procedure, and execution
Including reform of criminal justice administration
For works limited to a particular subject, see the subject
For works pertaining exclusively to the codes, see the codes
7971-7979 General (Table K9b)
Administration of criminal justice. Administration de la justice criminelle
History see KJV7962
Criticism and reform see KJV7967
7982 General (Table K11)
Judicial assistance. Assistance judiciaire
7984 General (Table K11)
7985 International judicial assistance (Table K11)
7987 Foreign judgments (Conflict of laws) (Table K11)
7988 Constitutional aspects (Table K11)
7990 Morality of criminal laws. Moralité des lois pénales (Table K11)
Applicability and validity. La règle de droit criminel
7992 General (Table K11)
Territorial applicability. Application des lois pénales dans l'espace
7994 General (Table K11)
7995 Conflict of laws (Table K11)
7996 Temporal applicability. Application des lois pénales dans le temps (Table K11)
Including works on retroactive (ex post facto) and intertemporal laws
Personal applicability
7998 General (Table K11)
Privileges and immunities. Privilèges et immunités

Criminal law. Droit penal
Applicability and validity. La règle de droit criminel
Personal applicability
Privileges and immunities. Privilèges et immunités -- Continued
7999 General (Table K11)
Parliamentary immunity see KJV4334
Right of asylum see KJV4189
8000 Interpretation and construction of criminal law (Table K11)
Criminal offense. Infraction
8002 General (Table K11)
Elements of crime. Statutory statement of facts. Qualification en matière criminelle
8003 General (Table K11)
Legal element. Elément légal
8004 General (Table K11)
8007 Trichotomy. Classification des infractions d'après leur gravité (Table K11)
Including felony, misdemeanor, and transgressions
8008 Classification of criminal offenses by distinction between criminal law, political criminal law and military criminal law (Table K11)
Material element. Elément matérial
8010 General (Table K11)
Incomplete criminal offense. Infraction inachevée
8011 General (Table K11)
8012 Attempted felony. Tentative punissable (Table K11)
8013.A-Z Other, A-Z
Subarrange each by Table K12
8015 Accomplished crime. Infraction consommée (Table K11)
Classification of criminal offenses based on material element. Classification des infractions fondée sur l'élément matériel
8016 General (Table K11)
8017 Criminal commission and criminal omission. Infraction de commission et infraction de omission (Table K11)
8018 Instantaneous and continuous criminal offenses. Infractions instanées et continues (Table K11)
8019 Simple, habitual, and complex offenses. Infractions simples, infractions d'habitude et infractions complexes (Table K11)
Cf. KJV8064 Compound offenses
Moral element see KJV8030
Criminal liability. Guilt. Responsabilité pénale. Culpabilité
8026 General (Table K11)

Criminal law. Droit penal
Criminal liability. Guilt. Responsabilité pénale. Culpabilité -- Continued
8030 Criminal intent. Mens rea. Dol criminel (Table K11)
8032 Criminal negligence. Négligence criminelle (Table K11)
8032.5 Criminal attempt (Table K11)
Principals of a criminal offense and accessories. Complices
8033 General (Table K11)
8034 Instigator. Instigateur (Table K11)
Accessory before and after the fact. Conspiracy. Complicité. Association des malfaiteurs
Including abettor
8036 General (Table K11)
Receiving and concealing stolen goods see KJV8357
Harboring of criminals see KJV8360
8038 Criminal liability of juristic persons. Responsabilité pénale des personnes morales
Circumstances excluding liability. Les causes de non-culpabilité
8040 General (Table K11)
Incapacity and limited capacity
8042 General (Table K11)
8043 Insanity. The mentally or emotionally disabled. Démence. Les troubles du système nerveux (Table K11)
8045.A-Z Special topics, A-Z
Subarrange each by Table K12
8045.I57 Intoxication. Ivresse (Table K12)
8047 Coercion. Contrainte (Table K11)
8048 Duty to act. Conflicting duties. Accomplissement d'un devoir (Table K11)
8049 Defense. Self-defense. Exercise d'un droit (Table K11)
8050 Necessity. L'état de nécesisté (Table K11)
8052 Victim's consent. Consentement de la victime (Table K11)
Punishment. Measures of rehabilitation and safety. La peine. Mesures de sûreté
8054 General (Table K11)
Criminal anthropology see HV6035+
8055 Criminal sociology (Table K11)
For non-legal works see HV6035+
Measurement of punishment. La mesure des peines
8057 General (Table K11)
Aggravating circumstances of a crime. Circonstances aggravantes de l'infraction
8059 General (Table K11)

Criminal law. Droit penal
Punishment. Measures of rehabilitation and safety. La peine. Mesures de sûreté
Measurement of punishment. La mesure des peines
Aggravating circumstances of a crime. Circonstances aggravantes de l'infraction -- Continued
8062 Recidivism. Recidive (Table K11)
8064 Compound offenses. Concurrence of sentences. Cumul d'infractions. Confusion des peines (Table K11)
Extenuating circumstances of a crime. Circonstances atténuantes de l'infraction
8066 General (Table K11)
8068 Excuses
e.g. Excuse of provocation
Causes barring prosecution or execution of sentence.
Suspension or extinction of punishment. Suspension ou extinction des peines
8069 General (Table K11)
Stay of execution. Sursis à l'exécution des peines
8072 General (Table K11)
8073 Simple stay of execution. Sursis simple à l'exécution (Table K11)
8074 Parole. Libération conditionnelle (Table K11)
Probation. Mise à l'épreuve
8076 General (Table K11)
8077 Probation of minors. Liberté surveillée (Table K11)
8079 Amnesty. Amnistie (Table K11)
8080 Pardon. Grâce (Table K11)
8082 Prescription (Table K11)
Obliteration of convictions. Effacement des condamnations
8084 General (Table K11)
Amnesty see KJV8079
8086 Rehabilitation. Réhabilitation (Table K11)
8090 Capital punishment. Peine du mort
Including question of abolition of capital punishment
For civil death see KJV8123
Imprisonment. Les peines privatives de liberté
8092 General (Table K11)
8094 Solitary confinement with hard labor. Réclusion criminelle (Table K11)
8096 Imprisonment with labor. Emprisonnement correctionnel (Table K11)
8098 Short-term sentence. Emprisonnement de police (Table K11)
8100 Fortress with loss of civil rights. Détention (Table K11)
Relegation to a penal colony. Relégation

Criminal law. Droit penal
Punishment. Measures of rehabilitation and safety. La peine. Mesures de sûreté
Imprisonment. Les peines privatives de liberté
Relegation to a penal colony. Relégation -- Continued
8102 General (Table K11)
Civil death see KJV8123
Penalties limiting freedom of movement. Les peines restrictives de liberté
8110 General (Table K11)
8112 Banishment from France. Banissement (Table K11)
8114 Local banishment. Interdiction de séjour (Table K11)
8118 Safety measures against drug addicts. Mesures de sûreté contre les toxicomanes (Table K11)
8120 Safety measures against alcoholics. Mesures de sûreté contre les alcooliques (Table K11)
Imposition of civil disabilities. Privation des droits civils, civiques et politiques
8122 General (Table K11)
8123 Civil death. Morte civile (Table K11)
8126 Professional disqualification. Privation des droits professionnels (Table K11)
Including deprivation of administrative permits, closing of business, etc.
Fines. Les peines pécuniaires
8130 General (Table K11)
8132 Fine imposed by court. L'amende (Table K11)
Confiscations
8134 General (Table K11)
Confiscation of illicit profits see KJV6777
Confiscation of collaborators' property see KJV7343
Individual offenses. Droit pénal spécial
Offenses against the person. Les infractions contre les personnes
Including aggravating circumstances
8144 General (Table K11)
Homicide
8150 General (Table K11)
Voluntary manslaughter. Homicide volontaire
8152 General (Table K11)
Murder. Meurtre
8154 General (Table K11)
8156 Capital murder. Meurtre aggravé (Table K11)
8157 Non-capital murder. Meurtre simple (Table K11)
8160 Poisoning. Empoisonnement (Table K11)
8164 Infanticide (Table K11)

Criminal law. Droit penal
Individual offenses. Droit pénal spécial
Offenses against the person. Les infractions contre les personnes
Homicide -- Continued
8166 Involuntary manslaughter. Homicide involontaire (Table K11)
8168 Euthanasia. Right to die. Living wills. Euthanasie. Droit à la mort. Volontés vivantes (Table K11)
Bodily injury. Dommage corporel
8170 General (Table K11)
Assault and battery. Coups et blessures
8173 General (Table K11)
Willful assault and battery. Les coups et blessures volontaires
8174 General (Table K11)
Rape see KJV8214
Indecent assault see KJV8216
8176 Castration (Table K11)
8180 Involuntary assault and battery. Les coups et blessures involontaires
8182 Duelling. Duel (Table K11)
8184 Failure to assist in emergencies. Refus d'assistance (Table K11)
Crimes against inchoate life
8186 General (Table K11)
8188 Criminal abortion. Avortement criminel (Table K11)
For birth control see KJV3648+
Moral injury. Dommage moral
8190 General (Table K11)
Illegal detention. False imprisonment. Arrestations illégales. Séquestrations de personnes
8192 General (Table K11)
8194 Committed by a public official. Commise par un fonctionnaire public (Table K11)
8196 Rifling of a burial place. Violation de sépulture (Table K11)
8197 Threats. Menaces (Table K11)
8198 False accusation. Dénonciation calomnieuse (Table K11)
Libel and slander. Insult. Diffamation. Injure
For works on civil liability for libel and slander see KJV2090
8200 General (Table K11)
8202 Disparagement of memory of the dead. Diffamations et injuries envers la mémoire des morts (Table K11)

Criminal law. Droit penal
Individual offenses. Droit pénal spécial
Offenses against the person. Les infractions contre les personnes
Moral injury. Dommage moral
Libel and slander. Insult. Diffamation. Injure -- Continued
8204 Immunities. Privileged comment. Immunités en matière de diffamation et d'injure (Table K11)
Offenses against personal privacy and secrets. Infractions contre l'intimité
8206 General (Table K11)
Violation of the privacy of correspondence. Violation de correspondence
8208 General (Table K11)
8210 Committed by a public official. Commise pa un fontionnaire public (Table K11)
8211 Eavesdropping. Wiretapping (Table K11)
Violation of confidential communication see KJV6342+
Offenses against chastity and public morality. Infractions contre les moeurs
Including works on legal implications of sexual behavior in general
8212 General (Table K11)
8214 Rape. Viol (Table K11)
8216 Indecent assault. Attentats à la pudeur (Table K11)
8218 Indecent exposure. Outrage aux bonnes moeurs (Table K11)
8220 Sodomy. Homosexual acts. Homosexualité (Table K11)
8222 Procuring. Proxénetisme (Table K11)
Seduction. Séduction
8224 General (Table K11)
8226 Seducing of children. Excitation de mineur à la débauche (Table K11)
Offenses against children and family. Infractions contre l'enfant et la famille
8230 General (Table K11)
Offenses against child's welfare. Infractions contre l'enfance
8233 General (Table K11)
8235 Abandonment, neglect, or abuse of a child. Abandon d'enfant (Table K11)
8236 Abduction of minors. Kidnapping. Détournement de mineurs. Enlèvement (Table K11)
Concealment of a child see KJV8347+

Criminal law. Droit penal
Individual offenses. Droit pénal spécial
Offenses against the person. Les infractions contre les personnes
Offenses against children and family ...
Offenses against child's welfare ...
Supposition d'enfant see KJV8352
8237 Desertion and non-support. Abandon de famille (Table K11)
8238 Adultery. Adultère (Table K11)
8239 Bigamy. Bigamie (Table K11)
Offenses against property. Infractions contre les biens
8240 General (Table K11)
Imprisonment for debt see KJV3985
Theft. Vol
Including aggravating circumstances (vol qualifié)
8242 General (Table K11)
8244 Theft from the fields. Vol champêtre (Table K11)
Larceny. Vol simple
8246 General (Table K11)
8247 Petty larceny. Vol insignificant (Table K11)
Fraud. Falsification. Fraude
8250 General (Table K11)
Fraudulent conveyances. Criminal bankruptcy see KJV3236
Forgery see KJV8364+
Breach of trust. Fraudulent conversion of funds. Abus de confiance
8256 General (Table K11)
Embezzlement see KJV8327
8258 Extortion (Table K11)
Receiving and concealing stolen goods see KJV8357
8260 Usury. Usure
Offenses against the state. Infractions contre l'Etat
8264 General (Table K11)
Political offenses. Offenses against security of the state. Infractions politiques. Infractions contre la sûreté de l'état
History
8268 General
World War II. Deuxième guerre mondiale, 1939-1945
8270 General
8272 Collaboration with the enemy
Cf. KJV7343 Emergency and wartime legislation
Confiscation of illicit profits see KJV6777
8281-8285.8 General (Table K10)

Criminal law. Droit penal
Individual offenses. Droit pénal spécial
Offenses against the state. Infractions contre l'Etat
Political offenses. Offenses against security of the state. Infractions politiques. Infractions contre la sûreté de l'état -- Continued
Offenses against external security of the state. Infractions contre la sûreté extérieure de l'état
8287 General (Table K11)
8289 Treason. Trahison (Table K11)
8292 Espionage. Espionnage (Table K11)
Offenses against internal security of the state. Infractions contre la sûreté intérieure de l'état
8294 General (Table K11)
8296 Anarchism. Anarchisme (Table K11)
8297 Terrorism. Terrorisme (Table K11)
Illegal associations and meetings see KJV8394+
8298 Rebellion. Rébellion (Table K11)
Offenses against the Constitution. Infractions contre la Constitution
8300 General (Table K11)
8302 Election crimes. Délits électoraux (Table K11)
Offenses against public finance. Infractions contre les finances publiques
8305 General (Table K11)
Tax and customs crimes see KJV7140+
8310 Counterfeit money. Monnaie contrefait (Table K11)
Criminal violations of public economic law see KJV5685
Commercial criminal law see KJV2281+
Offenses against public order. Infractions contre la paix et l'autorité publiques
8320 General (Table K11)
Offenses of public officials. Misconduct in office. Infractions des fonctionnaires publics. Forfaiture
8322 General (Table K11)
8325 Peculation. Concussion (Table K11)
8327 Embezzlement. Détournement (Table K11)
8329 Interference. Ingérance (Table K11)
Cf. KJV4745+ Abuse of administrative power
8332 Corruption (Table K11)
8335 Influence peddling. Traffic d'influence (Table K11)
8337 Usurpation of titles or authority. Usurpation de titre ou de fonction (Table K11)
Offenses against administration of justice. Infractions contre l'administration de la justice
8340 General (Table K11)

Criminal law. Droit penal
Individual offenses. Droit pénal spécial
Offenses against the state. Infractions contre l'Etat
Offenses against public order. Infractions contre la paix et l'autorité publiques
Offenses against administration of justice. Infractions contre l'administration de la justice -- Continued

8342 Perjury. Subornation of perjury. Parjure. Subornation de témoin (Table K11)

Concealments. Recels

8345 General (Table K11)

Concealment of a child. Recel d'enfant

8347 General (Table K11)

Concealment of pregnancy or birth. Suppression de part ou d'enfant

8349 General (Table K11)

8352 Setting up a child to displace a real heir. Supposition d'enfant (Table K11)

8355 Concealment of a due portion of inheritance. Recel d'un part d'héritage (Table K11)

8357 Receiving and concealing of stolen goods. Recel de choses (Table K11)

8360 Misprision. Harboring of criminals. Non-dénonciation de crime. Recel de malfaiteurs (Table K11)

False accusation see KJV8198

8362 Contempt of court. Infractions d'audience (Table K11)

Forgery. Faux

8364 General (Table K11)

Counterfeiting see KJV8310

8370 Forgery of documents. Faux documentaire (Table K11)

Offenses against public safety. Infractions contre la sûreté publique

8372 General (Table K11)

Mobs see KJV8398

8380 Affray. Bagarre (Table K11)

8384 Vagrancy and begging. Vagabondage et mendicité (Table K11)

8386 Arson. Incendie criminel (Table K11)

8390 Carrying weapons without a licence. Concealed weapons. Port d'armes prohibé. Port d'armes dissimulées (Table K11)

Traffic violations see KJV6009

8392 Offenses against public health (Table K11)

Criminal law. Droit penal
Individual offenses. Droit pénal spécial
Offenses against the state. Infractions contre l'Etat -- Continued
Illegal associations and meetings. Associations et réunions illicites
Cf. KJV4248 Religious congregations unauthorized by the state
8394 General (Table K11)
8398 Mobs. Attroupements (Table K11)
8400 Sacrilege (Table K11)
Class here disturbance of free exercise of cults
Labor law criminal provisions see KJV3480
8410 Contraventions (Table K11)
For works on a particular contravention, see the subject, e.g. KJV6009 , Traffic violations
Criminal courts and procedure. Tribunaux criminels et procedure pénale
8411-8415.8 General (Table K10)
8417 Criminal procedure and public opinion (Table K11)
Including trial by newspaper
Court organization
8420 History
8431-8435.8 General (Table K10)
8440 Criminal Division of the Court of Cassation. Chambre criminelle de la Cour de cassation (Table K11)
Including procedure
Cf. KJV3792+ Court of cassation
Courts of Assizes. Cours d'assises
Including procedure
8444 General (Table K11)
8446 President of the assizes. Président des assises (Table K11)
Juvenile court of assizes see KJV8850
8450 Single-judge sitting. Juge unique (Table K11)
8460 Tribunaux correctionnels (Table K11)
Class here works on tribunaux de grande instance (first instance courts of major jurisdiction, or second-instance courts of minor jurisdiction)
Including procedure
8464 Tribunaux de simple police (Police courts) (Table K11)
Including procedure
Cf. KJV5252.C75 Criminal police
Cf. KJV8608+ Police judiciaire
Tribunaux d'exception (Courts of special jurisdiction)
Including historical courts
8470 General (Table K11)

Criminal courts and procedure. Tribunaux criminels et procedure pénale
Court organization
Tribunaux d'exception (Courts of special jurisdiction) -- Continued
8474 Revolutionary Tribunal. Tribunal révolutionnaire (1789-1792) (Table K11)
Haute cour de justice see KJV8495
8480 Tribunal of the State. Tribunal d'Etat (Vichy Government, 1940-1944) (Table K11)
Cours de justice (1944-1951)
Class here courts for judging collaboration with the enemy during the war of 1939-1945
For Haute cour de justice see KJV8495
8485 General (Table K11)
8487 Civic divisions. Chambres, civiques (Table K11)
8489 Purging committees. Comités d'épuration (Table K11)
8495 Haute cour de justice. The court established by the constitution for judging high treason (Table K11)
Including Haute cour de la liberation (1944-1949)
Juvenile courts see KJV8850
Procedural principles
Civil matters before criminal courts. Matières civiles devant les juridictions répressives
8500 General (Table K11)
Civil actions before criminal courts see KJV3943
Evidence in terms of civil law before criminal courts see KJV8707
8504 Due process of law (Table K11)
8508 Orality and publicity of trial (Table K11)
Parties to action
8514 General (Table K11)
Prosecution. Poursuites en justice répressive
8516 General (Table K11)
Public prosecution. Public prosecutors. Poursuites publiques. Ministère public
8518 General (Table K11)
8520 Flagrant délit (Table K11)
Private prosecution. Poursuites par la victime
Including victim of a felony or misdemeanor
8524 General (Table K11)
8526 Private prosecution by associations. Poursuites par les associations (Table K11)
8528 Intervention (Table K11)
Defense. Défense
8530 General (Table K11)
The accused in preliminary procedure see KJV8614+

Criminal courts and procedure. Tribunaux criminels et procedure pénale
Parties to action
Defense. Défense
8532 Defendant in criminal court. Prévenu (Table K11)
Defendant before a jury see KJV8810
Pretrial procedure. Instruction préalable
8600 General (Table K11)
Criminal investigation
Including police judiciaire (Criminal investigation department)
8608 General (Table K11)
Techniques of criminal investigation see HV8073+
The accused in preliminary procedure. Inculpé
8614 General (Table K11)
Protection of human rights in cirminal proceedings see KJV8504
Compulsory and precautionary measures against the accused
8620 General (Table K11)
8624 Police surveillance. Surveillance de la police (Table K11)
8630 Detention under remand. Arrest. Détention préventive (Table K11)
8640 Searches and seizures. Perquisition et saisie (Table K11)
8643 Extradition (Table K11)
Including constitutional aspects
Judicial assistance see KJV7984+
Investigating jurisdictions. Juridictions d'instruction
8648 General (Table K11)
Examining magistrate. Juge d'instruction
8650 General (Table K11)
8654 Letters rogatory of examining magistrate. Commissions rogatoires du juge d'instruction (Table K11)
8660 La Chambre d'accusation (The indicting chamber) (Table K11)
8664 Remedies. Voies de recours (Table K11)
Trial. Plenary proceedings. Procès criminel
Including juridictions de jugement
8670 General (Table K11)
Orality and publicity of trial see KJV8508
Evidence. Preuve
8690 General (Table K11, modified)
History
8690.A8 General

Criminal courts and procedure. Tribunaux criminels et procedure pénale
Trial. Plenary proceedings. Procès criminel
Evidence. Preuve
General
History -- Continued
8690.A82 Ordeals
Including wager of battle (combat judiciaire), water ordeal, fire ordeal, etc.
8692 Burden of proof (Table K11)
Admission of evidence
8700 General (Table K11)
8704 Physical examination (Table K11)
Including blood tests, urine tests, etc.
8707 Evidence in terms of civil law before criminal courts. Preuve du droit civil devant les juridictions répressives (Table K11)
8720 Oath. Serment (Table K11)
Evidence by witnesses. Preuve par témoins
8740 General (Table K11)
Cross examination see KJV8760
8750 Expert testimony. Expertise (Table K11)
For forensic medicine, chemistry, psychology, psychiatry, toxicology see RA1001+
8760 Cross examination. Confrontation. Interrogatoire contradictoire (Table K11)
8770 Presumption. Présomption (Table K11)
Jury
8800 General (Table K11, modified)
History
8800.A8 General
8800.A82 Feudal assizes. Assises féodales
8810 Defendant before a jury. Accusé (Table K11)
8820 Default. Procedure du défaut (Table K11)
Including judgment by default (jugement par défaut)
Procedure at juvenile courts. Tribunaux pour enfants
8840 General (Table K11)
8850 Juvenile courts of assizes. Cours d'assises de mineurs (Table K11)
The juvenile delinquent
8858 General (Table K11)
8860 Liability and circumstances excluding liability. Justification. Les causes de non-culpabilité (Table K11)
Punishment. Correction. La peine
8890 General (Table K11)

Criminal courts and procedure. Tribunaux criminels et procedure pénale
Trial. Plenary proceedings. Procès criminel
Procedure at juvenile courts. Tribunaux pour enfants
Punishment. Correction. La peine -- Continued
Reformatory institutions for children. Maisons de correction pour jeunes détenus
8895 General (Table K11)
9000 Corporal punishment. Châtiments corporels (Table K11)
Judgment. Jugement
9010 General (Table K11)
Judgment by default see KJV8820
Conviction. Condamnation
9020 General (Table K11)
Concurrence of sentence see KJV8064
9025 Acquittal (Table K11)
Res judicata. Chose jugée
9030 General (Table K11)
Effect of criminal res judicata on civil judgment see KJV3962
Appellate procedure. Remedies. Procedure de recours. Voies de recours
9035 General (Table K11)
9040 Appeal to the Court of Cassation. Pourvoi en cassation (Table K11)
Execution of sentence
Including execution of sentence of juvenile court
For measures of rehabilitation and safety see KJV8118
9060 General (Table K11)
Penal institutions. Etablissements pénitentiaires
9070 General (Table K11)
9073 Corporal punishment. Châtiments corporels (Table K11)
9080 Prisons. Imprisonment. Prisoners (Table K11)
9085 Penal colonies. Colonies de déportation (Table K11)
9090 Compensation for judicial error. Indemnités aux victimes des erreurs judiciaires (Table K11)
9100 Criminal registration and registers. Casier judiciaire (Table K11)
Judicial assistance in criminal matters see KJV7984+
Extradition see KJV8643
9150 Costs. Frais de justice
Victimology
9155 General (Table K11)
9158 Compensation to victims of crimes (Table K11)
Criminology and penology see HV6001+

	French regions, provinces, departments, etc.
	Including extinct and mediated regions, provinces, etc.
51-59	Ain (Table KJV-KJW7)
81-89	Aisne (Table KJV-KJW7)
121-129	Allier (Table KJV-KJW7)
	Alpes, Hautes- see KJW2061+
151-159	Alpes-de-Haute-Provence (Table KJV-KJW7)
181-189	Alpes-Maritimes (Table KJV-KJW7)
211-219	Alsace (Table KJV-KJW7)
221-229	Alsace-Lorraine (Table KJV-KJW7)
	Cf. KJW2611+ Lorraine
251-259	Angoumois (Table KJV-KJW7)
281-289	Anjou (Table KJV-KJW7)
311-319	Aquitaine (Table KJV-KJW7)
341-349	Ardèche (Table KJV-KJW7)
371-379	Ardennes (Table KJV-KJW7)
401-409	Ariège (Table KJV-KJW7)
431-439	Artois (Table KJV-KJW7)
461-469	Aube (Table KJV-KJW7)
491-499	Aude (Table KJV-KJW7)
501-529	Auvergne (Table KJV-KJW7)
551-559	Aveyron (Table KJV-KJW7)
581-589	Bas-Rhin (Table KJV-KJW7)
611-619	Basque Provinces (Table KJV-KJW7)
641-649	Basse-Normandie (Table KJV-KJW7)
	Basses-Alpes see KJW151+
671-679	Béarn (Table KJV-KJW7)
701-709	Belfort, Territoire de (Table KJV-KJW7)
731-739	Berry (Table KJV-KJW7)
761-769	Bouches-du-Rhône (Table KJV-KJW7)
791-799	Bourbonnais (Table KJV-KJW7)
821-829	Brittany (Bretagne) (Table KJV-KJW7)
851-859	Burgundy (Bourgogne) (Table KJV-KJW7)
861-869	Calvados (Table KJV-KJW7)
871-879	Cambrésis (Table KJV-KJW7)
891-899	Cantal (Table KJV-KJW7)
921-929	Centre (Table KJV-KJW7)
951-959	Champagne (Table KJV-KJW7)
971-979	Champagne-Ardennes (Table KJV-KJW7)
1001-1009	Charente (Table KJV-KJW7)
1031-1039	Charente-Maritime (Table KJV-KJW7)
1061-1069	Cher (Table KJV-KJW7)
1091-1099	Corrèze (Table KJV-KJW7)
1111-1199	Corse-du-Sud (Table KJV-KJW7)
1121-1129	Corsica (Corse) (Table KJV-KJW7)
1151-1159	Côtes-du-Nord (Table KJV-KJW7)

1211-1219	Creuse (Table KJV-KJW7)
1241-1249	Dauphiné (Table KJV-KJW7)
1271-1279	Deux-Sèvres (Table KJV-KJW7)
1281-1289	Dombes (Table KJV-KJW7)
1301-1309	Dordogne (Table KJV-KJW7)
1331-1339	Doubs (Table KJV-KJW7)
1361-1369	Drome (Table KJV-KJW7)
1391-1399	Essone (Table KJV-KJW7)
1421-1429	Eure (Table KJV-KJW7)
1451-1459	Eure-et-Loire (Table KJV-KJW7)
1481-1489	Finistère (Table KJV-KJW7)
1511-1519	Forez (Table KJV-KJW7)
1541-1549	Franche-Comté (Table KJV-KJW7)
1571-1579	Gard (Table KJV-KJW7)
	Garonne, Haute- see KJW1751+
1601-1609	Gascony (Table KJV-KJW7)
1631-1639	Gers (Table KJV-KJW7)
1661-1669	Gironde (Table KJV-KJW7)
1691-1699	Guienne (Table KJV-KJW7)
1721-1729	Haute-Rhin (Table KJV-KJW7)
1741-1749	Haute-Corse (Table KJV-KJW7)
1751-1759	Haute-Garonne (Table KJV-KJW7)
1781-1789	Haute-Loire (Table KJV-KJW7)
1811-1819	Haute-Marne (Table KJV-KJW7)
1841-1849	Haute-Normandie (Table KJV-KJW7)
1871-1879	Haute-Saone (Table KJV-KJW7)
2001-2009	Haute-Savoie (Table KJV-KJW7)
2031-2039	Haute-Vienne (Table KJV-KJW7)
2061-2069	Hautes-Alpes (Table KJV-KJW7)
2091-2099	Hautes-Pyrénées (Table KJV-KJW7)
2121-2129	Hautes-de-seine (Table KJV-KJW7)
2151-2159	Hérault (Table KJV-KJW7)
2181-2189	Ile-de-France (Table KJV-KJW7)
2211-2219	Ille-et-Vilaine (Table KJV-KJW7)
2241-2249	Indre (Table KJV-KJW7)
2271-2279	Indre-et-Loire (Table KJV-KJW7)
2301-2309	Isère (Table KJV-KJW7)
2331-2339	Jura (Table KJV-KJW7)
2361-2369	Landes (Table KJV-KJW7)
2391-2399	Languedoc (Table KJV-KJW7)
2421-2429	Languedoc-Roussillon (Table KJV-KJW7)
2461-2469	Limousin (Table KJV-KJW7)
2491-2499	Loire-et-Cher (Table KJV-KJW7)
2521-2529	Loire (Table KJV-KJW7)
	Loire, Haute see KJW1781+
2551-2559	Loire-Atlantique (Table KJV-KJW7)

2581-2589 Loiret (Table KJV-KJW7)
2611-2619 Lorraine (Table KJV-KJW7)
Cf. KJW221+ Alsace-Lorraine
2641-2649 Lot (Table KJV-KJW7)
2671-2679 Lot-et-Garonne (Table KJV-KJW7)
2701-2709 Lozère (Table KJV-KJW7)
2731-2739 Maine (Table KJV-KJW7)
2761-2769 Maine-et-Loire (Table KJV-KJW7)
2791-2799 Manche (Table KJV-KJW7)
2821-2829 Marche (Table KJV-KJW7)
2851-2859 Marne (Table KJV-KJW7)
Marne, Haute- see KJW1811+
2881-2889 Mayenne (Table KJV-KJW7)
2911-2919 Meurthe-et-Moselle (Table KJV-KJW7)
2941-2949 Meuse (Table KJV-KJW7)
2971-2979 Midi-Pyrénées (Table KJV-KJW7)
3001-3009 Morbihan (Table KJV-KJW7)
3031-3039 Moselle (Table KJV-KJW7)
3061-3069 Navarre (Table KJV-KJW7)
3091-3099 Nièvre (Table KJV-KJW7)
3121-3129 Nord (Table KJV-KJW7)
3181-3189 Normandy (Table KJV-KJW7)
3211-3219 Oise (Table KJV-KJW7)
3241-3249 Orne (Table KJV-KJW7)
3251-3259 Paris (Dept.) (Table KJV-KJW7)
Paris Region see KJW3571+
3271-3279 Pas-de-Calais (Table KJV-KJW7)
3301-3309 Pays de la Loire (Table KJV-KJW7)
3331-3339 Picardy (Table KJV-KJW7)
3361-3369 Poitou (Table KJV-KJW7)
3391-3399 Poitou-Charentes (Table KJV-KJW7)
3421-3429 Provence (Table KJV-KJW7)
3451-3459 Provence-Alpes-Côte d'Azur (Table KJV-KJW7)
3481-3489 Puy-de-Dome (Table KJV-KJW7)
Pyrénées, Hautes- see KJW2091+
3511-3519 Pyrénées-Atlantiques (Table KJV-KJW7)
3541-3549 Pyrénées-Orientales (Table KJV-KJW7)
3571-3579 Region parisienne (Table KJV-KJW7)
Rhin, Bas- see KJW581+
Rhin, Haut see KJW1721+
3601-3609 Rhône (Table KJV-KJW7)
3631-3639 Rhône-Alpes (Table KJV-KJW7)
3661-3669 Roussillon (Table KJV-KJW7)
Saône, Haute- see KJW1871+
3691-3699 Saône-et-Loire (Table KJV-KJW7)
3721-3729 Sarthe (Table KJV-KJW7)

3751-3759 Savoie (Table KJV-KJW7)
Savoie, Haute see KJW2001+
Seine-Inférieure see KJW3811+
3781-3789 Seine-et-Marne (Table KJV-KJW7)
3811-3819 Seine-Maritime (Table KJV-KJW7)
3841-3849 Seines-Saint-Denis (Table KJV-KJW7)
Sèvres, Deux- see KJW1271+
3871-3879 Somme (Table KJV-KJW7)
3901-3909 Tarn (Table KJV-KJW7)
3931-3939 Tarn-et-Garonne (Table KJV-KJW7)
3961-3969 Touraine (Table KJV-KJW7)
3991-3999 Val-de-Marne (Table KJV-KJW7)
4021-4029 Val-d'Oise (Table KJV-KJW7)
4051-4059 Var (Table KJV-KJW7)
4081-4089 Vaucluse (Table KJV-KJW7)
4111-4119 Venaissin (Table KJV-KJW7)
4141-4149 Vendée (Table KJV-KJW7)
4171-4179 Vendôme (Table KJV-KJW7)
4201-4209 Vermandois (Table KJV-KJW7)
4231-4239 Vienne (Table KJV-KJW7)
Vienne, Haute- see KJW2031+
4261-4269 Vivarais (Table KJV-KJW7)
4291-4299 Vosges (Table KJV-KJW7)
4321-4329 Yonne (Table KJV-KJW7)
4351-4359 Yvelines (Table KJV-KJW7)
4550.A-Z Other regions, provinces, departments, etc., A-Z
Subarrange each by Table KJV-KJW9

French overseas departments. Départements d'outre-mer

Guadeloupe

see KGR

French Guiana (Guyane française)

see KGJ

Martinique

see KGT

Réunion

see KTC

French overseas territories. Territoires d'outre-mer
French Polynesia (Polynésie française)
see KVP
Mayotte
see KSV5000+
New Caledonia (Nouvelle Calédonie)
see KVW
Saint Pierre et Miquelon
see KDZ
Southern and Antarctic Territories (Terres australes et antarctiques françaises)
see KWX
Wallis and Futuna Islands
see KWV

French cities and communities

5201-5209 Agen (Table KJV-KJW8)
5231-5239 Aix-en-Provence (Table KJV-KJW8)
5261-5269 Albi (Table KJV-KJW8)
5291-5299 Alençon (Table KJV-KJW8)
5321-5329 Alès (Table KJV-KJW8)
5351-5359 Amiens (Table KJV-KJW8)
5381-5389 Angers (Table KJV-KJW8)
5411-5419 Angoulême (Table KJV-KJW8)
5441-5449 Annecy (Table KJV-KJW8)
5471-5479 Arles (Table KJV-KJW8)
5501-5509 Armentières (Table KJV-KJW8)
5531-5539 Arras (Table KJV-KJW8)
5561-5569 Aurillac (Table KJV-KJW8)
5591-5599 Auxerre (Table KJV-KJW8)
5621-5629 Avesnes (Table KJV-KJW8)
5651-5659 Avignon (Table KJV-KJW8)
5681-5689 Bar-le-Duc (Table KJV-KJW8)
5711-5719 Bastia (Table KJV-KJW8)
5741-5749 Bayonne (Table KJV-KJW8)
5771-5779 Beauvais (Table KJV-KJW8)
5801-5809 Belfort (Table KJV-KJW8)
5831-5839 Bellac (Table KJV-KJW8)
5861-5869 Bergerac (Table KJV-KJW8)
5890-5899 Besançon (Table KJV-KJW8)
5921-5929 Béthune (Table KJV-KJW8)
5951-5959 Béziers (Table KJV-KJW8)
5981-5989 Blois (Table KJV-KJW8)
6011-6019 Bordeaux (Table KJV-KJW8)
6041-6049 Boulogne-sur-Mer (Table KJV-KJW8)
6071-6079 Bourg-en-Bresse (Table KJV-KJW8)
6101-6109 Bourges (Table KJV-KJW8)
6131-6139 Brest (Table KJV-KJW8)
6141-6149 Briey (Table KJV-KJW8)
6161-6169 Brive-la-Gaillarde (Table KJV-KJW8)
6191-6199 Bruay-en-Artois (Table KJV-KJW8)
6221-6299 Caen (Table KJV-KJW8)
6251-6259 Calais (Table KJV-KJW8)
6281-6289 Cambrai (Table KJV-KJW8)
6311-6319 Cannes (Table KJV-KJW8)
6341-6349 Carcassonne (Table KJV-KJW8)
6371-6379 Castres (Table KJV-KJW8)
6401-6409 Ceyreste (Table KJV-KJW8)
6431-6439 Chalon-sur-Saône (Table KJV-KJW8)
6461-6469 Châlons-sur Marne (Table KJV-KJW8)
6491-6499 Chambéry (Table KJV-KJW8)
6521-6529 Charleville-Mézières (Table KJV-KJW8)

6551-6599	Chartres (Table KJV-KJW8)
6581-6589	Chateauroux (Table KJV-KJW8)
6611-6619	Cherbourg (Table KJV-KJW8)
6641-6649	Cholet (Table KJV-KJW8)
6671-6679	Clermont-Ferrand (Table KJV-KJW8)
6701-6709	Colmar (Table KJV-KJW8)
6731-6739	Compiègne (Table KJV-KJW8)
6761-6769	Condom (Table KJV-KJW8)
6791-6799	Creil (Table KJV-KJW8)
6821-6829	Dijon (Table KJV-KJW8)
6851-6859	Dole (Table KJV-KJW8)
6881-6889	Douai (Table KJV-KJW8)
6911-6919	Dreux (Table KJV-KJW8)
6941-6949	Dunkerque (Table KJV-KJW8)
6971-6979	Elbeuf (Table KJV-KJW8)
7001-7009	Epinal (Table KJV-KJW8)
7031-7039	Evreux (Table KJV-KJW8)
7061-7069	Forbach (Table KJV-KJW8)
7091-7099	Fréjus (Table KJV-KJW8)
7121-7129	Givors (Table KJV-KJW8)
7151-7159	Grenoble (Table KJV-KJW8)
7211-7219	La Rochelle (Table KJV-KJW8)
7241-7249	Laon (Table KJV-KJW8)
7271-7279	Laval (Table KJV-KJW8)
7301-7309	Le Creusot (Table KJV-KJW8)
7331-7339	Le Havre (Table KJV-KJW8)
7361-7369	Le Mans (Table KJV-KJW8)
7391-7399	Le Puy (Table KJV-KJW8)
7421-7429	Lens (Table KJV-KJW8)
7451-7459	Lille (Table KJV-KJW8)
7481-7489	Limoges (Table KJV-KJW8)
7511-7519	Longwy (Table KJV-KJW8)
7571-7579	Lorient (Table KJV-KJW8)
7601-7609	Lyon (Table KJV-KJW8)
7631-7639	Mâcon (Table KJV-KJW8)
7661-7669	Mantes-la-Jolie (Table KJV-KJW8)
7691-7699	Marseille (Table KJV-KJW8)
7721-7729	Martigues (Table KJV-KJW8)
7751-7759	Maubeuge (Table KJV-KJW8)
7781-7789	Meaux (Table KJV-KJW8)
7811-7819	Melun (Table KJV-KJW8)
7841-7849	Menton (Table KJV-KJW8)
7871-7879	Metz (Table KJV-KJW8)
7901-7909	Montargis (Table KJV-KJW8)
7931-7939	Montauban (Table KJV-KJW8)
7961-7969	Montbeliard (Table KJV-KJW8)
7991-7999	Montceau-les-Mines (Table KJV-KJW8)

8051-8059	Montluçon (Table KJV-KJW8)
8081-8089	Montpellier (Table KJV-KJW8)
8171-8179	Moulins (Table KJV-KJW8)
8201-8209	Mulhouse (Table KJV-KJW8)
8231-8239	Nancy (Table KJV-KJW8)
8261-8269	Nantes (Table KJV-KJW8)
8291-8299	Nevers (Table KJV-KJW8)
8321-8329	Nice (Table KJV-KJW8)
8351-8359	Nîmes (Table KJV-KJW8)
8381-8389	Niort (Table KJV-KJW8)
8411-8419	Orléans (Table KJV-KJW8)
8441-8449	Paris (Table KJV-KJW8)
8471-8479	Pau (Table KJV-KJW8)
8501-8509	Périgueux (Table KJV-KJW8)
8531-8539	Perpignan (Table KJV-KJW8)
8561-8569	Poitiers (Table KJV-KJW8)
8591-8599	Pontoise (Table KJV-KJW8)
8621-8629	Quimper (Table KJV-KJW8)
8651-8659	Reims (Table KJV-KJW8)
8681-8689	Rennes (Table KJV-KJW8)
8711-8719	Roanne (Table KJV-KJW8)
8741-8749	Romans-sur-Isère (Table KJV-KJW8)
8771-8779	Rouen (Table KJV-KJW8)
8801-8809	Saint-Amand (Table KJV-KJW8)
8831-8839	Saint-Brieuc (Table KJV-KJW8)
8861-8869	Saint-Chamond (Table KJV-KJW8)
8891-8899	Saint-Dié (Table KJV-KJW8)
8921-8929	Saint-Etienne (Table KJV-KJW8)
8951-8959	Saint-Malo (Table KJV-KJW8)
8981-8989	Saint-Nazaire (Table KJV-KJW8)
9011-9019	Saint-Omer (Table KJV-KJW8)
9041-9049	Saint-Quentin (Table KJV-KJW8)
9071-9079	Salies-de-Béarn (Table KJV-KJW8)
9101-9109	Senlis (Table KJV-KJW8)
9131-9139	Séte (Table KJV-KJW8)
9161-9169	Soissons (Table KJV-KJW8)
9201-9209	Strasbourg (Table KJV-KJW8)
9221-9229	Tarbes (Table KJV-KJW8)
9251-9259	Thonon-les-Bains (Table KJV-KJW8)
9281-9289	Toulon (Table KJV-KJW8)
9311-9319	Toulouse (Table KJV-KJW8)
9341-9349	Tours (Table KJV-KJW8)
9401-9409	Troyes (Table KJV-KJW8)
9431-9439	Valence (Table KJV-KJW8)
9461-9469	Valenciennes (Table KJV-KJW8)
9491-9499	Versailles (Table KJV-KJW8)
9521-9529	Vichy (Table KJV-KJW8)

9551-9559 Villefranche-sur-Saône (Table KJV-KJW8)

9600.A-Z Other cities, A-Z

Subarrange each by Table KJV-KJW9

.1 Indexes. Registers (General)

For indexes relating to a particular collection, see the publication

.2 Chronological indexes

.4 General collections. By initial date of period covered

.5 Selections. By editor, compiler, or title

.6 Summaries of judgments

TABLES

.x date Texts. By date, arranged chronologically from the earliest to the latest (most recent) edition

Class here unannotated and annotated editions

Including iconography, manuscript editions, and including modernized versions

.x3 General works on the source. Textual criticism. Controversy

Including early (contemporary) works

0 General (Table K11)
0.2 Authorship (Table K11)
0.3 Plagiarism. Infringement. Contrefaçon (Table K11)
0.32 Formalities. Formalités (Table K11)
Including registration of transfer, licenses, deposit, and notice
0.4 Protected works. Ouvres protegées (Table K11)
Including original works, subsequent rights, idea, and title
Scope of protection. Etendue de protection
0.5 General (Table K11)
0.6 Moral rights. Droit moral de l'auteur ou de l'artiste (Table K11)
Reproduction rights. Droit de production
0.62 General (Table K11)
0.622 Publishing right
see KJV3318+
0.63 Recording. Enregistrement (Table K11)
Including phonographs, magnetic recorders, and jukeboxes
Adaptations
0.7 General (Table K11)
0.72 Variations and arrangements. Variations et arrangements (Table K11)
0.8 Exhibition rights (Table K11)
Performing rights. Droit de représentation
0.82 General (Table K11)
0.83 Broadcasting. Droit d'emission radiophonique (Table K11)
0.84 Filming and photographing (Table K11)
0.9 Translations (Table K11)
0.92 Duration and renewal. Durée. Prolongation de la durée (Table K11)

TABLES

0 General (Table K11)
0.15 Trade practices. Price policy (Table K11)
0.2 Economic assistance. Price supports (Table K11)
0.3 Labeling (Table K11)
0.4 Quality inspection. Health standards. Purity (Table K11)
Including regulation of adulteration and additives
0.6 Sanitation. Plant inspection. Store inspection (Table K11)

0	General (Table K11)
0.2	Education. Licensing (Table K11)
0.3	Professional representation. Ethics. Discipline (Table K11)
0.5	Fees (Table K11)
0.7	Liability (Table K11)

TABLES

1 General (Table K11)
2 Military requisitions from civilians. Requisitioned land. Requisition militaire (Table K11)
Including contracts for work and labor
For damages and compensation see KJV-KJW6 16+
3 Control of property. Confiscations (Table K11)
Including enemy, collaborator and alien property
For damages and compensation see KJV-KJW6 16+
Control of manpower
4 General (Table K11)
5 Prisoners of war (Table K11)
6 Insolvent debtors. Wartime and crisis relief (Table K11)
For agricultural credits, see KJV5722+
7 Finances (Table K11)
For special levies, war taxes, etc., see KJV6910+
For confiscation of excess or illicit profits, see KJV6777
8 Procurement and defense contracts (Table K11)
Industrial priorities and allocations. Economic recovery measures
9 General (Table K11)
10.A-Z By industry or commodity, A-Z
Subarrange each by Table K12
Strategic material
11 General (Table K11)
12.A-Z By commodity, A-Z
Subarrange each by Table K12
Rationing. Price control
13 General (Table K11)
14.A-Z By commodity, A-Z
Subarrange each by Table K12
War damage compensation. Réparation des dommages de guerre. Spoliations et restitutions
Including damage caused by siege, and foreign claims settlement
Cf. KJV3670+ , Social services
16 General (Table K11)
18.A-Z Particular claims, A-Z
Subarrange each by Table K12
Confiscations see KJV-KJW6 18.R47
Military occupation damages see KJV-KJW6 18.R47
18.P47 Personal damage. Property loss or damage (Table K12)
Property loss or damage see KJV-KJW6 18.P47
18.R46 Reparations. Demontage (Table K12)
18.R47 Requisitions. Confiscations (Table K12)
19.A-Z Particular victims, A-Z
Subarrange each by Table K12

20 Military occupation. Les lois de l'occupation (Table K11)
Including legislation during state of siege
For damage caused by military occupation or siege see KJV-KJW6 16+

TABLES

1.A12 Bibliography

<1.A13> Periodicals

For periodicals consisting predominantly of legal articles, regardless of subject matter and jurisdiction, see K

For periodicals consisting primarily of informative material (Newsletters, bulletins, etc.) relating to a particular subject, see subject and form division for periodicals

For law reports, official bulletins or circular, and official gazettes intended chiefly for the publication of laws and regulations, see the appropriate entries in the text or Form Division Tables

1.A14 Monographic series

Official gazettes

Agency gazettes

see the issuing agency

City gazettes

see the issuing city

1.A145 Indexes (General)

1.A15A2-.A15A29 General

Arranged chronologically

Legislative and executive papers (including historical sources)

see J

Legislation

see J

1.A16 Indexes and tables. By date

1.A163 Early territorial laws and legislation. By date

Class here early sources not provided for elsewhere, e.g. custumals, royal ordinances, privileges, edicts, mandates, etc.

Collections. Compilations

1.A17 Serials

1.A173 Monographs. By date

Individual

see the subject

Remonstrances of the Provincial Sovereign Court (Parlement)

For remonstrances of the Sovereign Court of Paris (Parlement de Paris), see KJV273+

Collections. Compilations

Including official and private editions with or without annotations

1.A18 Serials

1.A183 Monographs. By date

Court decisions and related materials

Including historical sources, and authorized and private editions

For decisions on a particular subject, see the subject

1.A19 Indexes. Digests. Abridgments. By date

1.A193 Several courts. By date

Class here decisions of courts of several jurisdictions

Court decisions and related materials -- Continued
Particular courts and tribunals
Under each court or court system (Single "A" Cutter no.):
Reports
.xA2-.xA29 *Serials*
Arranged chronologically
.xA3 *Monographs. By date*
.xA4 *Indexes. Digests. Abridgments. By date*
For indexes to a particular publication, see the publication
Under each court or court system (Double-Cuttered):
Reports
x-x29 *Serials*
Arranged chronologically
x3 *Monographs. By date*
x4 *Indexes. Digests. Abridgments. By date*
For indexes to a particular publication, see the publication
Including historical courts and tribunals not provided for by subject
Trial courts
1.A194 General
1.A195A-.A195Z Particular courts. By city, province, department, etc., A-Z
Local courts
Including justices of the peace courts, magistrates' courts, etc.
1.A196 General
1.A197A-.A197Z Particular courts. By city, province, department, etc., A-Z
1.A198A-.A198Z Other courts. By place or name, A-Z
Dictionaries. Encyclopedias
see KJV115
Form books
see KJV119
Yearbooks
see KJV120
Judicial statistics
1.A2 General
1.A23 Criminal statistics
Including juvenile delinquency
1.A25A-.A25Z Other. By subject, A-Z
Directories
see KJV125+

Trials
see KJV128+
Legal research
see KJV140+
Legal education
see KJV150+
The legal profession
see KJV170+
Legal aid
see KJV229
Bar associations. Law societies and associations
see KJV230
1.A28 History of law
For the history of a particular subject (including historical sources), see the subject
1.A29 General works
Including compends, popular works, civics, etc.
Private law. Civil law
1.2 General works (Table K11)
1.22 Rights of civil law (Table K11)
1.25 Juristic facts and acts (Table K11)
Persons
1.3 General (Table K11)
Natural persons
1.32 General (Table K11)
1.33 Personality rights (Table K11)
1.34 Civil status (Table K11)
Domestic relations. Marriage. Husband and wife
Including dissolution and disintegration of marriage
1.35 General (Table K11)
1.36 Matrimonial property relationships (Table K11)
1.365 Dissolution and disintegration of marriage (Table K11)
Protection of incapables
1.37 General (Table K11)
1.38 Administration légale (Table K11)
1.39 Guardianship (Table K11)
1.4 Curatorship (Table K11)
1.42 Juristic persons (Table K11)
Property
1.44 General (Table K11)
1.45 Ownership and possession (Table K11)
1.47 Rights in rem upon another's property (Table K11)
Real property
1.5 General (Table K11)
1.52 Ownership and possession. Land tenure (Table K11)

Private law. Civil law
Property
Real property -- Continued
1.54 Rights and interests incident to ownership and possession (Table K11)
1.55 Encumbrances. Servitudes (Table K11)
1.56 Land registry. Registration of rights upon real property (Table K11)
Personal property
1.57 General (Table K11)
1.58 Tangible and intangible personal property (Table K11)
1.59.A-Z Other, A-Z
Subarrange each by Table K12
Succession upon death
1.6 General (Table K11)
1.62 Testate succession. Wills (Table K11)
1.63 Intestate succession (Table K11)
1.64 Order of succession. Classes of heirs (Table K11)
Gratuities
1.65 General (Table K11)
1.66 Charitable gratuities (Table K11)
1.68 Disguised gifts (Table K11)
Obligations
1.7 General (Table K11)
Contracts
1.72 General (Table K11)
1.73.A-Z Particular contracts, A-Z
Subarrange each by Table K12
1.74 Quasi contracts (Table K11)
1.75 Civil liability. Tortious liability (Table K11)
1.76 Security. Suretyship and guaranty
Commercial law. Commercial contracts
1.8 General (Table K11)
1.83 Chambers of commerce (Table K11)
2 Commercial registers (Table K11)
2.22 Brokerage. Brokers (Table K11)
2.23 Commercial sale (Table K11)
2.25 Commercial leases (Table K11)
2.3 Deposit (Table K11)
2.4 Securities (Table K11)
2.6 Banking. Credit (Table K11)
Contract of carriage of goods and passengers
2.7 General (Table K11)
2.75 Freight forwarders (Table K11)
2.8 Insurance (Table K11)
3 Business associations. Commercial companies

Insolvency
3.2 Judicial administration (Table K11)
3.23 Bankruptcy (Table K11)
3.24 Intellectual and industrial property (Table K11)
Social legislation
3.25 General (Table K11)
Labor law
3.26 General (Table K11)
3.27 Management-labor relations (Table K11)
3.28 Trade and professional associations (Table K11)
3.3 Collective labor agreements and disputes (Table K11)
3.32 Protection of labor (Table K11)
3.34 Social insurance (Table K11)
3.36 Social service. Public welfare (Table K11)
Courts and procedure
The administration of justice. The organization of the judiciary
3.4 General (Table K11)
3.42 Organization and administration (Table K11)
Including regional, provincial, departmental, and local department boards
Judicial statistics
see KJV121+
Courts
History
3.43 General
3.44.A-Z Particular courts, A-Z
3.44.F48 Feudal and servitary courts
Manorial courts see KJV-KJW7 3.44.P38
3.44.P38 Patrimonial and manorial courts
Servitary courts see KJV-KJW7 3.44.F48
3.44.S69 Sovereign court. Parlement
3.45 General (Table K11)
3.46.A-Z Particular courts and tribunals, A-Z
Subarrange each by Table K12
3.46.C68 Cours d'appel (Table K12)
3.47.A-Z Courts of special jurisdiction, A-Z
Subarrange each by Table K12
For courts of special jurisdiction not listed below, see the subject
3.47.C68 Courts of honor (Table K12)
3.47.J88 Justices of the peace (Table K12)
Judicial personnel
For legal profession in general, see KJV170+
3.48 General (Table K11)
3.5 Judges (Table K11)

Courts and procedure
Courts
Judicial personnel -- Continued
3.52.A-Z Other, A-Z
Subarrange each by Table K12
3.55 Judicial assistance (Table K11)
Procedure in general
Including all branches of law
3.6 General (Table K11)
3.62.A-Z Special topics, A-Z
Subarrange each by Table K12
Civil procedure
3.65 General (Table K11)
3.7.A-Z Special topics, A-Z
Subarrange each by Table K12
3.8 Noncontentious jurisdiction (Table K11)
4 Public law (Table K11)
Constitutional law
4.2 General (Table K11)
Constitutional history
4.23 General
Social orders
4.24 General
4.25.A-Z Particular, A-Z
Feudal system
4.26 General
4.27.A-Z Special topics, A-Z
Organs of government
4.3 General (Table K11)
The people
4.33 General (Table K11)
4.35 Election law (Table K11)
4.4.A-Z Other, A-Z
Subarrange each by Table K12
Administrative law
Administrative process
5 General (Table K11)
5.2 Administrative acts. Administrative contracts (Table K11)
5.24 Administrative courts and procedure (Table K11)
Administrative organization. Administrative divisions
5.25 General (Table K11)
5.3.A-Z Particular, A-Z
Subarrange each by Table K12
5.3.S87 Supramunicipal corporations. Municipal services and powers beyond corporate limits (Table K12)
5.32 Public services (Table K11)

Administrative law -- Continued
5.34 Civil service (Table K11)
Public property. Public restraint on private property
5.4 General (Table K11)
5.42 Roads and highways (Table K11)
Water resources
Including rivers, lakes, and water courses, etc.
5.46 General (Table K11)
5.5 Water resources development (Table K11)
5.55 Eminent domain (Table K11)
Regional planning
5.6 General (Table K11)
5.62 City planning and redevelopment (Table K11)
5.66 Building and construction (Table K11)
5.7 Public works (Table K11)
5.73 Police and public safety (Table K11)
Public health
6 General (Table K11)
6.2.A-Z Special topics, A-Z
Subarrange each by Table K12
Medical law
6.3 General (Table K11)
6.34.A-Z The health professions, A-Z
Subarrange each by Table K12
6.36 Auxiliary (paramedical) professions, A-Z (Table K12)
6.4 Pharmaceutical law (Table K11)
6.5 Veterinary medicine (Table K11)
Environmental law
6.55 General (Table K11)
Environmental pollution
6.56 General (Table K11)
6.6.A-Z Pollutants, A-Z
Subarrange each by Table K12
Cultural affairs
6.62 General (Table K11)
Education
6.63 General (Table K11)
6.65 Teachers (Table K11)
6.67 Elementary and secondary education (Table K11)
6.7 Education of children with disabilities (Table K11)
6.74 Vocational education (Table K11)
6.76 Higher education (Table K11)
6.8 Private schools (Table K11)
6.82 Adult education. Continuing education (Table K11)
6.86.A-Z Special topics, A-Z
Subarrange each by Table K12

Cultural affairs -- Continued
Science and the arts
7 General (Table K11)
7.2.A-Z Special topics, A-Z
Subarrange each by Table K12
Public collections
7.22 General (Table K11)
7.4 Archives (Table K11)
7.6 Libraries (Table K11)
7.7 Museums and galleries (Table K11)
7.8 Historic buildings and monuments (Table K11)
Economic law. Regulation of industry, trade, and commerce
8 General (Table K11)
Agricultural law. Rural law
8.25 General (Table K11)
8.27 Entail (Table K11)
8.28.A-Z Agricultural industries and trades, A-Z
Subarrange each by Table K12
8.3.A-Z Agricultural products, A-Z
Subarrange each by Table K12
8.35 Corporate representation. Agricultural societies (Table K11)
8.37 Viticulture (Table K11)
8.39 Apiculture. Beekeeping (Table K11)
8.4 Horticulture (Table K11)
8.42 Forestry (Table K11)
Including timber and game laws
8.45.A-Z Special topics, A-Z
Subarrange each by Table K12
8.47 Fishery (Table K11)
Mining and quarrying
8.5 General (Table K11)
8.52.A-Z By resource, A-Z
Subarrange each by Table K12
8.56.A-Z Special topics, A-Z
Subarrange each by Table K12
Manufacturing industries
8.6 General (Table K11)
8.62.A-Z Types of manufactures, A-Z
Subarrange each by Table K12
8.65.A-Z Special topics, A-Z
Subarrange each by Table K12
8.7.A-Z Other industrial and trade lines, A-Z
Subarrange each by Table K12
8.7.C66 Construction and building industry (Table K12)
8.8 Professions (Table K11)
Public finance

Public finance -- Continued
9 General (Table K11)
9.2 Budget. Accounting and auditing (Table K11)
9.25 Public debts. Loans (Table K11)
9.3 Fees. Fines (Table K11)
Taxation
9.35 General (Table K11)
9.4.A-Z Particular taxes, A-Z
Subarrange each by Table K12
9.45.A-Z Special topics, A-Z
Subarrange each by Table K12
Customs. Tariff
9.5 General (Table K11)
9.53.A-Z Special topics, A-Z
Subarrange each by Table K12
Tax and customs crimes and delinquency
see KJV7140+
Criminal law
9.6 General (Table K11)
9.62.A-Z Individual offenses, A-Z
Subarrange each by Table K12
9.62.S33 Seduction (Table K12)
Criminal courts and procedure
9.63 General (Table K11)
9.64.A-Z Courts, A-Z
Subarrange each by Table K12
Execution of sentence
9.65 General (Table K11)
Imprisonment
9.66 General (Table K11)
9.67.A-Z Penal institutions, A-Z
Subarrange each by Table K12
9.68.A-Z Special topics, A-Z
Subarrange each by Table K12

1.A1 Bibliography

<1.A15> Periodicals

For periodicals consisting predominantly of legal articles, regardless of subject matter and jurisdiction, see K

For periodicals consisting primarily of informative material (Newsletters, bulletins, etc.) relating to a particular subject, see subject and form division for periodicals

For law reports, official bulletins or circular, and official gazettes intended chiefly for the publication of laws and regulations, see the appropriate entries in the text or Form Division Tables

Official gazettes

1.A17A2-.A17A29 General

Arranged chronologically

Legislative documents

Including historical sources

Cf. JS4801+, Municipal documents of local governments

1.A2-.A24 Serials

Arranged chronologically

1.A25 Monographs. By date

1.A3 Statutes affecting cities. By date

Including historical sources

Charters (Privileges), ordinances and local laws

Including historical sources

1.A4-.A44 Serials

Arranged chronologically

1.A45 Collections. By date

1.A5 Individual charters or acts of incorporation. By date

Collections of decisions and rulings

Including historical sources

1.A6-.A64 Serials

Arranged chronologically

1.A65 Monographs. By date

Judicial statistics. Surveys of local administration of justice

1.A7A-.A7Z Serials

1.A75A-.A75Z Monographs

1.A8 Special agencies, courts, or topics, A-Z

Subarranged by date

Directories

see KJV126

Legal profession

see KJV170+

Legal aid

see KJV229

History

For biography, see KJV251+

For the history of a particular subject, see the subject

History -- Continued
1.A85A-.A85Z Sources
Class here sources not falling under one of the categories above
1.A86A-.A86Z Roman law. Reception
1.A9-Z General works
Particular subjects
Not to be further subarranged by form
Private law
Including civil and commercial law
1.12 General
Persons. Domestic relations. Marriage. Matrimonial property
1.13 General
1.14.A-Z Special topics, A-Z
1.15-.18 Property. Law of things. Real property
1.15 General
1.18 Land registry
Inheritance. Succession upon death
2 General
2.22 Special topics, A-Z
2.23 Gratuities
Obligations. Contracts
2.24 General
2.25.A-Z Special topics, A-Z
2.26 Merchant and business enterprise
2.27 Commercial registers
2.28 Banking. Negotiable instruments. Insurance
Labor law. Social insurance. Public welfare
3 General
3.32.A-Z Particular groups, A-Z
3.33.A-Z Particular agencies, institutions, or courts, A-Z
City constitution and government
3.34 General
3.35 Legislative functions. City council, etc.
Including elections
3.36 Executive functions. Mayor and administrative departments. Municipal civil service
Including elections
3.37 Judicial functions. City courts and procedure
4.A-Z Special topics, A-Z
Municipal civil service see KJV-KJW8 3.36
Police and public safety. Police forces
4.42 General
4.44.A-Z Particular safety hazards or preventive measures, A-Z
4.44.F57 Fire
4.46.A-Z Special topics, A-Z
Public property. Public restraint on private property

	Particular subjects
	Public property. Public restraint on private property -- Continued
4.47	General
5.A-Z	Special topics, A-Z
	Public health. Medical legislation
5.54	General
5.55	Burial and cemetery laws
5.58.A-Z	Special topics, A-Z
5.58.D74	Drinking water
6	Environmental laws
	Cultural affairs
6.63	General
6.64	Education. Schools. Institutions
6.65	Theater. Orchestra
6.66	Public collections
6.67.A-Z	Historic buildings and monuments, A-Z
	Industry, trade, and commerce
7	General
7.75.A-Z	Artisans, A-Z
7.76.A-Z	Professions, A-Z
	Health professions see KJV-KJW8 5.58.A+
7.78.A-Z	Corporate representation, A-Z
7.78.B63	Boards of trade
7.78.C43	Chambers of commerce
7.78.G85	Guilds
7.78.T73	Trade associations
8	Public utilities
	Public finance
8.83	General
8.85	Sources of revenue. Taxes, fees, and fines
9	Offenses (Violations of ordinances) and administration of criminal justice. Correctional institutions
	Supramunicipal corporations and organization
	see the appropriate region, province, department, etc., subdivided by Table KJW7, 5.3.S87

TABLES

.x date Legislation. By date

.x2 Decisions. Rulings. By date

.x3A-.x3Z General works

Including comprehensive legal works and works on specific legal topics

INDEX

A

Abandon de famille: KJV8237
Abandon d'enfant: KJV8235
Abandonment of a child: KJV8235
Abatement of gifts and legacies: KJV1428+
Abdication
  July monarchy: KJV4126.A23
Abduction of minors: KJV8236
Abeyance, Administration of estates in: KJV1442
Abordage maritime: KJV6118+
Abortion: KJV3648+
  Criminal abortion: KJV8188
Abroad, Rights and duties of Frenchmen residing: KJV378.R54
Abus de confiance
  Business association managers: KJV3009.B74
  Offenses against property: KJV8256+
Abus de droit
  Administrative law: KJV4682
Abus de droit en matiere de contrat
  Civil liability: KJV2097+
Abus de droit en matière de contrat
  Breach of contract: KJV1766.M57
Abuse of administrative power: KJV4745+
Abuse of contractual rights
  Civil liability: KJV2097+
Abuse of one's right
  Administrative law: KJV4682
Abutting property
  Roads and highways: KJV5146+
Academic secondary schools: KJV5452
Academies
  Public institutions: KJV5475.A+
Acceptance of contract: KJV1710+
Acceptance of gifts
  Civil law: KJV1496
Acceptance of inheritance: KJV1405+
Acceptance pure and simple
  Succession upon death: KJV1407+
Acceptance with the benefit of inventory
  Succession upon death: KJV1409+
Acceptation des dons
  Civil law: KJV1496
Acceptation des la succession: KJV1405+
Access to public records: KJV5111.5
Accession artificielle au profit d'un immeuble: KJV1249+
Accession au profit d'un immeuble: KJV1247+
Accession naturelle au profit d'un immeuble: KJV1248
Accession to real property: KJV1247+
Accessions to property: KJV1154
Accessory before and after the fact
  Criminal law: KJV8036+
Accident control: KJV5267+
Accident insurance: KJV2895+
Accidents
  Automobile accidents: KJV2100.A88
Accidents de chasse: KJV5804
Accidents de la circulation: KJV6005+
Accomplissement d'un devoir
  Criminal liability: KJV8048
Accoucheuses: KJV5353
Accountants: KJV6352+
  Expert evidence in commercial courts: KJV2223
Accounting: KJV323
  Business associations: KJV3010+
  Business enterprise: KJV2261+
  Joint stock companies: KJV3068+
  Military law: KJV7397
Accounts, Public
  Public finance: KJV6480+
Accréditifs: KJV2462
Achalandage
  Commercial law: KJV2252+
Aconier: KJV2797.2
Acquisition de la propriété immobiliers: KJV1238+
Acquisition de la propriété par la possession: KJV1161+
Acquisition of ownership
  Property: KJV1145+
Acquisition of ownership by possession
  Property: KJV1161+
Acquisition of real property: KJV1238+

Acquittal
  Criminal courts and procedure: KJV9025
Act conservatoire: KJV1114
Acte d'administration
  Civil law: KJV493
Acte de disposition
  Civil law: KJV494
Acte de naissance
  Natural persons: KJV556+
Actes à titre gratuit et actes à titre onereux
  Civil law: KJV490+
Actes administratifs: KJV4695+
Actes administratifs unilatéraux: KJV4711+
Actes bilatéraux et actes unilatéraux
  Civil law: KJV489
Actes de commerce: KJV2301+
Actes de gouvernement: KJV4707+
Actes de l'état civil
  Natural persons: KJV579+
Actes des officiers publics
  Conflict of jurisdictions: KJV418+
Actes notariés: KJV189+
  Conflict of jurisdictions: KJV420+
Actes solennels
  Civil law: KJV506
Actes sous signe privé
  Civil law: KJV505
Actes unilatéraux et actes bilatéraux
  Civil law: KJV489
Acteurs
  Labor law: KJV3475.A38
Acteurs cinématographiques
  Labor law: KJV3475.M69
Action against disturbance of possession
  Real property: KJV1258
Action aquilienne
  Civil liability: KJV2094.3
Action in rem verso: KJV1987
Action oblique
  Obligations: KJV1616
Action or writ of ejectment
  Real property: KJV1256+
Action rédhibitoire
  Sales contracts: KJV1797
Actions à droit de vote inégal
  Joint companies: KJV3118
Actions and defenses
  Courts and procedure: KJV3872+
Actions de la Banque de France: KJV2434
Actions de travail
  Joint stock companies: KJV3124
Actions directes
  Courts: KJV3874
Actions possessoires
  Real property: KJV1256+
Actions préventives
  Courts: KJV3876
Actors
  Labor law: KJV3475.A38
Acts in solemn form
  Civil law: KJV506
Acts of civil status
  Natural persons: KJV579+
Acts of public officials
  Conflict of jurisdictions: KJV418+
Acts of the executive: KJV4707+
Acts under private signature
  Civil law: KJV505
Adjoining landowners: KJV1228+
Administrateur provisoire
  Mentally ill: KJV1000
Administrateurs
  Business associations: KJV3006+
  Joint stock companies: KJV3051
Administration
  Church property: KJV4275
  Social legislation: KJV3382+
Administration consultative
  Administrative law: KJV4904
Administration de la justice criminelle: KJV7981.2+
Administration légale
  Incapables: KJV952
Administration of criminal justice: KJV7981.2+
Administration of justice: KJV3721+
Administrative acts: KJV4695+
Administrative contracts: KJV4722+

Air Force: KJV7530
Air law: KJV6145+
Air navigator: KJV6200
Air personnel: KJV6194+
Air pollution: KJV5420+
Air traffic rules: KJV6172+
Air way bill: KJV2702
Aircraft: KJV6147+
  Conflict of laws: KJV397.S55
  Noncontentious jurisdiction: KJV3994
Aircraft commander: KJV6198
Aircraft operator: KJV2697
Aircraft ownership: KJV2696
Airline creditors: KJV2696.3
Airlines: KJV2691+
Airports: KJV6176+
Alcohol industry: KJV5868
Alcoholic beverages: KJV5929+
Alcoholic beverages (Food processing)
  Overseas France: KJV4618
Alcoholics, Safety measures against
  Criminal law: KJV8120
Alcoholism
  Public health: KJV5326
Aleatory and commutative contracts: KJV1687
Aleatory contracts: KJV1970+
Alien labor
  Labor law: KJV3458
Alien property: KJV383.A44
Alienable and prescriptible communal property: KJV4990
Aliens
  Capacity and disability to inherit: KJV1337.A65
  Conflict of jurisdictions: KJV407+
  Labor law: KJV3477.A55
  Nationality and citizenship: KJV4198.A55
  Nuptial capacity: KJV652
Aliens in France
  Private international law: KJV382+
Alimony: KJV933+
Allocation de logement
  Labor standards: KJV3452
  Social insurance: KJV3569
Allowances
  Civil service: KJV5062+
    Overseas France: KJV4586.S35
  Soldiers: KJV7454+
Ambulance service: KJV5367.E43
Aménagement du territoire: KJV5200+
Amending process: KJV4164
Amnesty: KJV8079
Amnistie: KJV8079
Amortissements
  Business enterprises: KJV2274
Anaesthetists: KJV5347.A53
Anarchism: KJV8296
Anchorage: KJV5157
Ancien Régime (to 1789): KJV4081+
Anciens combattants
  Social services: KJV3670+
Anciens combattants de la Résistance: KJV3674
Ancrage: KJV5157
Anésthesistes: KJV5347.A53
Animal tuberculosis: KJV5404
Animals: KJV324+
Animals, Domestic
  Taxation: KJV6970+
Animaux: KJV324+
Animaux domestiques: KJV325+
  Taxation: KJV6970+
Animaux sauvage: KJV5795+
Annuities
  Income tax: KJV6845
  Personal property: KJV1294.A66
Annulation de mariage: KJV665+
Antenne collective: KJV6307+
Antenuptial contracts: KJV705+
  Gifts by antenuptial contracts: KJV1484+
Antichrèse: KJV2141
Antichresis: KJV2141
Anticipation, Personal property by: KJV1294.P47
Apartments
  Lease: KJV1824
Apiculture: KJV5770
Appareils de levage
  Labor safety: KJV3469.E56
Apparence: KJV317

Appeal to the Court of Cassation:
  KJV9040
Appealable judgments: KJV3914.A77
Appellate administrative courts:
  KJV4793
Appellate procedure: KJV3912+
  Civil procedure: KJV3972+
  Criminal courts: KJV9035+
Appellations d'origine
  Trademarks: KJV3354.M37
Application des lois pénales dans le
  temps: KJV7996
Application des lois pénales dans
  l'espace: KJV7994+
Appointment
  Civil service: KJV5032+
  Judges: KJV3840+
Apprenticeship tax
  Local taxes: KJV7120
Approved associations
  Contracts: KJV1906
Approvisionnement
  Military equipment: KJV7482+
Aqueduct: KJV5180
Arbitrage
  Administrative courts and procedure:
    KJV4875
  Courts and procedure: KJV4000
  Labor disputes: KJV3441+
Arbitration
  Administrative courts and procedure:
    KJV4875
  Labor disputes: KJV3441+
Arbitration and award
  Conflict of jurisdiction: KJV417
  Courts and procedure: KJV4000
Arbitration clause
  Courts and procedure: KJV4000
Archaeology and French law: KJV248.3
Architects: KJV6359+
Architectural landmarks: KJV5526+
Archives: KJV5516
Armateur: KJV2795
Armed Forces: KJV7408+
Armée de l'air: KJV7530
Armée de mer: KJV7510+
Armée de terre: KJV7486+
Armory
  French law: KJV250
Army: KJV7486+
  Criminal law and procedure:
    KJV7546+
Arrest: KJV8630
Arrestations illégales: KJV8192+
Arrhes
  Contracts: KJV1726
Arrondissements
  Administrative law: KJV4939.92+
Arson: KJV8386
Articles of association
  Business associations: KJV3004
Articles of incorporation
  Joint stock companies: KJV3042.5
Artificial accession to real property:
  KJV1249+
Artificial insemination: KJV5374
Artillerie
  Army: KJV7490
Artillery
  Army: KJV7490
Artisans: KJV6370
  Labor law: KJV3475.A78
  Taxation: KJV6704
Artistes: KJV6375
Artistic interest, Personal property of:
  KJV1294.P48
Artists: KJV6375
  Labor law: KJV3475.A79
Arts: KJV5470+
Arts figuratives: KJV5483
Ascendant, Partition by an
  Estates: KJV1437
Ascendants (Order of succession):
  KJV1390+
Ascenseurs
  Labor safety: KJV3469.E56
Assassinat de Sadi Carnot
  Trials: KJV131.A78
Assassination
  Trials: KJV129.M87
Assault and battery: KJV8173+
Assemblée générale
  Joint stock companies: KJV3047+
Assemblée nationale: KJV4342+

Assemblée nationale
  Elections: KJV4311
Assemblée of notables: KJV4088+
Assembly, Control of: KJV5285
Assembly of Notables: KJV4088+
Assessment
  National revenue: KJV6604+
    Income taxes: KJV6760
Assets
  Business associations: KJV3011+
Assignment of business concern: KJV2257
Assignment of inheritance rights: KJV1440+
Assistance judiciaire: KJV229
Assistance sociale: KJV3601+
Association and civil company
  Contracts: KJV1881+
Association des malfaiteurs
  Criminal law: KJV8036+
Association et société civile
  Contracts: KJV1881+
Association internationale des travailleurs, Procès de l': KJV131.A79
Association nationale des avocats de France et de Communauté: KJV180
Associations
  Overseas France: KJV4556+
Associations agrées
  Contracts: KJV1906
Associations and juristic persons of aliens in France: KJV385+
Associations déclarées
  Contracts: KJV1902
Associations et personnes morales des étrangers en France: KJV385+
Associations non déclarés
  Contracts: KJV1904
Associés
  Private companies: KJV3039.2
Assumption of risk by injured party: KJV2045.2
Assurance
  Seamen: KJV6078+
Assurance au profit d'un tiers: KJV2889
Assurance automobile: KJV2928
Assurance automobile obligatoire: KJV2930
Assurance contre la maladie: KJV2892
Assurance contre les accidents: KJV2895+
Assurance contre l'incendie: KJV2950
Assurance de responsabilité civile: KJV2957+
Assurance-group: KJV2879.G76
Assurance maladie et maternité: KJV3546+
Assurance sur la vie entre époux: KJV2887
Assurance-vol: KJV2940
Assurances
  Commercial law: KJV2871+
  Conflict of laws: KJV397.I56
Assurances aériennes: KJV2720
Assurances agricoles: KJV5742+
Assurances au voyage: KJV2897.T73
Assurances de dommages: KJV2900+
Assurances de personnes: KJV2884+
Assurances de responsabilité professionnelle: KJV2959
Assurances de transports: KJV2915+
Assurances maritimes: KJV2862+
Assurances multiples: KJV2908
Assurances mutuelles: KJV2879.M87
Assurances sociales: KJV3510.2+
  Agriculture: KJV5816+
Assurances sur la vie
  Commercial law: KJV2885+
  Conflict of laws: KJV397.L54
Astreinte (Fine for debtor's delay): KJV3980
Asylum, Right of: KJV4189
Attachment of current accounts: KJV2440
Attachment of real property
  Civil procedure: KJV3984
Attachment of wages
  Labor law: KJV3455.A88
Atteinte à la pudeur
  Civil liability: KJV2091
Atteinte à la reputation
  Civil liability: KJV2090

Atteinte à une autorité légitime
  Civil liability: KJV2089
Atteinte aux sentiments d'affection
  Civil liability: KJV2092
Atteintes (Civil liability): KJV2099
Attempted felony: KJV8012
Attendance list
  Stockholders' meeting: KJV3048
Attentats à la pudeur: KJV8216
Attorneys before commercial courts: KJV2222
Attribution integrale
  Estates: KJV1433+
Attribution préférentielle
  Estates: KJV1433+
Attroupements: KJV8398
Auction: KJV2329+
Auctioneers: KJV6377
  Economic law: KJV5682
Auditing: KJV323
  Business associations: KJV3010+
  Joint stock companies: KJV3068+
  Public finance: KJV6486+
Auditors: KJV6352+
  Supervisory auditors in commercial companies: KJV3013
Auteur et l'éditeur: KJV3318+
Author and publisher: KJV3318+
Authors
  Social insurance: KJV3545.A76
Automatic data processors: KJV333.C65
Automobile accidents
  Civil liability: KJV2100.A88
Automobile industry: KJV5864
Automobile insurance: KJV2928+
Automobiles: KJV328
  Commercial leases: KJV2361
Autonomie de la volonté
  Sources of obligations: KJV1544
Autonomy
  Sources of obligations: KJV1544
Autonomy and rulemaking power
  Municipal government: KJV4957
Autorisations administratifs: KJV4715+
Autorité parentale: KJV917+
Autorités administratives indépendantes: KJV4899
Autorités gouvernementales: KJV4280+
Auxiliaires medicaux: KJV5349+
Auxiliary medical professions: KJV5349+
Avancement d'hoire: KJV1427+
Avances sur marchandises
  Banking: KJV2464
Avarie
  Maritime law: KJV2838
Average
  Maritime law: KJV2838
  Transport insurance: KJV2919
Average in overland insurance: KJV2922
Aveugles
  Social services: KJV3642
Aviation civile: KJV6145+
Avis: KJV3906
Avocats: KJV173+
  Collective bargaining: KJV3438.L38
  Taxation: KJV6708
Avocats aux conseil: KJV176
Avocats Généraux: KJV3850
Avortement: KJV3648+
Avortement criminel: KJV8188
Avoués: KJV212+
Avril, Affaire d'
  Criminal trials: KJV131.A98
Award, Arbitration and: KJV417
Awards of honor: KJV4507+
Ayants cause du creancier: KJV1628+
Ayants cause du debiteur: KJV1640+
Ayants cause universels ou particuliers: KJV1624

B

Bagarre: KJV8380
Bail
  Contracts: KJV1814+
Bail à cheptel: KJV5714
Bail à ferme: KJV5710+
Bail à metaire: KJV5712
Bail commercial: KJV2341+
Bail de chasse: KJV5797

Buildings: KJV1232+
Buildings erected upon another's land: KJV1235+
Bullfights: KJV5292.B85
Burden of proof
Criminal courts: KJV8692
Burglary insurance: KJV2940
Burial laws: KJV5310+
Cities, etc: KJV-KJW8 5.55
Burial place, Rifling of a
Criminal law: KJV8196
Business associations
Commercial law: KJV2985+
Overseas France: KJV4562
Regions, provinces, etc: KJV-KJW7 3
Business concerns
Corporation tax: KJV6883
Business enterprises
Partition of estates: KJV1434.B87
Taxation: KJV6685
Business enterprises and merchant
Commercial law: KJV2235+
Cities, etc: KJV-KJW8 2.26
Business insurance: KJV2898
Business names: KJV2252.2
Business tax
Departmental and communal finance: KJV7100
Businessmen
Labor law: KJV3475.B88
Businesspeople
Manuals for: KJV240.B87
Businesswoman, Married: KJV677
By-roads: KJV5139+

C

Cable television: KJV6307+
Cadastral surveys: KJV1287
Cadastre: KJV1287
Caducité et revocation des legs: KJV1364
Caisse de retraited des marines: KJV6082
Caisse nationale de retraites des agents des collectivités locales: KJV5074
Caisses de sécurité sociale de la sécurité sociale: KJV3538
Caisses d'épargne: KJV2435
Calamités agricoles: KJV5740
Calcul de l'impôt
National revenue: KJV6604+
Campaign expenditures: KJV4319
Campaign financing
Elections: KJV4301
Campaign funds: KJV4319
Canning industry
Food processing: KJV5938.C35
Cantonal courts: KJV3813
Cantonal delegate: KJV4948
Cantons
Administrative law: KJV4946+
Canvassing
Retail trade: KJV5650
Capacité
Natural persons: KJV562+
Trade and professional associations: KJV3432+
Capacité de contracter: KJV1736
Capacité de disposer et de recevoir à titre gratuit: KJV1476
Capacité du testateur: KJV1341
Capacité et état des personnes: KJV397.S73
Capacité nuptiale: KJV649+
Capacity and disability to inherit: KJV1333+
Capacity and incapacity: KJV562+
Capacity and status of persons: KJV397.S73
Capacity to contract: KJV1736
Capacity to make a gratuitous disposition or to receive it: KJV1476
Capacity to make a will: KJV1341
Capiaux immobilisés
National revenue: KJV6789+
Capital
Insurance companies: KJV2880.3
Joint stock companies: KJV3066+
Capital-actions
Joint stock companies: KJV3089+
Capital d'emprunt
Joint stock companies: KJV3092+

Capital en numéraire
Joint stock companies: KJV3099+
Capital income tax (National revenue): KJV6787+
Capital murder: KJV8156
Capital punishment: KJV8090
Capital social (Joint stock companies): KJV3083+
Capitaux mobiliers (Income taxes)
National revenue: KJV6804+
Car repair stations: KJV5680
Career (Soldiers): KJV7440+
Carnot, Sadi: KJV131.A78
Carriage of passengers and goods (Railroads): KJV6020
Carriages and horses (Taxation)
National revenue: KJV6977
Cartels: KJV5598+
Cas fortuit ou de force majeure (Civil law): KJV482
Cash capital
Joint stock companies: KJV3099+
Casier judiciaire: KJV9100
Casinos: KJV5297
Castration: KJV8176
Catalogs
Copyright: KJV3313+
Catholic ethics and French law: KJV319.E84
Cattle: KJV5734.C38
Causalité
Civil law: KJV2040+
Causalité juridique
Civil law: KJV480+
Philosophy and theory: KJV310+
Causality (Civil liability): KJV2040+
Cause
Contracts: KJV1725
Obligations: KJV1545+
Caution bancaire: KJV2459
Caution judicatum solvi (Conflict of jurisdictions): KJV409
Cautionnement (Civil law): KJV2122+
Cautionnement solidaire: KJV2123
Cavalerie (Army): KJV7495
Cavalry (Army): KJV7495
Celebration du mariage: KJV659+
Cemetery laws: KJV5310+
Cities, etc: KJV-KJW8 5.55
Censorship
Theaters: KJV5489
Centrales nucléo-électriques: KJV5958
Centrales thermiques: KJV5954
Centralization and decentralization (Administrative organization): KJV4882
Centre national de la recherche scientifique: KJV5476.C46
Cereal products: KJV5906
Céréales
Customs and tariffs: KJV7026.G73
Food products: KJV5906
Cereals
Agricultural law: KJV5738.C47
Customs and tariffs: KJV7026.G73
Certainty of law: KJV289
Certificat de propriété (Real property): KJV1239
Certificates, Registered: KJV2385
Certification (Civil law): KJV507
Certificats médicaux: KJV5330+
Cession de droit d'autuer: KJV3262
Cession de fonds de commerce: KJV2257
Cession des droits successifs: KJV1440+
Chaînes de télévision: KJV6310+
Chambers of agriculture: KJV5752
Chambers of commerce (Commercial law): KJV2228+
Chambre criminelle de la Cour de cassation: KJV8440
Chambre d'accusation: KJV8660
Chambre des pairs: KJV4122.C46
Chambre des requêtes: KJV3793
Chambres civiles (Supreme courts): KJV3795+
Chambres d'agriculture: KJV5752
Chambres de commerce (Commercial law): KJV2228+
Change of name (Natural persons): KJV574
Changement de nom (Natural persons): KJV574

INDEX

Collatéraux (Order of succession): KJV1392+
Collation (Succession): KJV1429
Collective agreements and individual contracts: KJV1686
Collective bargaining and labor agreements: KJV3436+
Collective labor agreements (Publishing and printing): KJV5979+
Collective ownership (Property): KJV1143
Collectivités locales: KJV4910+
Collèges d'enseignement général: KJV5452
Collèges d'enseignement professionnel: KJV5453
Collision at sea: KJV6118+
Colonial law: KJV4638+
Colonies
  Overseas France: KJV4533+
Colonies de déportation: KJV9085
Colonies de vacances: KJV5287
Colportage
  Retail trade: KJV5650
Combinations
  Business associations: KJV3192+
Combustibles solides (Mining): KJV5860.S65
Comedie française: KJV5496.C65
Comités d'enterprise: KJV3427
Commandant d'aéronef: KJV6198
Commerçants et industrials (Labor law): KJV3475.B88
Commerce de gros (Economic law): KJV5640
Commerce des bois: KJV5788
Commerce d'exportation (Overseas France): KJV4620+
Commerce d'importation (Overseas France): KJV4620+
Commerce en détail (Economic law): KJV5642+
Commerce extérieur (Economic law): KJV5630+
Commercial agency: KJV2313+
Commercial art
  Copyright: KJV3313+
Commercial companies
  Regions, provinces, etc: KJV-KJW7 3
  Taxation: KJV6650+
Commercial companies with civil purpose: KJV3172
Commercial contracts
  Regions, provinces, etc: KJV-KJW7 1.8+
Commercial courts: KJV2218+
Commercial intelligencers: KJV6385
Commercial law: KJV2185+
  Overseas France: KJV4560+
  Regions, provinces, etc: KJV-KJW7 1.8+
Commercial leases: KJV2340+
Commercial mandate: KJV2312+
Commercial maritime courts: KJV2791
Commercial pledges and liens: KJV2470+
Commercial registers: KJV2232+
  Cities, etc: KJV-KJW8 2.27
Commercial sale: KJV2320+
Commercial transactions: KJV2301+
Commissaires aux comptes (Joint stock companies): KJV3076
Commissaires-priseurs: KJV5682
Commission merchants: KJV2316
Commission superieure des conventions collectives: KJV3437
Commissions rogatoires
  Conflict of jurisdictions: KJV404
Commodat (Loan contracts): KJV1958
Commodatum (Loan contracts): KJV1958
Communal finance: KJV7049+
Communal public works: KJV4996
Communauté: KJV4644+
Communication: KJV6220+
Communication par fil au public: KJV6307+
Community antenna television: KJV6307+
Community of inventors: KJV3339
Community property: KJV722+
Commutative and aleatory contracts: KJV1687

Confiscations
  Criminal law: KJV8134+
  Eminent domain: KJV5199+
Confiserie (Food processing): KJV5910
Conflict of interests
  Constitutional law: KJV4174
Conflict of jurisdictions: KJV401+
  Civil procedure: KJV3939
Conflict of laws
  Labor law: KJV3409
Conflict of laws (Overseas France): KJV4541+
Conflicting duties (Criminal liability): KJV8048
Conflits d'attribution (Administrative law): KJV4687
Conflits de jurisdictions: KJV401+
  Civil procedure: KJV3939
Conflits de lois en matière de filiation
  Conflict of laws: KJV397.F55
Conflits de lois (Overseas France): KJV4541+
Conflits de nationalité: KJV374.C65
Conflits du travail: KJV3439+
Confrontation
  Criminal courts: KJV8760
Confusion (Extinction of obligations): KJV1662
Congés
  Labor law: KJV3464+
Conjugal domicile: KJV679+
Connaissements: KJV2815+
Consanguinity and affinity: KJV870+
Conscientious objectors (Military draft): KJV7432.C65
Conscription
  Armed Forces: KJV7428+
Conseil constitutionnel: KJV4390+
Conseil d'administration
  Joint stock companies: KJV3051
Conseil d'arrondissement: KJV4942
Conseil de famille (Incapables): KJV972
Conseil de surveillance
  Joint stock companies: KJV3052
Conseil des ministres: KJV4362+
Conseil d'Etat: KJV4385+
Conseil économique et social actuel: KJV5556.C66
Conseil National du Travail: KJV3408
Conseil supérieur de la sécurité sociale: KJV3536
Conseils de guerre: KJV7568+
Conseils de préfecture: KJV4770
Conseils de prud'hommes: KJV3488
Conseils d'enquête (Military criminal law): KJV7568+
Consensual contracts: KJV1674+
Consent
  Contracts: KJV1710+
  Defects of: KJV500+
Consent by the family (Marriage): KJV658+
Consentement
  Contracts: KJV1710+
  Vices de (Civil law): KJV500+
Consentement de la victime (Criminal liability): KJV8052
Consentement des époux (Marriage): KJV655
Consentement des parents (Marriage): KJV658+
Consentement familial (Marriage): KJV658+
Conservation of environmental resources: KJV5410
Conservation of water resources: KJV5174+
Consideration
  Contracts: KJV1725
  Obligations: KJV1545+
Consignation (Deposit): KJV2366
Consignment (Deposit): KJV2367
Consolidation (Usufruct of property): KJV1172
Conspiracy
  Criminal law: KJV8036+
Constitutional aspects
  Administrative courts and procedure: KJV4800
  Criminal law: KJV7988
Constitutional Council: KJV4390+
Constitutional history: KJV4080.5+
Constitutional law: KJV4055.2+

Contrats à exécution instantanée et contrats successifs: KJV1688
Contrats administratifs: KJV4722+
Contrats aléatoires: KJV1970+
Contrats commutatifs et contrats aléatoires: KJV1687
Contrats consensuels, solennels et réels: KJV1674+
Contrats d'adhesion: KJV1682
Contrats de commerce: KJV2301+
Contrats de mariage: KJV705+
Contrats de transport des marchandises et des voyageurs: KJV2541+
Contrats des communes: KJV4994+
Contrats d'exportation: KJV2333+
Contrats enregistrés: KJV1690
Contrats immoraux et contrats illicites: KJV1746+
Contrats judiciaires (Civil procedure): KJV3964
Contrats nommés et contrats innomés: KJV1689
Contrats relatifs aux droits d'auteur: KJV3260+
Contrats synallagmatiques et unilatéraux: KJV1675+
Contrats-types: KJV1683
Contrats unilatéraux: KJV1678
Contraventions de grande voirie: KJV6009
Contre-lettres (Void and voidable contracts): KJV1750
Contrebande: KJV7155
Contrefaçon
  Patent law: KJV3360
Contributions
  Social security: KJV3544+
Contributory negligence: KJV2045
Control français des assurances: KJV2880.2
Control over abuse of administrative power (Administrative law): KJV4765
Contrôle de la régularité des élections: KJV4315+
Contrôle des banques et la direction dur crédit: KJV2424
Contrôle des monnaie des changes: KJV6510+
Contrôle des prix: KJV5575+
Contrôle juridictionnel de l'administration: KJV4840
Contrôle juridictionnel des réglement d'administration: KJV4830
Contrôlement des finances (Public finance): KJV6486+
Convention de prête-nom: KJV1939
Conventional sequestration (Contracts): KJV1870
Conventions collectives: KJV3436+
Conventions collectives de travail (Publishing and printing): KJV5979+
Conventions collectives et contrats individuels: KJV1686
Conventions collectives nationales de travail (Publishing and printing): KJV5980
Conventions de responsabilité (Civil liability): KJV2080+
Conventions entre époux: KJV801+
Convertible bonds (Joint stock companies): KJV3125
Conviction (Criminal courts): KJV9020+
Cooperative societies
  Business associations: KJV3174+
  Income tax: KJV6879+
  Taxation: KJV6670
Coopératives agricoles: KJV5756
  Taxation: KJV6692
Copropriété
  Property: KJV1137+
  Real property: KJV1236+
Copropriété des immeubles divisés par étage ou par appartements: KJV1236.3
Copyhold: KJV1182+
Copyright: KJV3252+
Corn
  Tariff: KJV7026.C67
Corporal punishment: KJV9073
  Juvenile courts: KJV9000
Corporate bodies of public law: KJV4051

INDEX

Cultural affairs
  Cities, etc: KJV-KJW8 6.63+
  Regions, provinces, etc: KJV-KJW7 6.62+
Cultural exchanges: KJV5530
Cultural policy: KJV5428
Curatelle: KJV985+
Curatorship: KJV985+
Currency
  Public finance: KJV6496+
Current account: KJV2439+
Curricula
  Educational law: KJV5462+
Custody (Parental power): KJV919
Customs: KJV7012+
  Overseas France: KJV4630
Customs law, Violations of: KJV7150+
Custumals: KJV256+

D

Dairy farming: KJV5736
Dairy products (Food processing): KJV5918+
Damage insurance: KJV2900+
Damage to the aesthetic physical appearance of a person (Civil liability): KJV2087
Damages
  Civil liability: KJV2072+
  Commercial sale: KJV2323+
  Evaluation of: KJV2079+
Dangerous goods, Transport of
  Aircraft: KJV6164
  Roads: KJV6000
  Ships: KJV6044.D35
Databases
  Communication: KJV6328
Dation en paiement: KJV1656
Day care centers for infants and children
  Medical law: KJV5367.D39
Days of grace (Payment): KJV1590
De facto companies
  Contracts: KJV1916
De facto tutorship (Incapables): KJV973
Dead bodies (Public health): KJV5310+
Deadlines (Legal concept): KJV322.T56
Death
  Natural persons: KJV560+
Death by wrongful act (Civil liability): KJV2088+
Deathbed marriages: KJV662
Débiteur and créancier: KJV1571+
Debtor
  Detention of debtor: KJV3985
Debtor and creditor: KJV1571+
Debtor's business, Charge registered against: KJV2251.2
Debts and claims, Commercial: KJV2201+
Deceased, Creditors of: KJV1412+
Deceit related to contracts (Civil liability): KJV2095
Decentralization: KJV4882
Déchéance de brevets: KJV3343
Décis (Natural persons): KJV560+
Decisions, Court: KJV80+
Décisions des juridictions administratives: KJV4860+
Décisions judicaires: KJV3898+
  Civil procedure: KJV3959+
Declaration
  Real property by: KJV1205+
Déclaration
  Immeubles par: KJV1205+
Déclaration de de volonté
  Philosophy and theory: KJV312
Déclaration de revenu
  Income taxes: KJV6764
Déclaration de volonté
  Civil law: KJV499+
  Public contracts: KJV4726
Declaration of death (Natural persons): KJV560+
Declaration of intention
  Civil law: KJV499+
  Philosophy and theory: KJV312
  Public contracts: KJV4726
Declaratory judgments (Courts): KJV3904.D43
Déconcentration: KJV4912
Déconfiture (Courts and procedure): KJV4002

District council: KJV4942
Districts
  Administrative law: KJV4939.92+
Divertissements (Taxation)
  National revenue: KJV6980
Dividends fictives (Joint stock companies): KJV3127
Dividends (Joint stock companies): KJV3126+
Divisible and indivisible obligations: KJV1560
Division of Preliminary Examination: KJV3793
Divorce
  Civil law: KJV831+
  Conflict of laws: KJV397.D59
Divorced people
  Taxation: KJV6638
Divorced woman's name: KJV573
Doctorat en droit: KJV164
Doctorate in law: KJV164
Documentary credit: KJV2460+
  Commercial sale: KJV2321
  Maritime transactions: KJV2837
Documentary evidence (Trials): KJV3890
  Civil procedure: KJV3953+
Documents of title: KJV2412+
Dogs
  Civil liability: KJV2066.D65
  Legal aspects: KJV326
  Taxation (National revenue): KJV6974
Dol
  Civil law: KJV502+
Dol criminel: KJV8030
Domaine de la couronne: KJV5094+
Domaine privé de la propriété publique: KJV5122+
Domaine public
  Public property: KJV5116+
Domaine public maritime: KJV5152+
Domestic animals: KJV325+
  Taxation: KJV6970+
Domestic relations: KJV608+
  Cities, etc: KJV-KJW8 1.13+
Domestic relations
  Regions, provinces, etc: KJV-KJW7 1.35+
Domestic trade: KJV5638+
Domestics
  Labor law: KJV3475.D66
  Labor standards: KJV3459.D66
Domicile
  Double taxation: KJV6570
  Legal concept: KJV322.D65
  Natural persons: KJV578
Domicile conjugal: KJV679+
Domiciled documents of title: KJV2414+
Dommage
  Civil liability: KJV2013+
Dommage corporel
  Criminal law: KJV8170+
Dommage de guerre (Architects): KJV6364.W37
Dommage direct et dommage indirect (Civil liability): KJV2042
Dommage écologique: KJV5424+
Dommage matériel à des biens corporels: KJV2023
Dommage moral
  Civil liability: KJV2022+
  Criminal law: KJV8190+
Dommages-intérêts
  Commercial sale: KJV2323+
  Evaluation des (Civil liability): KJV2079+
Dommages pécuniaire (Material and moral injuries): KJV2024
Donations à cause de mort: KJV1491
Donations de biens a venir (Civil law): KJV1474
Donations déguisées (Civil law): KJV1469
Donations entre époux: KJV1485+
Donations entre vifs: KJV1480+
Donations par contrats de mariage: KJV1484+
Donations rémunératoires (Civil law): KJV1473
Dons manuels (Gifts inter vivos): KJV1482
Dotal system: KJV780+

Droits civiques et libertés publiques
  Armed Forces: KJV7414
Droits corporels (Civil law): KJV479
Droits de douane: KJV7012+
Droits de la minorité (Joint stock companies): KJV3132
Droits de la personnalité
  Juristic persons: KJV588
  Natural persons: KJV570+
Droits de l'auditeur (Broadcasting): KJV6317
Droits de vote (Joint stock companies): KJV3130+
Droits des créanciers (Dissolution of companies): KJV3028.2
Droits des riverains: KJV5166
Droits et devoirs respectifs des époux: KJV672+
Droits incorporels (Civil law): KJV479
Droits réels: KJV476+
Droits seigneuriaux: KJV4094+
Droits subjectifs (Philosophy and theory): KJV308+
Drug addiction: KJV5324
Drug addicts, Safety measures against
  Criminal law: KJV8118
Drugs
  Pharmaceutical law: KJV5377+
Due process of law (Criminal courts): KJV8504
Duelling: KJV8182
Duration of patents: KJV3344
Duress (Civil law): KJV502+
Duty to act (Criminal liability): KJV8048
Dwelling, Inexpensive (Partition of estates): KJV1434.D94
Dwellings, Employee (Labor standards): KJV3455.E66

E

Earnest
  Contracts: KJV1726
Earthworks: KJV5232.E37
Eau-de-vie
  Food processing: KJV5936
Eau potable: KJV5182
Eaux courantes: KJV5164+
Eaux de sources (Water resources): KJV5168
Eaux minerales (Food processing): KJV5927
Eaux non domaniales: KJV5162
Eavesdropping: KJV8211
Ecclesiastical law, Secular: KJV4234+
Echange (Contracts): KJV1791+
Echange de biens immobiliers: KJV1246
Ecological aspects
  Regional planning: KJV5204+
Ecological damage: KJV5424+
Economic crises
  Government measures: KJV7180+
Economic law: KJV5541+
  Regions, provinces, etc: KJV-KJW7 8+
Economy, Municipal: KJV4985+
Ecoulement de valeurs: KJV2491+
Ecrivains: KJV6415+
Edifices (Real property by nature): KJV1203
Edition: KJV5973+
Education: KJV5434+
  Legal education: KJV150+
  Soldiers: KJV7440+
Education physique: KJV5465+
Educational exchanges: KJV5530
Effets (Commercial law): KJV2371+
Egalité en droit: KJV4206+
Egg products
  Food processing: KJV5916
Election contest: KJV4317
Election crimes: KJV8302
Election law: KJV4295+
Election to particular offices: KJV4305+
Elections, Municipal: KJV4970+
Elections municipales: KJV4970+
Electric current accidents: KJV5269
Electric equipment (Labor safety): KJV3469.E54
Electricité et gaz: KJV5947+
Electricity: KJV5947+
Electrification rurale: KJV5962

Electronic data processing
Legal research: KJV142+
Electronic funds transfer
Banking: KJV2465
Elementary education: KJV5444+
Elementary school teachers: KJV5446
Elevator accidents: KJV5270
Elevators
Labor safety: KJV3469.E56
Emancipated minors (Curatorship): KJV986
Embezzlement (Public officials): KJV8327
Emergency measures
Contracts: KJV1670
Lease contracts: KJV1828+
Emergency medical services: KJV5367.E43
Emigration: KJV4190
Eminent domain: KJV5190+
Emotionally disabled (Criminal liability): KJV8043
Emphytéose: KJV5713
Emphyteusis: KJV5713
Empire deuxième: KJV4130+
Emploi réservé: KJV3446+
Employee dwellings (Labor standards): KJV3455.E66
Employee ownership: KJV3454
Employee participation in management: KJV3423.5+
Employees
Municipal government: KJV4967+, KJV6016
Social insurance: KJV3542
Employees' inventions: KJV3340
Employer's liability: KJV2071.E66
Employers' unions: KJV3435
Employés de banque (Labor law): KJV3475.B35
Employés de commerce: KJV6390
Labor law: KJV3475.M47
Employés des assurances (Labor law): KJV3475.I67
Employés des entreprises nationalisées (Labor law): KJV3475.N38
Employés d'exploitation forrestiere (Labor law): KJV3475.L86
Employés d'industrie hotelière
Labor law: KJV3475.I55
Employés d'industrie hôtelière: KJV5670
Employment, Free choice of: KJV3404+
Empoisonnement: KJV8160
Emprisonnement correctionnel: KJV8096
Emprisonnement de police: KJV8098
Enchère: KJV2329+
Encumbrances (Real property): KJV1271+
Endorsement (Negotiable instruments): KJV2384+
Endossement en blanc
Negotiable instruments: KJV2384.3
Endossement (Negotiable instruments): KJV2384+
Energie atomique: KJV5972+
Energy policy: KJV5941+
Enfants adultérins: KJV900
Enfants de parents divorcées ou separés: KJV897.C45
Enfants et les parents, Rapports entre: KJV397.P37
Enfants légitimes: KJV1389
Enfants naturels (Heirs): KJV1400+
Enforced performance: KJV1606+
Enforcement
Administrative law: KJV4762+
Courts and procedure: KJV4015
Enforcement of judgment (Civil procedure): KJV3978+
Engagement unilatéral (Obligations): KJV1545.2+
Enlèvement
Offenses against child's welfare: KJV8236
Enlèvement des ordures: KJV5306
Enlistment
Sailors: KJV7526
Soldiers: KJV7452
Enquêtes parlementaires: KJV4330
Enquêtes publiques
Administrative process: KJV4693

INDEX

Enregistrement
Business associations: KJV3005+
Civil law: KJV527
Enregistrement de fonds de commerce: KJV2254+
Enrichissement sans cause (Quasi contracts): KJV1985+
Enrôlement
Sailors: KJV7526
Soldiers: KJV7452
Enseignants: KJV5439+
Enseignement primaire: KJV5444+
Enseignement secondaire: KJV5448+
Enseignement supérieur: KJV5456+
Enseignement technique: KJV5463
Entail: KJV1359
Entailed estate: KJV1359
Entertainers
Labor law: KJV3475.E57
Entertainment (Taxation)
National revenue: KJV6980
Entraves au commerce: KJV5595+
Entreprise commerciale ou industrielle et commerçant
Commercial law: KJV2235+
Partition of estates: KJV1434.B87
Taxation: KJV6685
Entreprises de service public: KJV5012+
Entreprises gazières: KJV5970
Entreprises nationalisées: KJV5594
Entreprises publiques (Labor law): KJV3475.G68
Environmental law: KJV5406+
Cities, etc: KJV-KJW8 6
Mining: KJV5858
Regions, provinces, etc: KJV-KJW7 6.55+
Environmental planning: KJV5410
Environmental pollution: KJV5412+
Envoi en possession: KJV1397.W75
Epoux (Civil law): KJV622+
Equality before the law: KJV4206+
Equipage d'aéronef: KJV6196
Equipement (Armed Forces): KJV7480+
Equipment
Armed Forces: KJV7480+
Equity (Philosophy and theory): KJV288
Equivalence, Theorie d': KJV472
Equivalence, Theory of: KJV472
Equivalents non pécuniaires (Civil liability): KJV2076
Erreur
Civil law: KJV501
Erreur judiciaire: KJV3910
Error (Civil law): KJV501
Escheat (Irregular successors): KJV1396
Escompte (Banks): KJV2457
Espionage: KJV8292
Espionnage: KJV8292
Essential oils (Food processing): KJV5922
Estate, Liabilities of: KJV1412+
Estate taxes: KJV6922+
Estates-General: KJV4086+
Estates, Partition of: KJV1430+
Etablissements de bienfaisance (Social services): KJV3660+
Etablissements de Saint Louis: KJV269
Etablissements d'utilité publique: KJV594+
Etablissements pénitentiaires: KJV9070+
Etablissements publics d'assistance: KJV3664
Etat
Irregular successors: KJV1396
Public law: KJV4052+
Etat civil (Soldiers): KJV7420+
Etat de necessité (Criminal liability): KJV8050
Etat et capacité des personnes (Conflict of laws): KJV397.S73
Etats étrangers
Taxation: KJV6648+
Etats généraux: KJV4086+
Ethics
Catholic ethics and French law: KJV319.E84
Legal: KJV220+
Professional: KJV6340+

Ethics in government
  Constitutional law: KJV4174
Etrangère, Paiement en monnaie
  (Money obligations): KJV1554+
Etrangers
  Capacity and disability to inherit:
    KJV1337.A65
  Conflict of jurisdictions: KJV407+
  Labor law: KJV3477.A55
  Nationality and citizenship:
    KJV4198.A55
  Nuptial capacity: KJV652
Etrangers en France
  Private international law: KJV382+
Etudiants (Labor law): KJV3475.S89
Euthanasia (Criminal law): KJV8168
Euthanasie (Criminal law): KJV8168
Evaluation d l'incapacité
  Workers' compensation: KJV3552
Evaluation de l'incapacité
  Permanent disability pensions:
    KJV3562
Evaluation des fonds de commerce:
  KJV2251.3
Evaluation des sociétés par actions:
  KJV3071
Evaluation of damages (Civil liability):
  KJV2079+
Evasion fiscale: KJV7146
Eviction (Business premises): KJV2359
Evidence
  Civil law: KJV525+
  Philosophy and theory: KJV313+
  Social insurance: KJV3520+
Evidence in court: KJV3882+
  Administrative courts: KJV4850
  Civil courts: KJV3949+
Ex parte jurisdiction (Courts and
  procedure): KJV3992+
Examining magistrate: KJV8650+
Exception d'illégalité (Administrative
  power): KJV4749
Exchange and sale contracts:
  KJV1791+
Exchange of apartments: KJV1824
Exchange of real property: KJV1246
Excitation de mineur à la débauche:
  KJV8226
Exclusive license (Commercial sale):
  KJV2326
Exclusive rights clause (Contracts):
  KJV1758.E93
Execution
  Commercial courts: KJV2226+
  Courts and procedure (Costs):
    KJV4015
  Criminal courts: KJV9060+
Exécution
  Administrative law: KJV4762+
  Choses in action: KJV1584+
Exécution d'un jugement (Civil
  procedure): KJV3978+
Exécution en nature: KJV1591
Exécution forcée: KJV1606+
Exécution pendant la guerre: KJV1600
Exécution provisoire: KJV3987
Exécution testamentaire: KJV1363
Executive advisory bodies
  Administrative law: KJV4904
Executive power: KJV4360+
Executives
  Joint stock companies: KJV3049+
  Labor law: KJV3475.E94
Exemptions
  Income tax: KJV6775+
  Nuptial capacity: KJV654
Exercise d'un droit (Criminal liability):
  KJV8049
Exhérédation: KJV1362
Exhibitions: KJV5282+
Exonération de responsabilité, Causes
  d': KJV2043+
Exonerations d'impôt
  Income tax: KJV6775+
Expatriation: KJV4194
Expédition (Deposit): KJV2367
Expenses of the last sickness (Creditors
  of the deceased): KJV1413.E97
Expert evidence (Commercial courts):
  KJV2223
Expert medical evidence (Social
  insurance): KJV3522
Expert testimony: KJV3892+

INDEX

INDEX

G

INDEX

I

Juges: KJV3838+
Juifs
  Equality before the law: KJV4207.J49
  Nationality and citizenship:
    KJV4198.J49
July monarchy: KJV4124+
Juridiction arbitrale (Conflict of
  jurisdictions): KJV417
Juridiction des référés
  Administrative courts and procedure:
    KJV4853
Juridiction gracieuse (Courts and
  procedure): KJV3992+
Juridictions consulaires (Commercial
  law): KJV2220+
Juridictions maritimes: KJV6130+
Jurisdiction
  Administrative law: KJV4810+
  Civil procedure: KJV3936+
  Courts: KJV3869+
    Civil courts: KJV3810+
    Commercial courts: KJV2219
Jurisdiction of secular courts over
  church matters and the clergy:
  KJV4262+
Jurisdictions
  Conflict of: KJV401+
  Inland water carrier: KJV2690+
Juristic facts and acts
  Civil law: KJV480+
  Philosophy and theory: KJV310+
Juristic personality
  Capacity: KJV4897
  Trade and professional associations:
    KJV3432+
Juristic persons
  Nationality of: KJV374.J87
  Taxation: KJV6640+
Juristic persons of private law:
  KJV584+
Juristic persons of public law:
  KJV4895+
Jury
  Criminal courts: KJV8800+
Jury civil: KJV3923
Justice
  Administration of justice: KJV3721+
Justice and law (Philosophy and theory):
  KJV285+
Justice, Evaluation de l'indemnité par
  (Civil liability): KJV2079.2
Justices of the peace: KJV3813
Justices seigneuriales: KJV3758
Juvenile courts: KJV8840+
  Child welfare: KJV3635
Juvenile courts of assizes: KJV8850
Juvenile delinquents: KJV8858+

K

Kidnapping: KJV8236
Kravchenko, Procès (Trials):
  KJV131.K73

L

Labeling
  Food processing: KJV5902
Labels
  Copyright: KJV3313+
Labor
  Contract for: KJV1841+
Labor and Employment Board:
  KJV3407
Labor contracts: KJV3410+
Labor courts: KJV3485+
Labor discipline: KJV3456
Labor disputes: KJV3439+
Labor law: KJV3384+
  Agricultural workers: KJV5812+
  Cities, etc: KJV-KJW8 3+
  Mining: KJV5850+
  Overseas France: KJV4568+
  Regions, provinces, etc: KJV-KJW7
    3.26+
Labor-management councils: KJV3427
Labor-management relations:
  KJV3420+
Labor standards: KJV3445+
Labor supply: KJV3457+
Labor unions: KJV3434+
  Delegates of: KJV3425
Laboratory assistants (Auxiliary medical
  professions): KJV5355

Land
  Rights incident to ownership of: KJV1227+
Land reclamation
  Mining: KJV5858
Land reform: KJV5690+
Land register: KJV1283+
Land registry
  Regions, provinces, etc: KJV-KJW8 1.18
Land subdivisions: KJV5208
Land tenure: KJV1208+
  Overseas France: KJV4550
Landlord and tenant contracts: KJV1814+
Landowners, Adjoining: KJV1228+
Language: KJV5432
Lapse and nullity of patents: KJV3343
Lapse and revocation of legacies: KJV1364
Larceny: KJV8246+
Law
  Object of law: KJV285+
  Philosophy and theory: KJV290+
  Students: KJV155
Law and justice (Philosophy and theory): KJV285+
Law as a career: KJV170+
Law dictionaries: KJV115
Law making (Overseas France): KJV4578
Law reform: KJV320
Law reporting: KJV147
Law schools: KJV156+
Lawyers
  Collective bargaining: KJV3438.L38
Lease
  Farming lease: KJV5710+
Lease contracts: KJV1804+
Lease litigation: KJV1827.3
Lease of business concern: KJV2258
Lease of business premises: KJV2341+
Lease of fishing waters: KJV5828
Lease of hunting grounds: KJV5797
Lease of urban property: KJV1822
Lease-purchase: KJV2327
Lease renewal (Business premises): KJV2358
Leave of absence
  Labor law: KJV3464+
Lectures publiques (Literary copyright): KJV3290.P83
Legacies: KJV1352+
Legal advertising: KJV316
Legal aid: KJV229
Legal capacity
  Trade and professional associations: KJV3430
Legal composition: KJV145
Legal deposit (Contracts): KJV1875
Legal education: KJV150+
Legal ethics: KJV220+
Legal implications of sexual behavior: KJV8212+
Legal maxims: KJV118
Legal profession: KJV170+
Legal remedies: KJV3912+
Legal research: KJV140+
Legal status
  Married women: KJV673+
Legal status of inventors: KJV3339
Legality (Constitutional principles): KJV4167
Legatee's mortgage: KJV1356.3
Legatees' security: KJV1356.2+
Légion d'honneur: KJV4512
Legion of honor: KJV4512
Legislation: KJV30+
  Civil law: KJV442.92+
  Regions, provinces, etc: KJV-KJW7 1.A16+
Législation de la sépulture: KJV5310+
Législation du batiment
  Regional planning: KJV5226+
Législation pénale (Economic law): KJV5685
Législation vétérinaire: KJV5396+
Legislative documents
  Cities, etc: KJV-KJW8 1.A2+
Legislative initiative: KJV4324+
Legislative power: KJV4321+
Legislators: KJV4332+
Legislature: KJV4321+

Legislature
  Elections: KJV4307+
Legitimacy (Parent and child): KJV894+
Legitimate children (Order of succession): KJV1389
Legitimate descendants: KJV1388+
Legitime and disposable portion of an estate: KJV1372+
Legitime in kind: KJV1374+
Legs à titre universel: KJV1354
Legs interdits: KJV1356+
Legs (Succession upon death): KJV1352+
Légumes
  Agricultural law: KJV5738.F78
  Food processing: KJV5908
Lesion
  Immoral and unlawful contracts: KJV1748
  Liquidation of property: KJV1141
Lesnier: KJV131.I58
Lessors liens (Farming lease): KJV5717
Letters
  Literary copyright: KJV3273+
Letters of credit: KJV2462
Letters rogatory
  Conflict of jurisdictions: KJV404
Lettre de change: KJV2391+
Lex causae: KJV391.2
Lex fori: KJV391
Liabilities of the estate: KJV1412+
Liability
  Airlines: KJV2698
  Barristers: KJV174
  Business association managers: KJV3008+
  Business enterprises: KJV2276+
  Civil liability: KJV2001+
  Civil servants: KJV5056
  Electric power: KJV5966
  Founders of joint stock companies: KJV3044
  Government liability: KJV5080+
  Incapables: KJV947
  Innkeepers' liability: KJV5669
Liability
  Joint stock companies
    Organs: KJV3061+
  Journalists: KJV6279
  Juristic persons: KJV589
  Lawyers: KJV219
  Legal concept: KJV322.L53
  Maritime law: KJV2866+
  Mentally ill and their guardians: KJV1003
  Notaries: KJV190
  Private companies: KJV3039.5
  Relief from: KJV2043+
  School liability: KJV5442
  Shipowners' liability: KJV2793+
  Social insurance: KJV3524+
  Solicitors: KJV214
  Tort liability: KJV2030+
  Tortious liability: KJV397.T67
  Work and labor contracts: KJV1855
Liability for damage caused by public works: KJV5245
Liability for one's own action: KJV2048
Liability for the acts of things: KJV2062+
Liability insurance: KJV2957+
Liability limitation and non-liability clauses: KJV2082
Liability of members of magistracy: KJV3862
Liability of railway companies: KJV2672+
Liability without fault: KJV2059+
  Government liability: KJV5083+
Libel and slander: KJV8200+
Liberal professions
  Taxation: KJV6710
Libéralités (Civil law): KJV1461+
Liberalités pieuses: KJV1467+
Libération conditionnelle: KJV8074
Liberté de circulation: KJV4227+
Liberté de la pensée: KJV4210+
Liberté de la presse: KJV6258
Liberté de l'enseignement: KJV4216
Liberté de réunion et d'association: KJV4224+, KJV5048+
Liberté de tester: KJV1341

INDEX

Misdemeanor: KJV8007
Mise à l'épreuve: KJV8076+
Misfeasance and negligent omission (Civil liability): KJV2019+
Misinformation (Journalists): KJV6283+
Missing persons (Natural persons): KJV560+
Mistrial: KJV3910
Misuse of one's right (Breach of contract): KJV1766.M57
Mitoyenneté
  Real property: KJV1230
Mobilization (Military draft): KJV7436
Mobs: KJV8398
Modalités de la force obligatoire: KJV1758.A+
Modèles (Figurative arts and photography)
  Copyright: KJV3312+
Models (Figurative arts and photography)
  Copyright: KJV3312+
Modes (Clothing): KJV5884
Modesty, Injury to: KJV2091
Monarchie de Juillet: KJV4124+, KJV4126.A23
Monetary clauses (Money obligations): KJV1553+
Money
  Compensation (Civil liability): KJV2077+
  Loan of (Contracts): KJV1960+
  Public finance: KJV6496+
Money obligations: KJV1551+
Moniteur universel: KJV12
Monnaie contrefait: KJV8310
Monopoles: KJV5604+
Monopolies: KJV5604+
Monsieur Bill, Procès de (Trials): KJV131.M65
Monuments historiques: KJV5526+
Moral and material injuries: KJV2022+
Moral injury
  Criminal law: KJV8190+
Moral rights
  Intellectual and industrial property: KJV3250
Moralité des lois pénales: KJV7990
Morality of criminal law: KJV7990
Morals, Good, and public policy: KJV287+
Moratoire
  Lease contracts (Wartime): KJV1829
  Payment: KJV1590
Moratorium
  Lease contracts (Wartime): KJV1829
  Payment: KJV1590
Morte civile: KJV8123
Mortgage bonds (Joint stock companies): KJV3138
Mortgage lodged for security of current accounts: KJV2443
Mortgage registration: KJV1285
Mortgages and privileges: KJV2151+
Mothers (Order of succession): KJV1391
Motion pictures: KJV5500+
  Copyright: KJV3316+
Motor vehicle drivers
  Labor law: KJV3475.M68
Motor vehicles (Carriage of goods and passengers): KJV2650+
Mountaineering: KJV5292.M68
Movie actors
  Labor law: KJV3475.M69
Moving expenses (Civil service): KJV5064
Moyens of paiement (Commercial law): KJV2203+
Multi-national corporations
  National revenue
    Income taxes: KJV6886+
Multi-national corporations (Taxpayers)
  National revenue
    Double taxation: KJV6574.M85
Multiple line insurance: KJV2908
Multiple shares (Joint stock companies): KJV3119
Municipal and international law: KJV304+
Municipal government: KJV4953+
Municipal markets: KJV5000
Municipal police: KJV4982
Municipal reforms: KJV4955

Navigation
Inland water transportation: KJV6096+
Navigation aérienne: KJV6168+
Navigation and pilotage: KJV6090+
Navigation intérieure: KJV6096+
Navires
Conflict of laws: KJV397.S55
Transportation: KJV6035+
Navires de commerce: KJV6048.M47
Navires de haute mer: KJV6048.O23
Navy: KJV7510+
Necessary deposit (Contracts): KJV1868
Necessité (Relief from liability): KJV2046
Necessity
Criminal liability: KJV8050
Relief from liability: KJV2046
Neglect of a child: KJV8235
Negligence (Contracts): KJV2019+
Négligence criminelle: KJV8032
Negligent omission: KJV2019+
Negotiable instruments: KJV2371+
Cities, etc: KJV-KJW8 2.28
Negotiated settlement: KJV3996+
Negotiorum gestio (Quasi contracts): KJV1980
Net charter
Maritime law: KJV2813
Newspaper reporting (Courts-martial): KJV7570.N49
Nobility: KJV4090+
Nobility (Ancien Regime): KJV4090+
Noblesse: KJV4090+
Noblesse (Ancien Regime): KJV4090+
Noise control: KJV5422
Nom
Civil law: KJV570+
Nom commercial: KJV2252.2
Nom de famille (Natural persons): KJV572+
Nom de la divorcée: KJV573
Nom de la femme mariée: KJV573
Nomades
Equality before the law: KJV4207.G96
Nominal capital (Joint stock companies: KJV3083+
Nominate and innominate contracts: KJV1689
Nominations (Civil service): KJV5032+
Non-capital murder: KJV8157
Non-commercial profits
Income taxes: KJV6778+
Non-competition clause (Labor contract): KJV3412
Non-contentious jurisdiction (Courts and procedure): KJV3992+
Non-merchant's insolvency (Courts and procedure): KJV4002
Non-pecuniary compensation (Civil liability): KJV2076
Non performance (Extinction of obligations): KJV1664+
Non-retroactivité des lois, Principe de la: KJV307.2
Non salariés (Labor law): KJV3475.S45
Non-supervisory employees (Labor law): KJV3475.N66
Non-support: KJV8237
Noncash funds transfer
Banking: KJV2465
Nonprofit corporations
Taxation: KJV6652
Nonretroactivity, Principle of: KJV307.2
Norms
Economic law: KJV5614
Notaires: KJV187+
Notarial acts
Conflict of jurisdictions: KJV420+
The legal profession: KJV189+
Notarial wills: KJV1344
Notaries: KJV187+
Notice
Labor contract: KJV3414+
Legal concept: KJV322.N68
Notification (Legal concept): KJV322.N68
Novation: KJV1658
Nuclear energy: KJV5972+
Nuclear power: KJV5262
Nuclear-power plants: KJV5958
Nuclear waste disposal: KJV5262

Nuisances (Civil liability): KJV2099
Nullité et inefficacité (Civil law): KJV497+
Nullités absolues et nullités relatives des contrats: KJV1740+
Nullités de sociétés (Contracts): KJV1907
Nullités du mariage: KJV665+
Nullity and ineffectiveness
  Civil law: KJV497+
  Conflict of laws: KJV397.N85
Nuptial capacity: KJV649+
Nurses and nursing: KJV5352
Nursing expenses, Privilege of: KJV1413.N87
Nursing homes
  Medical law: KJV5367.O42

O

Oath
  Evidence (Criminal courts): KJV8720
  Political oath: KJV4502
Object
  Real property: KJV1205+
Object of contracts: KJV1696
Object of law: KJV285+
Objecteurs de conscience (Military draft): KJV7432.C65
Objective and subjective negligence: KJV2021
Objet auquel ils s'appliquent, Immeubles par: KJV1205+
Obligation alimentaire (Family law): KJV931+
Obligation to do or refrain from doing: KJV1557
Obligations
  Cities, etc: KJV-KJW8 2.24+
  Civil law: KJV1529+
  Conflict of laws: KJV397.C76
  Overseas France: KJV4554+
  Regions, provinces, etc: KJV-KJW7 1.7+
Obligations à sujets complexes: KJV1576+
Obligations civiles ou naturelles: KJV1549
Obligations conjointes: KJV1578+
Obligations convertibles (Joint stock companies): KJV3125
Obligations de donner: KJV1550+
Obligations de donner des choses de genre: KJV1550.2
Obligations de faire ou de ne pas faire: KJV1557
Obligations de résultat et les obligations de moyen: KJV1562
Obligations divisibles et indivisibles: KJV1560
Obligations hypothécaires (Joint stock companies): KJV3138
Obligations in kind: KJV1550.2
Obligations legislatives: KJV1567
Obligations patrimoniales ou extra-patrimoniales: KJV1563
Obligations pécuniaires: KJV1551+
Obligations plurales: KJV1564+
Obligations positives: KJV1561
Obligations précontractuelles: KJV1704+
Obligations solidaires: KJV1579+
Obligations to give: KJV1550+
Oblique action
  Obligations: KJV1616
Occupancy (Possession of property): KJV1163
Occupation (Possession of property): KJV1163
Occupational diseases: KJV3550+
Ocean-going vessels (Transportation): KJV6048.O23
Oeufs (Food processing): KJV5916
Oeuvres cinématographiques et télévision (Copyright): KJV3316+
Oeuvres de caractère scientifique (Literary copyright): KJV3275+
Oeuvres des arts figuratifs et photographie (Copyright): KJV3310+
Oeuvres musicales (Copyright): KJV3292+
Oeuvres théatrales (Copyright): KJV3292+

Procédure criminelle (Overseas France): KJV4635
Procedure de recours
Criminal courts: KJV9035+
Procédure de recours: KJV3912+
Civil procedure: KJV3972+
Procédure de révision de la constitution: KJV4164
Procédure d'urgence: KJV3968+
Administrative courts and procedure: KJV4853
Procedure in chambers: KJV3968+
Administrative law: KJV4853
Procédure judiciaire (Conflict of jurisdictions): KJV403+
Procédure par défaut (Commercial courts): KJV2225
Proceeds of husband's and wife's work: KJV804.P76
Procès (Courts): KJV3880+
Military courts: KJV7578+
Processions and manifestations, Control of: KJV5285
Procuration (Mandate): KJV1937
Procurement, Military: KJV7482+
Procureur Général à la Cour de Cassation: KJV3799
Procureurs de la République: KJV3806+
Procureurs Généraux: KJV3848
Procuring (Moral offense): KJV8222
Prodigals, Judicial counsel and curator of: KJV1010
Prodigues, Conseil judiciaire et curateur des: KJV1010
Producers' cooperatives: KJV3176
Production primaire: KJV5687+
Products liability (Commercial sale): KJV2324
Produits alimentaires (Overseas France): KJV4614+
Produits de la pêche: KJV5924
Produits du travail des époux: KJV804.P76
Produits laitiers (Food processing): KJV5918+
Professional associations: KJV3429+
Professional associations
Overseas France: KJV4572
Professional corporations: KJV6334+
Professional-liability insurance: KJV2959
Professional misconduct: KJV6342+
Professional premises
Lease: KJV1824
Professional secrets (Practice of law): KJV222
Professions: KJV6330+
Cities, etc: KJV-KJW8 7.76.A+
Regions, provinces, etc: KJV-KJW7 8.8
Professions disqualification (Criminal law): KJV8126
Professions libérales
Taxation: KJV6710
Professions medicales: KJV5338+
Profit sharing
Labor law: KJV3453
Profits exceptionnels (Joint stock companies): KJV3128+
Programme de construction d'habitation: KJV5222+
Programming (Broadcasting): KJV6320+
Prohibited legacies: KJV1356+
Projets d'immeubles d'habitation: KJV5222+
Promesse de contrat: KJV1705+
Promesse de contrat (Taxation)
National revenue: KJV6990
Promesse de mariage: KJV645+
Promise of contract: KJV1705+
Promise of marriage: KJV645+
Promises of contract (Taxation)
National revenue: KJV6990
Promissory note: KJV2410
Promoters (Building and construction industry): KJV5894
Promotion sociale (Education): KJV5468
Proof of ownership (Real property): KJV1260
Property
Alien property: KJV383.A44

Public health: KJV5302+
Cities, etc: KJV-KJW8 5.54+
Offenses against: KJV8392
Regions, provinces, etc: KJV-KJW7 6+
Public housing agencies: KJV5220
Public institutions of relief: KJV3664
Public interest (Administrative law): KJV4675
Public land law: KJV5125+
Public law: KJV4050+
Overseas France: KJV4576+
Public lectures (Literary copyright): KJV3290.P83
Public libraries: KJV5520.P83
Public maritime resources: KJV5152+
Public Ministry: KJV3845+
Public Ministry at the Court of Cassation: KJV3798+
Public offices: KJV5020+
Public officials, Acts of: KJV418+
Public officials, Offenses of: KJV8322+
Public policies in research: KJV5472
Public policy
Conflict of laws: KJV393
Copyright contracts: KJV3266
Public policy and good morals: KJV287+
Public policy and police power (Constitutional law): KJV4180+
Public property: KJV5090+
Cities, etc: KJV-KJW8 4.47+
Regions, provinces, etc: KJV-KJW7 5.4+
Public prosecution (Criminal courts): KJV8518+
Public prosecutors (Criminal courts): KJV8518+
Public restraints on private property: KJV5090+
Public safety: KJV5255+
Public services (Administrative law): KJV5008+
Public servitudes: KJV5129+
Public utilities: KJV5012+
Cities, etc: KJV-KJW8 8
Public welfare: KJV3601+
Public welfare
Cities, etc: KJV-KJW8 3+
Public works: KJV5238+
Publicité
Business associations: KJV3005.5
Publicité fonciere: KJV1283+
Publicité légale: KJV316
Publicity
Business associations: KJV3005.5
Trials (Criminal courts): KJV8508
Publicity of trial (Criminal courts): KJV8508
Publishing: KJV5973+
Contracts: KJV3318+
Punishment
Criminal law: KJV8054+
Juvenile courts: KJV8890+
Purity
Food processing: KJV5904
Putative marriage: KJV666

Q

Qualifications (Conflict of laws): KJV390+
Qualités requises pour succéder: KJV1333+
Quality control
Economic law: KJV5614
Quarrying: KJV5830+
Quasi contracts: KJV1978+
Quasi délit: KJV2019+
Quasi-martial relationships: KJV865
Quasi matrimonial relationship: KJV663+
Quasi offense (Civil liability): KJV2013+
Quasi personality (Personal property): KJV1294.P47
Quatrième République: KJV4158+
Quotations: KJV118
Quotité disponible entre époux: KJV1486

R

Radio communication: KJV6290+
Radio interference: KJV6312

INDEX

INDEX

Self-liquidation of an estate: KJV1437
Semantics
History of law
France: KJV248
Senat: KJV4336+
Elections: KJV4309
Senior Council on Social Security: KJV3536
Sentences arbitrale (Conflict of jurisdictions): KJV417
Separation
Marriage law: KJV840+
Conflict of laws: KJV397.D59
Séparation des églises et de l'état: KJV4239+
Séparation des pouvoirs (Constitutional principles): KJV4170+
Separation of church and state: KJV4239+
Separation of patrimonies: KJV1410
Separation of powers (Constitutional principles): KJV4170+
Separation of property: KJV770+
Sequestration
Contracts: KJV1869+
Séquestrations de personnes: KJV8192+
Séquestre
Contracts: KJV1869+
Séquestre conventionnel (Contracts): KJV1870
Séquestre judiciaire: KJV1874
Serfdom: KJV4095
Serment (Evidence)
Criminal courts: KJV8720
Servage: KJV4095
Service and labor, Contract of: KJV1837+
Service d'assistance médicale d'urgence: KJV5367.E43
Service postal: KJV6238+
Service stations: KJV5676+
Service trades: KJV5664+
Services du logement: KJV5220
Services publics (Administrative law): KJV5008+
Servitudes
Real property: KJV1277+
Telecommunication lines: KJV6302
Servitudes aériennes: KJV6170
Servitudes de droit public: KJV5129+
Servitudes légales (Real property): KJV1280.S73
Servitudes réelles (Real property): KJV1278+
Set-off (Extinction of obligation): KJV1660
Settlement market: KJV2506
Sexual behavior
Legal implications: KJV8212+
Share capital
Joint stock companies: KJV3089+
Shares of stock of the Bank of France: KJV2434
Shares of stocks and bonds
Joint stock companies: KJV3106+
Taxation (National revenue): KJV6998
Double taxation: KJV6574.S52
Ship brokers: KJV2797.4
Ship operator: KJV2795
Ship ownership: KJV2792
Shipmaster: KJV6050+
Shipping documents (Railroads): KJV2668
Ships: KJV6037+
Conflict of laws: KJV397.S55
Shop stewards: KJV3424
Short-term sentence: KJV8098
Shows (Copyright): KJV3300+
Sick (Curatorship): KJV988
SIDA: KJV5316.A53
Signes distinctifs (Patent law): KJV3352+
Silent partners (Business associations): KJV3036
Simulated marriage: KJV656
Simulation (Void and voidable contracts): KJV1750
Simulations (Civil law): KJV1469
Single women (Capacity and incapacity): KJV568
Skiing: KJV5292.S55

Sociétés travaillant en France
  Taxation: KJV6680
Sodomy: KJV8220
Solde
  Soldiers: KJV7454+
Soldes
  Civil service: KJV5060+
    Overseas France: KJV4586.S35
Soldiers: KJV7418+
  Estates of deceased: KJV1356.3
  Nuptial capacity: KJV651
Sole general manager (Joint stock companies): KJV3059
Solicitors: KJV212+
  Commercial courts: KJV2222
Solid universal fuels (Mining): KJV5860.S65
Solidarité active: KJV1580
Solidarité passive: KJV1582
Solidarity between creditors: KJV1580
Solidary obligations: KJV1579+
Solitary confinement with hard labor: KJV8094
Sollicitation de commandes
  Retail trade: KJV5650
Sources non volontaires (Obligations): KJV1548
Sources volontaires (Obligations): KJV1545+
Sous-entreprise (Work and labor): KJV1853
Sous-location: KJV1825
Sous-louage: KJV1825
Sous-préfets (Districts)
  Administrative law: KJV4944
Souvenirs de famille (Partition of estates): KJV1434.H45
Sovereign Court of Paris: KJV3747
Specifications
  Building and construction industry: KJV5897
Spectacles
  Copyright: KJV3300+
  Taxation (National revenue): KJV6980
Spéculation illicite (Business enterprises): KJV2283.I55
Splits
  Business associations: KJV3020+
  Joint stock companies: KJV3146
Sport activities: KJV5290+
Sports: KJV5286+
  Sports de montagne: KJV5292.M68
Sports accidents
  Civil liability: KJV2100.S66
Springs (Water resources): KJV5168
Staff shares
  Joint stock companies: KJV3124
Stamp duties (National revenue): KJV6956
Standardized terms of contract: KJV1683
Standards
  Agricultural law: KJV5730
  Economic law: KJV5614
State
  Irregular successors: KJV1396
  Offenses against: KJV8264+
  Public law: KJV4052+
State and the theatre: KJV5489
State Audit Office: KJV6492+
State bonds: KJV6528
State monopolies: KJV5606
State supervision of banks: KJV2424
Stations de sports d'hiver: KJV5292.S55
Stations d'hiver: KJV5288+
Statistics
  Criminal statistics: KJV122
  Judicial statistics: KJV121+
    Regions, provinces, etc: KJV-KJW7 1.A2+
Status and capacity of persons: KJV397.S73
Status and capacity of persons (Conflict of laws): KJV397.S73
Statut juridique de la femme mariée: KJV673+
Statutes (Legislation): KJV50+
Statutory mortgage: KJV2168+
Statutory obligations: KJV1567
Statutory servitudes (Real property): KJV1280.S73
Stay of execution: KJV8072+

Supplies
Military equipment: KJV7482+
Supplies, Military: KJV7482+
Support, Obligation of (Family law): KJV931+
Supra-municipal corporations and cooperation: KJV5004+
Supreme Council of French Union: KJV4648
Supreme courts: KJV3790+
Surenchère (Auction): KJV2330
Sûreté
Mesures de (Criminal law): KJV8054+
Sûreté de l'État: KJV4200+
Sûretés
Civil law: KJV2111+
Sûrétés des légataires: KJV1356.2+
Sûretés personnelles (Civil law): KJV2122+
Sûretés réelles: KJV2130+
Sûretés réelles sur les immeubles: KJV2132
Sûretés rélles sur les meubles: KJV2134
Suretyship and guaranty
Regions, provinces, etc: KJV-KJW7 1.76
Suretyship and guaranty (Civil law): KJV2122+
Surgeons: KJV5347.S87
Sursalaires familiaux (Labor standards): KJV3450
Sursis à exécution des décisions administratives: KJV4764
Sursis à l'exécution des peines: KJV8072+
Surtaxes
Income tax: KJV6890+
Surveillance de la police: KJV8624
Surviving spouse (Heirs): KJV1403+
Suspension
Military service: KJV7430+
Suspensive conditions (Civil law): KJV514
Swine: KJV5734.S85
Swiss civil judgments in France, Execution of: KJV428.E93
Sylviculture: KJV5786+
Symbolism and French law: KJV248.3
Synallagmatic contracts: KJV1675+
Syndic (Business associations): KJV3001
Syndicat de communes: KJV4950
Syndicats de fonctionnaires: KJV5050
Syndicats d'employeurs: KJV3435
Syndicats des salariés: KJV3434+
Syndicats professionnels: KJV3429+
Overseas France: KJV4572

T

Tabac: KJV5738.T63
Tabagisme: KJV5421
Tangible personal property (Conflict of laws): KJV397.T35
Tangible rights (Civil law): KJV479
Tariffs: KJV7012+
Tax collection: KJV6600+
Tax collector (Local taxes): KJV7064
Tax courts: KJV6614+
Tax evasion: KJV7146
Tax on furnished accommodations (Local taxes): KJV7082
Tax returns
Income tax: KJV6764
Taxable income: KJV6775+
Taxation
National revenue: KJV6547.2+
Overseas France: KJV4630
Taxe d'apprentissage
Local taxes: KJV7120
Taxe d'habitation (Local taxes): KJV7082
Taxe sur la valeur ajoutée (National revenue): KJV6966
Agriculture: KJV6700
Taxe sur le chiffre d'affaires (National revenue): KJV6960+
Taxe sur les salaires (Local taxes): KJV7110
Taxes
Cities, etc: KJV-KJW8 8.85
Local taxes: KJV7060+

Travaux publics: KJV5238+
  Municipal government: KJV4996
Travel agencies: KJV2555
Travel expenses (Civil service): KJV5064
Travel insurance: KJV2897.T73
Treason: KJV8289
  Criminal trials: KJV129.T74
Treasury Division: KJV6465+
Treasury liens: KJV6536+
Trial: KJV3880+
  Civil procedure: KJV3948+
  Criminal procedure: KJV8670+
Trial by newspaper: KJV8417
Trials: KJV128+
  Military courts: KJV7578+
Tribunal de la connétablie: KJV4768
Tribunal des conflits: KJV3820
  Decisions: KJV90
Tribunal d'Etat: KJV8480
Tribunal révolutionnaire: KJV8474
Tribunaux administratifs: KJV4795
Tribunaux cantonaux: KJV3813
Tribunaux civils: KJV3808+
Tribunaux correctionnels: KJV8460
Tribunaux criminels et procedure pénale: KJV8411+
Tribunaux de baux ruraux: KJV5719
Tribunaux de commerce et procédure commerciale: KJV2218+
Tribunaux de commerce maritime: KJV2791
Tribunaux de grande instance: KJV3804+
  Decisions: KJV105
Tribunaux de paix: KJV3813
Tribunaux de simple police: KJV8464
Tribunaux des successions: KJV1442
Tribunaux d'exception: KJV8470+
Tribunaux d'instance: KJV3812+
  Decisions: KJV108
Tribunaux du travail: KJV3485+
Tribunaux en matière testamentaire: KJV1371
Tribunaux pour enfants
  Child welfare: KJV3635
  Criminal courts: KJV8840+
Tribunaux révolutionnaires: KJV3760
Troisieme République: KJV4134+
Truck lines (Carriage of goods and passengers): KJV2650+
Trucks (Commercial leases): KJV2361
Trustees (Commercial agency): KJV2313+
Trusts, Industrial: KJV3192+
Tuberculose animale: KJV5404
Tutelle (Incapables): KJV961+
Tutorship (Incapables): KJV961+

U

Unauthorized practice (Legal profession): KJV223
Unborn children: KJV558
Uncovered checks: KJV2405
Unemancipated minors (Tutorship): KJV974+
Unequal voting shares (Joint stock companies): KJV3118+
Unfair competition: KJV5610+
Unforseeability (Extinction of obligations): KJV1661
Unilateral administrative acts: KJV4711+
Unilateral and bilateral acts
  Civil law: KJV489
Unilateral contracts: KJV1678
Unilateral engagement (Obligations): KJV1545.2+
Unintentional faults: KJV2015
Union française: KJV4646+
Union libre (Marriage): KJV663+
Universal profit partnership (Contracts): KJV1914
Universal property partnership (Contracts): KJV1912
Universités: KJV5457+
Universities: KJV5457+
Unjust enrichment (Quasi contracts): KJV1985+
Unlawful contracts: KJV1746+
Unlawful interference (Administrative power): KJV4747
Unpaid seller, Right of: KJV1798+

V

GPO U.S. GOVERNMENT PRINTING OFFICE: 2008-330-111/60012